THE EUROPEAN PARLIAMENT AND THE EUROPEAN COMMUNITY

Also by Valentine Herman

PARLIAMENTS OF THE WORLD: A Reference Compendium

CABINET STUDIES (*with James E. Alt*)

THE BACKBENCHER AND PARLIAMENT (*with Dick Leonard*)

WORKBOOK FOR COMPARATIVE GOVERNMENT (*with Jean Blondel*)

Also by Juliet Lodge

THE EUROPEAN POLICY OF THE SPD

SMALL STATE DIPLOMACY: New Zealand and the European Community (*forthcoming*)

AMERICAN BEHAVIOUR DURING THE BERLIN CRISIS OF 1948–49 (*with Avi Shlaim*) (*forthcoming*)

THE EUROPEAN PARLIAMENT AND THE EUROPEAN COMMUNITY

Valentine Herman
Juliet Lodge

St. Martin's Press   New York

10010
Printed in Great Britain
Library of Congress Catalog Card Number 77-26889
ISBN 0-312-27074-7
First published in the United States of America in 1978

Library of Congress Cataloging in Publication Data

Herman, Valentine.
The European Parliament and the European community.

Bibliography: p.
Includes index.
1. European Parliament. I. Lodge, Juliet, joint
author. II. Title.
JN36.H4   341.24′2   77-26889
ISBN 0-312-27074-7

To

SUSANNAH

and to

CHRIS, TERRY-ANITA AND NEIL

Contents

Preface   ix

1 Introduction   1

PART ONE

2 The Functions, Powers and 'Decline' of Parliaments   13

3 The Legislative and Financial Powers of the European
  Parliament   24

4 The Control Powers of the European Parliament   44

5 The Powers and Functions of the European Parliament   64

PART TWO

6 Democratic Legitimacy and Direct Elections   73

7 Citizens and the Elections   94

8 The European Parliament and the Media   120

9 The Dual Mandate   141

10 The Case for a Bicameral Parliament   157

Bibliography   179

Index   191

Preface

This book grew out of a conversation over wine in the café of the European Parliament in Luxembourg. It was written over a six-month period while Herman was at the Universities of Aarhus, Essex and Erasmus, and Lodge at the London School of Economics and Political Science, and the Universities of Auckland and Hull. During this time more wine was consumed: our contribution to alleviating Community wine lake problems.

We have attempted to clarify aspects of the debate about the nature and extension of the European Parliament's powers, their relationship to direct elections, problems arising out of these, and the position of the Parliament in the Community's institutional balance.

We wish to thank officials of the Directorate-Generals of Research and Documentation, and Information and Public Relations, in Luxembourg and London, for their assistance. The views in this book do not imply their endorsement but represent instead only those of the two authors who, while collectively accepting responsibility for errors of fact and interpretation, individually are quite prepared to attribute them to each other.

Several people – whom it would be invidious to name – commented on various chapters of the book, and we are grateful to them for making our lives more difficult. We also owe an intellectual debt to a number of colleagues who, in their infinite wisdom, refused invitations to read parts of the draft manuscript.

We should also like to thank Peter Lodge for his exacting reading of the manuscript, and Anne-Marie Christiansen and Joanne Brunt for typing it. Football provided by Darlington and Chelsea, and music by the Who, the Rolling Stones and Vivaldi, were also of considerable assistance.

Our gratitude also goes to our families for their almost infinitesimal forbearance, interruptions, backrubs and provision of light relief. And finally, we should like to thank each other for making collaboration both great fun and absolute hell.

V.H., J.L.

London, October 1977

1 Introduction

> A consequence of the Parliament's new authority will be an increase in its powers, which will take place gradually in the course of the progressive development of the European Union, notably through a growing exercise of the legislative function. It goes without saying that the Parliament should assume an important responsibility in the construction of the Union.
>
> Tindemans Report (1976) p. 29

Why have direct elections to the European Parliament? The answers to this question have raised anxiety among member governments of the European Community (EC) for it has been recognised that direct elections hold the key to the future of the EC. They have been seen as confirming and defining the existence, nature and political form of the Community – as resolving its ontological problems in favour of federalism. The elections would thus undermine any illusions that the Community was (and would remain) an apolitical, functionally specific international organisation, inspired by functionalist premises, and devoid of political import or implications for the exercise of power by the component member states' governments.[1]

As Emilio Colombo, President of the European Parliament, points out:

> By solemnly signing in Brussels on 20 September 1976 the Act on the Election in May–June 1978 of the European Parliament by Direct Universal Suffrage, the Nine responded to one of the most enduring and popular European aspirations. The most *enduring* because, since it was first put forward at the Hague Conference in 1948, the idea of a European Parliament elected by direct universal suffrage has never lost its attraction. Although it has frequently been disparaged and held up to derision, it could never be completely stifled. The most *popular*, because the present organisation of Europe – although a necessary stage in its development – has none the less failed to elicit the whole-hearted support of its peoples who saw it as something remote from their everyday life. The election of the European Parliament by direct universal suffrage provides an opportunity of bringing the debate on Europe into the public forum and of enlisting the active support of the man in the street for the construction of

1

Europe. Is the direct election of the European Parliament an end in itself? Obviously not; no more than the election of a national assembly, but certainly no less. The eternal question of the purposes of the Parliament is no more relevant to the European Parliament than to a national assembly.[2]

Apart from the political and constitutional questions raised by the holding of direct elections, logistical problems (campaigning regulations, synchronising the day(s) on which the election is held, determining electoral procedures, and so on) have often been regarded by the member governments as so extensive as to justify deferment of the elections pending the accretion of the Parliament's powers. It was argued that the very limited nature both of the European Parliament's powers and the part it played in EC decision-making, indicated that its role in the Community was not strictly analogous to that of national parliaments in the member states. Thus, notwithstanding Members of the European Parliament's (MEPs') aspirations, there would be little point in holding elections to the Parliament in the same manner as elections to national parliaments. Since the elections would be neither concerned with the election of politicians to form a supranational government, nor with the election of politicians to exercise significant decision-making powers, they would be tantamount to an elaborate and costly way of filling seats in the European Parliament that could be adequately filled by other indirect methods. It was argued that MEPs could continue to be selected from among the members of national parliaments, or that this indirect method of selection was perfectly adequate. It was further implied that only if the European Parliament had more extensive powers could the election of its members by direct universal suffrage be justified.

The opponents of this view argued that only a directly elected European Parliament would justify the extension of the chamber's powers. This argument derived from the belief that only directly elected MEPs could legitimately seek an extension of the Parliament's powers – especially its legislative powers – so that, like national MPs, they could act on behalf of, and be directly accountable to, their electorate. The argument was predicated on four principles. Firstly, in the name of 'democracy', citizens should be given the right to elect their representatives by direct suffrage. Secondly, these representatives should be subjected to periodic elections and thereby held accountable for their actions. Thirdly, these representatives should protect and further the interests of those whom they represented. And fourthly, there should be respect for the principle of no taxation without representation. Of these, the second and third could not be realised without first extending the powers of the European Parliament. So long as the European Parliament was devoid of legislative power, MEPs could expect neither to protect nor advance, like their national counterparts, the interests of voters. For what, then, were they to be held accountable to electors?

Given that the European Parliament was regarded as the chamber representing the interests of the people (as opposed to the member governments), and that the holding of elections was regarded as an essential facet of democracy, it was argued that it was more important initially to secure the democratic basis of the Parliament, and subsequently work from this to extend its powers.[3]

Suspicion that this was indeed the intention of MEPs and exponents of direct elections led the member governments to prevaricate over the issue. The dilemma of deciding whether first to increase the Parliament's powers, and then to elect it directly, or vice versa, came to be seen in terms of the chicken and the egg. Even the gradualist strategy for introducing a new method for the selection of MEPs, advanced in 1960 by a working party chaired by Ferdinand Dehousse of the Parliament's Committee on Political Affairs and Institutional Questions, was not seriously examined by the member governments.[4]

Since the Rome Treaty empowers the Parliament to draw up proposals for elections by direct universal suffrage in accordance with a uniform procedure in all member states, failure on the part of the member governments to agree to the holding of direct elections could be interpreted as violation of the Treaty. In May 1969 the Parliament debated the failure of the Council of Ministers to consider the 1960 Convention, and the legal terms (under Article 175) to remedy this omission. The threat led the Council of Ministers to instruct the Committee of Permanent Representatives to consider the matter.[5] Even so, it was not until September 1976 that the member governments agreed to direct elections, and even then they were not to be held in accordance with a uniform electoral procedure, but in accordance with national provisions. Pressure for the Council to agree to the holding of elections had grown in view of the accretion of the Parliament's budgetary powers in 1975. Yet the basic dilemma remained largely unresolved, as became apparent in early 1977 when both the British and French governments indicated their opposition to the Parliament acquiring either extended powers or legislative competence following its direct election.

Irresolution over direct elections has been born of two main assumptions concerning the implications of such elections for firstly the Council of Ministers, secondly, the 'sovereignty' of the member states, and thirdly the nature of 'union' in the Community – should it be inter-governmental or supranational? Let us consider these in greater detail.

The first assumption is that direct elections to the Parliament will lead to its demanding increased powers. Any such powers would have to be approved by the Council of Ministers. Since the type of powers sought by the Parliament have been concerned with the acquisition of legislative authority, and since the EC's supreme legislative body is the

Council of Ministers, any legislative authority granted to the European Parliament would limit, if not compete with, that of the Council, and hence of the member governments represented in it.[6] For a number of reasons associated with the composition and functions of the Council of Ministers, all measures likely to restrict its autonomy and that of the member governments vis-à-vis supranational bodies have been resisted. These reasons are worth listing briefly. They hinge on the notion of the MEPs being inferior to members of the Council of Ministers – 'inferior' in that, in national terms, MEPs have lesser status than members of the Council. It has therefore been argued that it would be improper to grant powers to a body comprising junior, part-time and backbench politicians that would curtail, even by co-decision, the autonomy of a body (also part-time) of government ministers. Similarly, it has been reasoned that senior politicians and ministers are more capable (because they are more experienced and familar with the exigencies and needs of national governments) of taking decisions for the EC, than a body comprising both government and opposition members. In addition, it has been argued that if the dual mandate should be abolished, opposition members (of any of the member states) might secure more seats than the governments in the European Parliament, and ·then pursue policies conflicting with the 'national interest' as defined by the governments.

Moreover, in the past, parliamentary parties tended to appoint to the European Parliament lacklustre backbench MPs. Hence in opposing accretion of the Parliament's powers, government argued that junior, subordinate and sometimes opposition politicians should not be afforded rights over their national and governmental seniors at a supra-national level in EC bodies.

In addition, it was felt that if MEPs argued that they directly represented EC citizens, then the Council of Ministers' claims to represent national interests – and by definition those of citizens within each of the member states — would be undermined. This in turn, it was argued, would lead to pressure for the Council of Ministers to be relegated to the role of an upper chamber in a bicameral, federal parliament. It was feared that the Council's powers would become limited – as have those of the House of Lords – and that it would be little more than a token and ineffectual representative of the member states. While such fears may have been unrealistic, they were closely linked with concern lest the holding of direct elections would alter the EC's institutional balance, and herald the demise of the Council of Ministers.[7] The latter, having the sole power to determine whether or not to approve the holding of direct elections (and by implication having the power to deliberate upon its own role in EC decision-making), demurred.

To summarise the first assumption, the holding of direct elections was thought likely to lead to demands for the accretion of the Parliament's powers. This could only be accomplished at the expense of the Council of Ministers, the body which exercised legislative powers in the EC. The question became one of whether the expense of holding elections could be justified prior to a significant increase in the Parliament's powers. Would it be possible to motivate voters to elect a body devoid of effective power? If not, should the powers of a body comprising backbenchers be increased, when its members lacked either the experience or status of their counterparts in the Council of Ministers, many of whom could claim that they were directly elected in national elections, and the legitimate representatives of the people and governments of the member states, something which MEPs (although members of national parliaments and hence representatives of voters in the member states) could not claim to be in respect of EC citizens.

In other words, it was assumed that the concomitants of direct elections would be, firstly, the development of the European Parliament as the EC's legislature; secondly, that this development could (and would) be justified in terms of the need for EC citizens to be able to rely on their representatives to protect and advance their interests; thirdly, that the directly elected and democratically legitimate European Parliament would claim similar powers and functions to those of the member states' legislatures. The second assumption concerning the implication of direct elections is linked both to the notion of the possession of democratic legitimacy by the EC and the European Parliament, and also to the concept of parliamentary sovereignty.

It has been suggested that the European Parliament would acquire democratic legitimacy through being directly elected by EC citizens, and that through the elections the Parliament would not only be seen as the locus of sovereignty but that the EC would become sovereign and acquire an existence independent of the member states. This argument is couched in terms of sovereignty being expressed through the consent of the people to the exercise of certain powers on their behalf by their parliamentary representatives. We return to this later. Suffice it here to note that the idea of European elections leading to the acquisition of sovereignty by the EC has resulted in competitive situations existing on the one hand between the European Parliament and the national parliaments, and on the other between the Community and the member states.

The competition between the European and national parliaments can be envisaged in terms of the struggle for legislative powers, and as the expression of popular sovereignty.[8] It is often erroneously thought that any acquisition of legislative competence by the European Parliament must be at the expense of the national parliaments.[9] This presupposes that if the European Parliament were to acquire legislative powers, it would exercise them in identical spheres to the national parliaments – that it would, therefore, seek to usurp the authority of the national parliaments. Not only does this overlook the scope of authority and the limits of the competence of EC bodies as defined by the Rome Treaty, but it assumes that national parliaments would be obliged to conform to whatever prescriptions or legislative programmes were placed before the European Parliament. There are no grounds for supposing that this would or could be the case even if the European Parliament were to be invested with extensive powers and authority. However, it probably derives from the fact that in areas of the EC's activities where there is a clash between national and Community laws, the latter take precedence; but this is only the case in areas specified by the Treaty of Rome.

The notion of competition between the powers of the European and national parliaments is also born out of a tendency to conflate and identify the latter with national governments, and hence with the body in which they are represented at the supranational level, the Council of Ministers. It would, in fact, be correct to assume that competition for the exercise of legislative powers at the supranational level would take place between the Council and the European Parliament, especially in view of the latter having acquired limited co-decision powers with the Council. In this respect, members of the Council of Ministers clearly have an interest in curtailing the powers of the European Parliament.

In addition to anxiety over the exercise of legislative power by parliamentary organs at the supranational level, the national parliaments' fears of being usurped or having their authority diminished by the European Parliament also derives from concern over the extent to which they have effective powers to scrutinise and supervise the legislative activities of EC bodies, in particular the Council of Ministers. For the most part, national parliaments have no direct role in EC decision-making and the amount of time they devote to scrutiny of EC proposals and the supervision of ministers in the Council of Ministers is extremely limited. By contrast, the European Parliament is, theoretically at least, in a position to effect some control at the supranational level over legislative outputs. It will only be able to do so in practice, however, if it is granted that right. Were this to be acquired, there can be little doubt that its role in scrutinising EC proposals would appear to be more significant than that of the national parliaments. In this regard, the national parliaments might indeed suffer not only a sense of, but also an actual, deprivation of competence.

This is a particularly sensitive issue given that the other assumption – concerning the implications of direct elections on the sovereignty of the national parliaments and member states – seems to underscore misapprehensions that the overall effect would be to deprive both of autonomy and competence, and to relegate them to inferior roles in the Community. Such apprehensions derive from the notion that, firstly, only the member states are, and can be, sovereign and independent; and secondly, that the joint exercise of power in pursuit of a common good in the Community is tantamount to limiting the independence of the member states in those spheres where joint decisions are taken on the basis of pooled, rather than transferred, sovereignty. So long as the member states are sovereign, the EC has no independent right of existence, for the EC is not sovereign. However, since the concept of sovereignty has become associated with the idea of parliament being the popular repository of sovereignty, it has been suggested that if the citizens of the member states who elected national MPs were also to elect representatives to a supranational parliamentary body, there would be a transfer of popular sovereignty from the national parliaments to the European Parliament. As a result, the national parliaments would lose sovereignty and authority, and become subordinate to the supranational body.

Here two issues once again become intermingled. On the one hand there is incertitude over the nature of sovereignty, and on the other incertitude over the effects on the standing of the national parliaments viv-à-vis the EC following the direct election of the European Parliament.

What the two issues come down to is a suspicion that direct elections will herald the advent of a federal Community.[10] Indeed, in the past the elections have been advanced by federalists and seen as part of a 'federalist plan'. However, to the extent that they are associated with federalist tendencies in the Community today, national parliaments and governments fear that they are but the first step in a process likely to culminate in the creation of a federal union in which the member governments and national parliaments will be relegated to roles akin to those of regional governments and regional parliaments in federations like the Federal Republic of Germany. If this were to prove to be the case, then it is clear why they should associate the elections with losses of sovereignty, autonomy and power for themselves, and why competition vis-à-vis the European Parliament should be envisaged. Similarly, it is easy to understand the member governments' reticence over the years to approve the holding of direct elections. However, since the Council of Ministers ultimately has the power to decide whether or not to agree to any extensions of the European Parliament's powers, such accretions can be almost indefinitely postponed. Thus, it is clear that notwithstanding arguments concerning the transfer of popular sovereignty, power ultimately lies with the member governments. In other words, the implications of direct elections being detrimental to the autonomy and authority of the member states and national parliaments have been exaggerated.

This exaggeration has two sources. Firstly, concern on the part of member governments to ensure that the Community should be founded on intergovernmental, rather than federal or supranational, practices has led them to eschew the introduction of measures or bodies likely to curtail the autonomy of the Council of Ministers (such as majority voting which is only gradually gaining acceptance). Secondly, the traditional functionalist premises concerning the desired goal of inter-national co-operation within functionally specific supranational organisations – the withering away of the nation-state[11] – has led governments to view integration suspiciously, and to regard it as a process that has to be carefully managed if it is not to result in nation-states – and specifically member governments in the EC – being divested of autonomy and sovereignty. Consequently, direct elections have been associated with a number of myths concerning the EC and the powers of its institutions. A good deal of confusion persists.

Somewhat paradoxically, given the limited nature of the European Parliament's powers, it has been implied that the role of the Parliament in the Community, after direct elections, and its role vis-à-vis EC citizens will be more extensive and all-embracing than it in effect can be. For instance, the notion of the European Parliament taking powers away from national parliaments not only presupposes that it has such aspirations but also that it has the power to intervene in the legislative processes of the member states. Furthermore, it assumes that the European Parliament has the ability to decree that it will exercise certain legislative powers in respect of EC matters even though it lacks the basic powers to initiate and pass legislation – those powers being invested in the Commission and Council of Ministers respectively. The Parliament cannot even extend its own legislative competence without the acquiescence of these other bodies, and also action taken by them to facilitate it.

Similarly, the European Parliament's impact on EC publics is paradoxically evaluated. On the one hand there have been suggestions that direct elections would be a waste of time and would not lead to an increase in the European Parliament's legitimacy because the public are unaware of its existence and powers, and would not, in any case, bother to vote for a body devoid of effective decision-making power.[12] On the other hand, it is implied that if the EC public turn out in large numbers to elect their representatives to the European Parlia-ment, the overall effect would be tantamount to a transfer of popular sovereignty from the member states to the Community. Such notions completely overlook the problem associated with conducting direct elections in the member states, and particularly overlook the difficulties associated with making the public aware of the existence, functions and powers of the European Parliament and its Members. They also confuse the notions of allegiance to the nation-state as based on the concept of national identity, and the act of voting for a supranational parliament.[13] In other words, they presuppose that a European citizenry exists and as a body wishes to give expression to a European identity transcending the nation-states. This does not, in fact, exist, and even the member governments have recognised the need for developing public awareness of the EC's dimensions and giving EC citizens some tangible expression of the fact that their state is a member of the EC. However, not even the long-mooted EC passport is an expression of EC nation-hood, and the EC Citizens' Charter has still to be drafted.[14]

Clearly, both the opponents and advocates of direct elections have confused a number of distinct and separate issues. They exhibit a lack of understanding of both the short-term implications of, and problems associated with, the actual conduct of direct elections vis-à-vis EC citizens, member governments, national parliaments, MEPs, national party groups and the European Parliament's party groups. They also exhibit a lack of understanding of the long-term implications of direct elections, and their concomitants, for the nature and scope of the European Parliament's powers and the position of the Parliament in, and the balance of, the EC's institutional arrangements. In Part One we shall attempt to clarify the nature and extent of the European Parliament's present powers; and in Part Two we shall explore problems associated with the elections and with the Parliament's acquisition of democratic legitimacy. Then we shall examine the impact of the elections on the institutional balance of the Community by advancing changes that could be made to enable decision-making to become more effective. Thus, although it is often said that direct elections will 'democratise' the EC (an argument that presupposes that EC decision-making is not democratic, when what is in fact meant is that until now citizens have not directly elected representatives to the European Parliament), a number of additional measures must be taken before this can be accomplished, or before the EC can attain democratic legitimacy.

Notes

1. These notions recur in most of the literature on European institutions which is too vast to cite here.
2. Directorate-General for Research and Documentation, *Elections to the European Parliament by Direct Universal Suffrage* (Luxembourg: European Parliament, 1977) p. 5.
3. Ibid., p. 7.
4. Directorate-General for Parliamentary Documentation and Information, *The Case for Elections to the European Parliament by Direct Universal Suffrage* (Luxembourg: European Parliament, 1969).
5. For details see W. Clark, *The Politics of the Common Market* (Englewood Cliffs, N. J.: Prentice-Hall, 1967) p. 81, and J. Lodge, 'The Reform of the European Parliament', *Political Science*, XXV (1973) 63–66.
6. *Elections to the European Parliament by Direct Universal Suffrage*, p. 7.
7. Dr Hallstein (then President of the Commission) indicated as much in 1963. See M. Forsyth, *The Parliament of the European Communities* (London: PEP, 1964) p. 88.
8. K. von Lindeiner-Wildau, *La Supranationalité en tant que Principe de Droit* (Leiden: Sijthoff, 1970) pp. 137 ff.

10   *The European Parliament and the European Community*

. See *Direct Elections to the EEC Assembly or European Parliament* (London: Safeguard Britain Campaign, 1977).
10. F. Cardis, *Fédéralisme et Intégration Européenne* (Lausanne: Centre de Recherches Européennes, 1964) pp. 42–56, 190–4, 225–31.
11. See D. Mitrany, *The Functional Theory of Politics* (London: Martin Robertson, 1975).
12. See M. Steed, 'The European Parliament: The Significance of Direct Election', *Government and Opposition*, VI (1971) 462–76.
13. J. Lodge, 'Loyalty and the EEC: The Limitations of the Functionalist Approach', *Political Studies*, XXVI (1978) (forthcoming).
14. See the Copenhagen Summit Declaration.

Part One

2 The Functions, Powers and 'Decline' of Parliaments

There is ... an increasingly important and influential school of thought which maintains that the problem of legitimacy in the Communities is intimately associated with the functions of Parliament, and that in this respect it is necessary to increase the powers of the European Parliament until that function is properly performed. This reasoning is based, not only on the view that legitimacy is lacking in the Community institutions as they are now but also on the related view that the transfer of functions from a national to a Community level weakens the National Parliaments and that some substitute parliamentary function must be provided at a Community level. What is needed in this argument, however, is a much more precise and realistic understanding of the role of National Parliaments. What has been particularly lacking is an articulation of what parliamentary functions really are.

David Coombes, 'Introductory Study to Papers on National Parliaments', in Directorate-General for Research and Documentation of the European Parliament (ed.), *Symposium on European Integration and the Future of Parliaments in Europe* (European Parliament, 1975) pp. 23–6, at p. 23.

With a few exceptions the Nine's national parliaments adopted both their constitutional role and their legislative procedures many years ago. Then, both the parliaments and the political systems within which they operated faced vastly different problems from those which challenge them today. Since the end of the Second World War the following – and this is no more than a partial catalogue of such events – have radically affected the viability of legislative institutions: the increase of bureaucratic involvement in the initiation and implementation of public policy; the increased size and ever-expanding role of central government; the increasing importance of international organisations, agencies and bodies and the implications these have had for national sovereignty; the growth of multinational corporations and the problems of controlling their activities and ensuring their responsibility; the tendency of governments to consult with pressure groups and interested organisations before a measure is drafted and introduced into the legislature; and so on. By far the most important of these events lies in the fact that governments have, over the years, taken on an ever-expanding array of tasks: this point is typically illustrated by reference to increase in phenomena such as the level of government expenditure, the quality and quantity of enacted legislation and delegated legislation, the number of local and national civil servants, etc.[1]

These developments, and especially the growth of governments, have given rise to a number of basic problems which are central to the structure and functioning of legislative institutions.[2] The most important of these are:

- to establish what, if anything, a parliament can contribute to a system of government in an advanced industrial society; that is, to adapt the idea of a representative institution which was conceived many centuries ago to the needs of the present day;

- to determine what the nature of the relationship between the legislative and executive branches of government should be. A misunderstanding of the historical dimension of this relationship has frequently led to claims that the powers of legislatures have 'declined' and those of 'executives' have grown;[3]

- to adapt constitutional provisions, which might have been drawn up in a pre-technological era, to the pressures, demands and pace of contemporary society and, especially, to decide whether legislative bodies should attempt to tackle the problems of law-making in the last quarter of the twentieth century;[4]

- to establish and maintain a legitimate role for the legislative branch of government, 'legitimate' in the sense that the tasks it performs and the decisions which emanate from it are accepted by the people over whom it has some authority.[5]

Frequently, most or all of these points are grouped together by commentators who use them to demonstrate the 'crisis of parliamentary democracy', and/or to illustrate 'the decline of legislatures, and the growth of executives' thesis. There is widespread acceptance by those who are disillusioned with the performance of political institutions that, *vis-à-vis* executives, parliaments have declined in power because of the way that they perform – or, more accurately, fail to perform – a number of functions which are believed to be central to the legislature's role. Before it is possible to evaluate the strength of such claims it is necessary to examine what the functions of parliaments are.

(i) The Functions of Parliaments

Almost all scholars of legislative institutions adopt – usually explicitly, occasionally implicitly – a functional approach, and the relevant literature contains a plethora of functions attributed to parliaments.[6] Indeed, it has been suggested that 'In part, this diversity is due to variations in national political structures and constitutional practices, but no less to differences in vocabulary, conceptualisation, and perspectives of the authors'.[7] Some indication of the extent of this diversity can be obtained from a consideration of a number of attempts to delineate the functions of parliaments.

Over one hundred years ago, in his classic work *The English Constitution*,[8] Walter Bagehot set out the following six functions of the House of Commons:

1. The elective function (with regard to the executive), 'the main function of the House of Commons'.
2. The expressive function, 'to express the mind of the English people on all matters which come before it'.
3. The teaching function, Parliament being 'a great and open council of considerable men [which] . . . ought to teach the nation what it does not know'.
4. The informing function, 'to lay . . . the grievances and complaints of particular interests . . . before the nation, which is the present sovereign'. This, Bagehot was 'disposed to reckon as the second function of Parliament in point of importance, that to some extent it makes us hear what otherwise we should not'.
5. The legislative function, for 'the annual legislation of Parliament is a result of singular importance; were it not so, it could not be, as it often is considered, the sole result of its annual assembling'.
6. The financial function, which was considered as part of the legislative function.[9]

Evidence of the contemporary validity of Bagehot's list of functions is provided by the way in which recent authors have adapted them to an examination of opposition in the European Communities,[10] and to a study of the German Bundestag.[11]

Klaus von Beyme has advanced the following related set of 'six principal functions of Parliament in the input and output sectors of the political systems' of Western Europe:

1. The representation and articulation function.
2. The communication function.
3. The controlling function.
4. The function of participation in the appointment and dismissal of the executive.

5. The legislative function.
6. The recruiting function.[12]

A third catalogue of functions comes from Colette Flesch and Michel Delvaux who in a recent study of the Luxembourg Chamber of Deputies proposed the following:

1. Law-making, that is, the right to initiate legislation, the right to vote on it, and 'the auxiliary rights to consider individual items of a bill and propose amendments'.
2. Information and warning, 'the traditional parliamentary function of "the voice of the people" and [drawing] the government's attention to the complexities of a problem or the inopportuneness of a proposal'.
3. Organisation of the Chamber.
4. Making and breaking governments.[13]

For our present purposes we draw on a final check-list of the functions of parliament in a 'liberal state' as set out by Donald Chapman:

1. The power to decide over the duration of government.
2. Providing members of the government and determining government membership.
3. The power to make rules binding on the government – legislative power, power over the budget, power to receive and approve the general and detailed policy of the government.
4. Confrontation between government and opposition, focusing political choice for the electorate, through the party system.
5. The focal point also for interest groups and expression of grievances, acting as a point of communication between citizen and government.[14]

While these lists of parliamentary functions emphasise the different approaches to the subject, it must be noted that, somewhat paradoxically, there are quite distinct similarities between them. For example, Bagehot's legislative function is shared by von Beyme, expressed as a 'law-making' function by Flesch and Delvaux, and seen as a component part of 'the power to make rules binding on the government' by Chapman; Bagehot's elective function is rephrased by von Beyme as 'the function of participation in the appointment and dismissal of the executive', as the 'making and breaking' of governments by Flesch and Delvaux, and as 'providing members of the government and determining government membership' by Chapman.

It would not be particularly fruitful for us to try and synthesise the various approaches. Instead, some general observations concerning the functional approach are in order. In any consideration of what a parliament does it is essential to distinguish between its 'powers' and its 'functions', a point to which we return in detail below and in later chapters. Whereas the powers of a parliament (legislative, financial, control, etc.) can be viewed as components of the functions of that parliament, the opposite is not the case. Although the powers of a parliament can almost universally be found in the neatly numbered articles and clauses of a constitution, basic law, or similar documents, it is difficult, if not impossible, to locate the functions of parliament in an equally convenient source. It follows from this that the *functions* of a parliament are more difficult to determine, wider in scope, and more likely to vary from one constitutional system to another, than are the *powers* of a parliament. While this distinction between the powers and functions of a parliament might seen commonsensical, it is noticeable that much of the literature on legislative institutions (including that of some of the authors quoted above) has failed to grasp it. This can be seen from a brief consideration of the 'decline of parliaments' thesis.

(ii) The 'Decline' of Parliaments

Classical theorists of representative democracy placed a common emphasis on the representative function and the legislative, financial and control powers of parliaments. The creation of parliaments was meant to achieve two objectives: on the one hand to ensure that the executive behaved within the constraints outlined by the legislature; and, on the other hand, to ensure that the general rules established by the legislature were produced collectively by men who had the people's confidence.[15] According to Blondel, it was originally held as axiomatic that the function of legislatures was to make laws, that is, to pass the most general rules under which countries were to be governed, the argument being that, 'if the "people" are to be sovereign, or at least as powerful as possible, their representatives should be concerned primarily with the most general rules. Executives are needed to keep the country going, but legislatures could and should decide on the general rules.'[16]

Because of various political, economic, social and technological developments over the last century, the nature of laws is very different from what it once was. In Blondel's words:

Locke and Montesquieu looked at societies in which state involvement in social and economic matters was minimal if not non-existent. For them, statutes did not mean education or housing acts; they covered problems of private property, individual rights, family law – in short the regulation of private relationships between individuals. Slowly the balance tilted, through the nineteenth and twentieth centuries, toward public legislation establishing new agencies and regulating social and economic matters. But no one drew the conclusion that this entailed a different type of involvement for legislatures.[17]

These developments have given rise to a considerable literature which laments the 'decline' of parliaments. This decline is viewed in terms of the way parliaments now perform their legislative, financial and control powers and their representative function, compared to the way that they performed them some hundred or so years ago in a supposed 'golden age' of parliamentary government. It is necessary for us to give some consideration to the 'decline' thesis as it will provide a backcloth against which we can evaluate the performance of the European Parliament's power and functions.

Firstly, it is argued that a number of factors have led to a decline in parliament's performance of its *legislative* powers. Changes in the nature of the law from an emphasis on the rights and duties of citizens to national and international matters relating to all aspects of the organisation of society are important in this respect. Attention must also be drawn to the volume, scope and complexity of contemporary legislation which is now prepared – and possibly only fully understood – by large-scale bureaucracies, whereas once it was drafted by individual Members of Parliament. Limitations imposed by the parliamentary time-table, the increasing claims on this time made by governments, and the importance that governments attach to implementing their election manifestoes combine to make parliamentary time a scarce resource, and one that is distributed to individual MPs only on rare occasions and only under exceptional circumstances. Furthermore, the ponderousness of parliaments and the slow and deliberative nature of the legislative process act as obstacles to the making of swift and firm decisions needed in the present technocratic era. Finally, it is argued that the performance of the legislative power has declined because of various constitutional and other limitations affecting the introduction of legislation by MPs which has financial implications – as many, if not most, such legislative items have financial implications, these limitations seriously reduce the MPs' ability to introduce legislation which will have any impact on society.

A second set of facts illustrate the way in which parliaments' *financial* powers have declined. These derive from the magnitude and intricacy of contemporary budgets which in their totality are beyond the understanding of both individual legislators, and even perhaps a committee of non-financial experts. This state of affairs is worsened by the fact that while, in theory, budgets contain expenditure and revenue figures for the coming financial year, in practice such expenditure and revenue are part of the ongoing financial commitments of the state. This makes their review, when conducted on a yearly basis, problematical, and furthermore contributes towards a lack of understanding of medium- and long-term economic goals and commitments. To this it must be added that a very high percentage of the expenditure and revenue contained in any single budget is committed to the existing obligations of the state and, as a consequence, the resultant amount of legislative – and for that matter executive – manoeuvre for alternative or innovative policies is extremely limited. Finally, although parliaments have, in conjunction with non-parliamentary agencies (such as Audit Offices and Comptroller and Auditors-General) established various procedures to approve the accounts of expenditure of the state, the existence of several instances of waste, misuse of funds, corruption of public figures, etc., has led to serious doubts being cast on the efficacy of such auditing procedures.

Thirdly, various additional factors have contributed to a decline in parliaments' *control* powers. The major cause of this is the growth of mass, organised and disciplined parties which have led to parliamentary debates and votes becoming a mock struggle or formality containing few elements of surprise or drama. Most matters are now decided in party caucus in advance of being publicly debated on the floor of the chamber or in a committee of the legislature. Consequently, the proceedings of parliament and the outcome of its debates and votes are often predictable and of little interest to the public. A closely related point is that, for various reasons mainly concerned with the party basis of governments, parliaments are unable or unwilling to use their major procedural controlling devices – such as votes of confidence, motions of censure, impeachment, etc. – and these have ossified and taken on the nature of 'nuclear' weapons (never to be used, but kept only for threatening purposes) in parliament's procedural arsenal. Also, the control power of parliament has declined because the mass media perform a number of important tasks – including agenda-setting, conducting investigations and providing a forum for political debate – originally performed by parliament. Lastly, the expansion of the activities of the state has been, at best, very imperfectly matched by an expansion of the instruments of parliamentary control.

Finally, it is argued that parliament and especially MPs' *representative* function has declined for a number of reasons. One is the development (already referred to) of the media: MPs can now communicate effectively with the public and their constituencies through the media; the public can use the media to bring matters to the attention of MPs; and, as a result of this, the personal links between an MP and his constituents have largely declined in importance. Opinion polls and the emphasis placed on them by MPs reinforce this trend as MPs no longer have to rely on personal and direct contacts with the public; 'public opinion' can now be gauged more easily, more accurately and with less personal cost to the MP through opinion polls than it could in earlier times. The decline of the representative function has been further exacerbated by the development of pressure and interest groups which provide an alternative – and often more effective – avenue to the government than the parliament or its individual members. In addition, such groups have come to place increasing reliance on direct action to press their cases – again, often effectively – when conventional, parliamentary methods have failed. And a final reason for the decline of the representative function is the increasing apathy, and alienation from the business of government, of the public, many of whom place very little importance on, and show very little interest in, politics, politicians or parliament.

It is not our intention to give much further consideration to these arguments. Indeed, in spite of the various trends already noted it is in fact problematical to evaluate the scale and import of the decline of parliaments. While some writers seek to locate this decline in a historical setting, others try to support the thesis by normative and abstract arguments. Moreover there is no consensus as to what parliaments have declined from or what they have declined to. Furthermore, considerable confusion exists as to whether the decline of parliaments' powers and functions vis-à-vis the executive and other political, social and economic forces is a relative or an absolute phenomenon. Indeed, as Loewenberg notes, 'Decline, in short, is in the eye of the beholder and depends on his analytical perspective'.[18]

Before leaving this subject, it is necessary to note that in recent years an additional element has been added to the more traditional aspects of the 'decline of parliaments' thesis. Membership of the European Community has involved a transfer of certain law-making powers on a range of social and economic matters from the national authorities of the member states to the executive institutions of the Community. Whether this involves a 'pooling', a 'limitation' or a 'loss' of sovereignty for the member states is not a matter which need detain us. However, the import of EC membership for our current argument is that the powers of the individual countries' national parliaments have been reduced over various legislative and financial matters without a corresponding – let alone compensatory – increase being made in the powers of the European Parliament.[19] Whereas national governments have maintained control over European legislation through the Committee of Permanent Representatives (CPR) and the Council of Ministers, neither the national parliaments nor the European Parliament have managed to exercise effective control over such legislation. It is argued that the national parliaments are becoming impotent, and while the European Parliament does not have authority over Community affairs comparable to that of the national parliaments over national affairs, there is a reduction in the amount of legislative influence and parliamentary democracy in the Community. The argument sometimes put to the European Parliament is that 'There is no cause to create a new mode of parliamentary control since each of us is accountable to his own national parliament'. However, the scrutiny procedures of the national parliaments afford rudimentary surveillance over the activities of the EC executive – specifically the Council. In most instances such surveillance is of a *post hoc* nature and is not tantamount to a control function. Similarly, the argument that individual Council members are accountable to national parliaments does not meet the criticism of inadequate parliamentary control. While it is often alleged that increasing the European Parliament's control powers will increase national parliaments' loss of sovereignty, this need not be the case, since, on the one hand, the abolition of existing scrutiny committees is not advocated and, on the other hand, effective democratic control of the Council can only be ensured at the supranational level by a supranational body.

(iii)   The Powers and Functions of the European Parliament

Our discussion has isolated important factors associated with the functioning of legislative institutions, and our unit of analysis has been primarily the national parliament. We shall now consider the powers and functions of the European Parliament.

The European Parliament claims that it has three main *powers*:[20]

1. A *legislative* power, 'to tell the Council of Ministers what it thinks of the Commission's legislative proposals'.[21]
2. A *financial* power, 'with the Council, to hammer out the Community budget'.[22]
3. A *control* power, 'to exert some political control over the Council and the Commission'.[23]

In Chapters 3 and 4 we shall examine the legislative, financial and control powers of the European Parliament. By making comparisons with the national parliaments of the member states we shall subject the European Parliament's claim to be a parliament to close scrutiny. Chapter 5 will consider the European Parliament in the light of the 'decline of parliaments' thesis and the basic problems of legislative institutions mentioned above.

In Part Two a detailed examination of the functions of the European Parliament will be undertaken. From our discussions so far it should be apparent that no list of functions which can be advanced for the European Parliament can be considered definitive, exhaustive or unchallengeable. However, it is our contention that the European Parliament performs, or has the potential for performing, the following five *functions*:

1. The *information* function.

2. The *communication* function.
3. The *education* function.
4. The *legitimation* function.
5. The *representation* function.

From the above it is evident that the European Parliament has more functions than powers. Furthermore, its potential for increasing its influence in the EC following elections lies in its exploiting its existing functions rather than seeking to extend or develop new powers. But our ideas run ahead of our arguments, and we shall not return to such matters until later.

Notes

1. See K. D. Bracher, 'Problems of Parliamentary Democracy in Europe', *Daedalus*, XCIII (1964) 179–98.
2. These developments have given rise to a sizeable literature on the concept of 'government overload'. See, for example, A. King (ed.), *Why is Britain Becoming Harder to Govern* (London: BBC, 1976) esp. chap. 1; J. Douglas, 'The Overloaded Crown', *British Journal of Political Science*, XLVI (1976) 483–505; and M. Crozier, S. P. Huntington and J. Watanuki, *The Crisis of Democracy* (New York: New York Univ. Press, 1975).
3. This thesis was first expressed in A. Lowell, *Governments and Parties in Continental Europe* (Cambridge, Mass.: Harvard Univ. Press, 1896), and in Lord Bryce, *The American Commonwealth* (London: Macmillan, 1888) vol. I. For more recent treatments see J. Blondel, *Comparative Legislatures* (Englewood Cliffs, N.J.: Prentice-Hall, 1973) chaps. 1–2; G. Loewenberg (ed.), *Modern Parliaments: Change or Decline?* (New York: Aldine-Atherton, 1971); and K. Wheare, *Legislatures*, 2nd ed. (London: Oxford Univ. Press, 1968) chap. 2.
4. See V. Herman 'Who Legislates in the Modern World?', *The Parliamentarian*, LVII (1976) 93–9.
5. 'A problem of legitimacy arises when the procedures and methods by which political authority is exercised are not acceptable to its subjects.' D. Coombes, 'Introductory Study to Papers on National Parliaments', in Directorate-General for Research and Documentation of the European Parliament (ed.), *Symposium on European Integration and the Future of Parliaments in Europe* (hereinafter *Symposium*) (Luxembourg: European Parliament, 1975) pp. 23–6, at p. 23.
6. See R. Packenham, 'Legislatures in Political Development', in A. Kornberg and L. D. Musolf (eds.), *Legislatures in Developmental Perspective* (Durham, N.C.: Duke Univ. Press, 1970) pp. 521–82.
7. E. Damgaard, 'Functions of Parliament in the Danish Political System', in *Symposium*, pp. 38–48, at p. 39.
8. W. Bagehot, The English Constitution (London: Fontana, 1963 ed.) chap. 4.
9. Ibid., chap. 4. It is necessary to quote Bagehot's exact words on the last function: 'Some persons will perhaps think that I ought to enumerate a sixth

function of the House of Commons – a financial function. But I do not consider that, upon broad principle, and omitting legal technicalities, the House of Commons has any special function with respect to other legislation. It is to rule in both, and to rule in both through the Cabinet. Financial legislation is of necessity a yearly recurring legislation; but frequency of occurrence does not indicate a diversity of nature or compel an antagonism of treatment.'

10. G. Zellentin, 'Form and Functions of Opposition in the European Communities', *Government and Opposition*, II (1967) 416–35.

11. U. Thaysen, 'The German Bundestag – the Guardian of Democratic Stability', in *Symposium*, pp. 49–60, at p. 49.

12. K. von Beyme, 'Basic Trends in the Developments of the Functions of Parliament in Western Europe', in *Symposium*, pp. 11–22, at p. 11.

13. C. Flesch and M. Delvaux, 'The Luxembourg Chamber of Deputies: A Microcosmic Image of a Small Country', in *Symposium*, pp. 114–32, at pp. 121–4.

14. D. Chapman, 'Parliament and European Union', in *Symposium*, pp. 180–97, at p. 180.

15. See Damgaard, in *Symposium*, p. 40.

16. Blondel, *Comparative Legislatures*, p. 4.

17. Ibid., p. 13.

18. G. Loewenberg, 'The Role of Parliaments in Modern Political Systems', in Loewenberg, *Modern Parliaments*, pp. 1–21, at p. 15.

19. See J. Taylor, 'British Membership of the European Communities: The Question of Parliamentary Sovereignty', *Government and Opposition*, X (1975) 278–93; and M. Kolinsky, 'Parliamentary Scrutiny of European Legislation', *Government and Opposition*, X (1975) 46–69.

20. Directorate-General for Information and Public Relations, *The European Parliament* (Luxembourg: European Parliament, 1976) pp. 15–19.

21. Article 137, Treaty Establishing the European Economic Community.

22. Article 203, ibid.

23. Articles 140, 143 and 144, ibid.

3 The Legislative and Financial Powers of the European Parliament

If an improvement of efficiency is defined in terms of what parliament accomplishes in its committees and sub-committees, we should realise that everything it does there could be done by other institutions. The polishing of legislative details and – *horribile dictu* – even law-making itself could be accomplished by a council of state composed of highly qualified experts on legislation, as long as the cabinet remains democratically responsible to the people. Parliament is not even necessary to supervise the bureaucracy. Everybody knows that parliamentary supervision has become merely a part of a much larger system of supervision. To be sure, no one who appreciates the blessings of a parliamentary system would like to live in a community in which parliament had no legislative or supervisory functions. What I want to point out is that so-called productive work is not the basic justification of parliamentary activity. But what is?

Wilhelm Hennis, 'Reform of the Bundestag: The Case for General Debate', in Gerhard Loewenberg (ed.), *Modern Parliaments: Change or Decline?* (1971) pp. 68–9

(i) Is the European Parliament a Parliament?

Curiously, the body which has come to be known as the European Parliament is referred to as the 'Assembly' in the Treaties – often referred to, and thought of, as the 'Constitution of the EC' – which established the European Economic Community; even though these Treaties have been amended on a number of occasions the name of the Assembly has not been changed to accord with its common usage.[1]

It is instructive to document the way in which the original Assembly of the European Coal and Steel Community (ECSC) evolved into the Parliament of the European Economic Community (EEC).[2] The ECSC, established by the Treaty of Paris in 1951, whose executive institution was known as the High Authority, was the first of the European communities. In view of the principles underlying the establishment of the ECSC, a decision was taken to establish a Common Assembly ideally to exercise democratic control over the High Authority in the same general way as the parliaments in the six member states of the Community exercised democratic control over their governments. However, as Buerstedde notes, 'from the start the Common Assembly saw its role not merely as the exercise of an *a posteriori* control of the High Authority. It sought rather to intervene fully in the decision-making process of the ECSC'.[3]

The treaties of Rome which established the EEC and the European Atomic Energy Community (Euratom) were signed in 1957. As the Common Assembly had by that time proved its effectiveness, it was decided to continue and extend the role of the parliamentary body to the three Communities. The 'Convention relative to certain Institutions common to the European Communities' established one single Assembly for the three Communities. However, as Fitzmaurice points out, 'this was not the original intention and was only conceded at the last minute after energetic pressure from the Common Assembly and the Consultative Assembly of the Council of Europe'.[4] The Common Assembly of the ECSC was replaced on 19 March 1958 by a 'single Assembly' which at its first sitting in Strasbourg adopted the title 'European Parliament' or 'European Parliamentary Assembly' to mark the 'fact that it now enjoyed more effective powers' as set out in Articles 137 to 144 of the Treaty of Rome. As Cocks has noted, 'those powers emphasise[d] the new concept in international affairs that the executive organs of the Communities [were] no longer the sole or paramount authority on international questions'.[5] The role of the Assembly was further defined in the first Annual Report of the EEC in 1958:

> The Assembly, composed of representatives of the various peoples, exercises democratic control over the activities of the Community. It has the right to pass a vote of Censure on the Commission. This control, however, is not negative in character, but rather a spur, an inspiration and a help for the activities of the institutions and it brings public opinion of the Community to the support of all steps or endeavours made in the service of Europe.[6]

On 30 March 1962 the Assembly resolved to change its name to the 'European Parliament'.

This brief incursion into the history of the European Parliament reveals, then, that it began life as a 'Common Assembly', six years later it informally changed its name to a 'European Parliament' or 'European Parliamentary Assembly', and some four years later formally adopted its present name which it has had for the last fifteen years. In attempting to answer our question 'Is the European Parliament a parliament?' its changes in nomenclature remind us of a passage from *Alice through the*

Looking Glass:

> 'when I use a word,' Humpty Dumpty said in a rather scornful tone,
> 'it means just what I choose it to mean – neither more nor less.'[7]

Political institutions are not named at random and we take it that their titles do have some greater intrinsic and, of more importance, greater symbolic meaning than Humpty Dumpty's use of words; we also take it as a matter of some significance that over the last twenty-five years the institution has changed its name from an 'Assembly' to a 'Parliament', and has come to be widely known by that name. In the words of Juliet,

> O! be some other name:
> What's in a name? that which we call a rose
> By any other name would smell as sweet'.[8]

While such a loose use of words might be satisfactory to the romantic and/or the non-specialist horticulturalist, it causes problems in the context of political institutions.

Our main task in this and the next chapter is to see whether or not the European Parliament has comparable powers to those of the parliamentary institutions of the EC's nine member states. Indeed, one way to determine whether the European Parliament *is* a parliament is to compare it with other bodies which are widely accepted as being parliaments. Comparison should obviously be made in this regard with the national parliaments of the member states which comprise the Community. An argument could be made, we concede, that the European Parliament should be compared to international bodies such as the Consultative Assembly of the Council of Europe or the Nordic Assembly. We reject this argument, however, basically on two grounds: firstly, that the relationships between the national parliaments and the European Parliament are of a different, special and unique nature from those between the national parliaments and other international bodies; and secondly, on the grounds that the nature of the sharing, or pooling, of sovereignty in the Community is not similar to that in other international organisations, even though they might contain an assembly, council or similarly named body.

Our purpose is, then, to attempt to evaluate the European Parliament's claim to be a parliament by drawing a series of comparisons between its powers on the one hand, and the powers of the national parliaments on the other.[9] As we saw in the last chapter, the European Parliament itself claims that it performs three main tasks: the first is 'to tell the Council of Ministers what it thinks of the Commission's legislative proposals', i.e. a legislative power; the second is 'with the Council to hammer out the Community budget', i.e. a financial power; and the third is 'to exert some political control over the

Council and the Commission', i.e. a control, or oversight, power.[10] On the basis of the way in which the European Parliament performs these powers we shall attempt to answer the question, 'Is the European Parliament a parliament?'[11]

(ii) The Legislative Powers of the European Parliament

Article 189 of the Treaty of Rome sets out four types of EC legislation. In accordance with this Article the Council of Ministers and the Commission may make regulations, issue directives, take decisions, make recommendations or deliver opinions.[12] The nature of, and differences between, these types of legislation are as follows:

1. 'A regulation shall have general application. It shall be binding in its entirety and directly applicable in all Member States.'[13]

Regulations are normally described as laws, and regarded as the most comprehensive legislative instrument of the Community.

2. 'A directive shall be binding, as to the result to be achieved, upon each Member State to which it is addressed, but shall leave to the national authorities the choice of form and methods.'

Directives are generally issued when the different constitutional structures of the member states make it impossible or impracticable for a binding regulation to be issued; they allow national authorities to choose the form and method of their implementation.

3. 'A decision shall be binding in its entirety upon those to whom it is addressed.'

A decision is often equated with an administrative act of a national government because it regulates specific practical matters and is addressed to specific recipients. Decisions are enforceable in national courts.

4. 'Recommendations and opinions shall have no binding force.'

These merely state Community views on certain matters. An indication of the volume of legislation enacted by the Council and the Commission in recent years can be seen from Table 3.1.[14]

Two different legislative procedures are followed in the Community. On the one hand there exists legislation adopted by the Commission, sometimes in consultation with the Management Committees in which the member states are represented; such legislation is frequently of the

TABLE 3.1. Rule-making* in the European Community, 1974–6†

	Regulations	Directives	Decisions	Recommendations and opinions
Council of Ministers:				
1974	357	44	21	99
1975	423	48	107	23
1976†	237	23	20	18
Commission:				
1974	455	14	205	14
1975	580	6	222	7
1976†	259	7	187	4

*Excludes extraordinary instruments, and also daily administrative rules concerning agricultural policy.
†To 1 July 1976.
Source: Compiled from the Register of the EEC *Official Journal*.

nature of either administrative decisions or subordinate legislation. On the other hand there exist Council acts (mainly regulations) adopted on proposals of the Commission after consultation with the European Parliament. It is important to stress that the Parliament plays no role whatsoever in the adoption of Commission acts, and is only marginally involved in the case of Council acts.

Concerning Commission acts, it is necessary to emphasise the similarity between this aspect of the legislative process in the Community and the process of delegated legislation in the member states.[15] One feature of this is the fact that in several instances the Commission is empowered by the Treaty to act independently of the Parliament and the Council;[16] another that many of the Council's legislative items do not receive consideration by the Parliament. However, one difficulty in drawing too close a parallel between legislation of this sort in the Community and delegated legislation in the member states, is that while in the latter case the national parliaments must authorise some body to legislate in their place,[17] in the Community such authorisation stems from the Treaty.[18] None the less, the legislative powers of the Council and the Commission, the volume of legislation enacted,[19] and the often very specific nature of this legislation, all combine to face the European Parliament with certain general problems concerning the performance of the legislative functions. These are similar to those caused by the growth of delegated legislation in the member states.[20]

The main steps in the legislative process concerning Council acts are the following:[21]

1. The Commission draws up proposals for the Council of Ministers after consultation with national officials, experts, representatives of interest groups and other bodies.
2. The Commission's proposal is forwarded to the Council of Ministers and sent – for information – to the Parliament.
3. The Council also sends a copy to the Parliament; a study of the proposal is undertaken by one or more of the Parliament's committees.
4. The Council is obliged to consult the European Parliament, or the Economic and Social Committee, or both, on most matters concerning legislation. In practice it consults the Parliament on all major items even if the Treaties do not specifically provide for such consultation.
5. A committee of the Parliament reports on the matter. This – together with the Commission's proposal – is debated in plenary session. Following the debate, Parliament gives its opinion which may call for amendments to the proposal; this opinion is sent to the Council and the Commission.
6. The Commission may alter its proposal in accordance with Parliament's opinion, or for other reasons. The final decision on the proposal is taken by the Council of Ministers after discussion of the Commission's amended or original proposal.
7. If, for proposals having substantial financial implications, the Council wishes to depart from Parliament's opinion, the 'concertation procedure' is followed. This may result in Parliament giving a second opinion on the proposal. The final decision on the proposal is taken by the Council of Ministers.

What is immediately noticeable about the EC's legislative process is the minimal involvement of the European Parliament. This contrasts with the roles that national parliaments play in the legislative processes of the member states. The main difference between the legislative roles of the European Parliament and the national parliaments can be understood in terms of the separation of powers model, under which

... the Legislature is the most important branch of Government; it lays down basic principles which the Executive has to apply in the implementation of laws and which the Judiciary has to use as its frame of reference in adjudicating cases relating to these laws. The Legislature, then, takes precedence over the other two branches of government since, according to the classical tradition of representative government, the power to legislate resides in Parliament, which alone represents the sovereign people, and which is competent to express the will of the people in the form of law.[22]

By contrast, as Fitzmaurice has noted, in the EC,

> ... an institutional structure somewhat different from that in the Member States has been adopted. Executive power is shared between two independent bodies, one of which is subject to direct parliamentary control and supervision. Legislative power as a separate element, in the sense developed by Montesquieu, is absent. The power to enact Community law resides in the two executive bodies acting in co-operation, subject to the consultation of the European Parliament. Only the judicial power is separate in the classical sense.[23]

The unique institutional structure of the EC has two effects on parliament's role in the legislative process; the first of these concerns the initiation of legislation, the second the right to amend legislation. Although in all of the Nine the power to initiate legislation is shared between the parliament and the executive,[24] in practice the latter is the dominant authority in the formative stages of the legislative process. Indeed, 'it is implicit in the concept of democracy that the initiative in law-making should rest with the elected Parliament'.[25] In the EC, however, the European Parliament has no power whatsoever to initiate legislation, and the absence of this power cannot solely be accounted for by the fact that the Parliament has been (to date) a non-elected body. In the paraphrased and much-used words of Altiero Spinelli, 'The Commission proposes, the Council disposes',[26] and the Parliament plays only a consultative role in legislative matters as we shall see later. As Fitzmaurice has argued:

> The Council has become the legislature and, through its reticence in delegation and the fact that the Commission lacks powers of decision and action, has in reality become the executive of the Communities. The traditional dialogue between Parliament and the Executive has been replaced by the dialogue between the Commission and the Council. The position of the European Parliament in the decision-making process of the Community has not been logically considered.[27]

And a similar conclusion has been reached by Coombes:

> The supreme legislative decision-making body of the Community is, without doubt, the Council of Ministers, but even the Council refuses to fit ordinary constitutional classifications. Strictly speaking, it is neither a legislative nor an executive body, for it consists simply of ministers representing their respective governments and has no means of implementing Community legislation. ... Thus Community legislation results from a kind of dialogue between the

Commission, on the one hand, and the member governments as represented in the Council on the other.[28]

A second noticeable deficiency of the European Parliament is its power to amend Commission proposals. In other parliamentary systems, 'The right to submit amendments to legislation is universally recognised as one of the prerogatives of Members of Parliament. It derives from their right to introduce a bill; if a Member is entitled to initiate a complete bill he is, *a fortiori*, entitled to propose an amendment to a bill.'[29] By contrast, the European Parliament and its Members cannot amend Community legislation but can only propose amendments for the Council of Ministers' consideration. In this connection – and again drawing parallels with the separation of powers model – Allott argues:

In the Community system, legislation is prepared by a clearly Executive-type body (the Commission) and is proposed to another Executive-type body (the Council) by the Commission. The Council then 'consults' the European Parliament, which means that it transmits the proposal to the Parliament and receives an 'opinion' from it. The Council may legally . . . ignore the opinion; it adopts the act finally and merely refers to the 'opinion of the European Parliament' in a preambular paragraph.[30]

The absence of the European Parliament's power either to initiate or to amend EC legislation results in it playing a much lesser role in the legislative process of the Community than the member states. Concerning the performance of the legislative power, the European Parliament is *not* a parliament in the same sense that the national parliaments are. Indeed, the role of the European Parliament is a consultative one which is mainly exercised at the 'pre-decision' stages of the legislative process.[31]

In these stages the Parliament, through its committee meetings (which are attended by representatives of the Commission) and through general debate, is able to exert some, albeit often indirect, influence on the form and content of draft legislation proposed by the Commission (see steps 2 and 3, p. 29). Later, when the Council receives a proposal from the Commission, in almost all cases it submits it to the Parliament for an opinion (step 4). The proposal is then discussed in one or more of the Parliament's specialised committees,[32] in whose work the Commission, and sometimes the Council, participates. The report of the committee forms the basis of a motion for a resolution and is debated in plenary session again with Commission and/or Council participation. The subsequent resolution, if adopted, is forwarded to the Council to be considered alongside the Commission proposal (steps 5 and 6).

A major way in which the Parliament increased its role in the legislative process followed from the introduction of the 'concertation procedure' in 1975.[33] This significantly changed, and strengthened, the Parliament's consultative role. Under the former procedures the Council could ignore or reject the opinion and the proposed amendments of the Parliament. However, under the new procedures, although the power of the Council has not formally been reduced, it has agreed to meet with the Parliament when differences of opinion exist between the two bodies on Community acts having financial implications.[34] When such differences occur, a 'conciliation committee'[35] comprising Council representatives, members of Parliament's political groups and Commission participants is established (step 7). If this committee decides that the Council and the Parliament are in a position to make agreement probable, the proposal is resubmitted to the Parliament which delivers a second opinion on it. After this is given, the proposal is returned to the Council which then has the right to take the final decision on the matter.

Although it is difficult to assess with any exactness the role that the Parliament plays in the legislative process, some idea of it can be obtained from the statement that former Commissioner George Thomson made to the Parliament concerning its legislative work in the years 1975 and 1976:

'During this period of two years, Parliament has given 281 opinions on the Commission's proposals. The vast majority of these – 207 – have been favourable ones. In 74 of its reports Parliament has proposed amendments, and in 52 out of these 74 cases the Commission has been able to accept them either partly or wholly. In only 22 cases has the Commission been unable to follow Parliament's amendments. Moreover, during the course of the debates on these 22 issues Parliament has very often shown that it appreciated the Commission's reasons for being unable to follow Parliament's advice'.[36]

Although the Treaties do not give the European Parliament formal powers to initiate legislation (except in the case of direct elections under Article 138(3) when even then passage of the legislation was subject to action – and hence delay – by the Council of Ministers) it is apparent from George Thomson's statement that the Parliament does have a means of influencing Commission proposals informally. Moreover, its own specialised committees can and do produce reports on their 'own initiative' calling for Commission action in specified areas. The Commission is not obliged to respond but nor is it predisposed to ignoring the Parliament's views. This is because the Commission and the Parliament have been considered to be 'on the same side', and because the prospect of direct elections has resulted in a commitment in principle to accord the Parliament's views greater attention on the part of the Commission.

At this stage we can draw attention to three similarities which exist between the role of the European Parliament in the legislative process of the Community, and the role of the national parliaments in the legislative process of the member states. The first of these is based upon the use of the concertation procedure and the way that agreement is reached between the two Houses of Parliament in two of the original (France and Germany), and one of the subsequent (Ireland), national bicameral legislatures of the member states.[37]

The second similarity concerns the European Parliament giving a second opinion on a proposal following the reduction of differences between the Parliament and the Council of Ministers in a conciliation committee. In this instance, the parallel is where national parliaments are requested by the executive to reconsider a bill, a procedure that exists in France, Italy and Germany.[38]

A third, and final, similarity concerns the power of the Council of Ministers to take the final decision on legislative matters, and reject amendments proposed by the European Parliament. This has parallels with the veto powers (or refusal to grant assent or sign a bill) over legislation granted to some of the executives of the member states.[39] Two points concerning this need to be emphasised: the first is that not only can the Council of Ministers reject or ignore the European Parliament's views; secondly, the European Parliament has no way of changing the Council's decision which is at all times final.

Thus a number of similarities can be traced between the legislative processes in the EC and in the member states. Although the closeness of such similarities must be approached with caution, parallels do appear to exist between the following:

1. The legislative process in the Community and the process of delegated legislation in the member states.
2. The use of the concertation procedure in the Community, and the way that agreement is reached between the two chambers in some of the member states' national bicameral legislatures.
3. The second opinion given on a legislative measure by the European Parliament and the right of the executive in some of the member states to request the national parliament to reconsider a measure.
4. The power of the Council of Ministers to take the final decision on legislative matters (and reject the amendments proposed by the European Parliament) and the power of the executive in some of the member states to veto a bill passed by the national parliaments.

Returning to our main theme – the nature and performance of the legislative power in the Community and parallels with the performance of the legislative power in the member states – we have attempted to show that the European Parliament is *not* a parliament in the way that the term is conventionally used. This we attribute to the following:

1. There is no clear-cut separation of powers between the legislative and executive branches of the Community's institutions.
2. The legislative power is not exercised wholly or even partly by the European Parliament which has neither the power to initiate nor to amend legislation.
3. The European Parliament is not involved in the passage of all of the Community's legislative items.
4. Notwithstanding recent changes, the European Parliament's legislative role is largely consultative and is limited to the pre-decisional stages of the legislative process.

(iii)   The Financial Powers of the European Parliament

The second way in which we shall evaluate the European Parliament's claim to be a parliament is by considering its financial powers. As the Parliament has no legislative powers, its claim for budgetary powers is especially important as it is through these that it can exercise some control over legislative items and can approve appropriations only for those arrangements which it considers sufficiently close to the opinions it expressed when consulted. The importance of financial powers in the evolution of parliamentary government is patent:

> In the history of Parliaments the powers to be won from the Executive were powers over finance and it was around these that modern constitutional systems gradually took shape. The legislative powers of Parliament were acquired after Parliament had gained its powers over finance; the people demanded and won the right to consent to the levy of taxes before they began to demand a role in the law-making process.[40]

According to Coombes, 'the power of the purse' in Western European parliaments is 'at least as important as other powers of Parliament (like that to approve ordinary legislation) and is certainly indispensable to effective government in open, pluralist societies'.[41] The power can be expressed in the following three statements:

1. 'in some way parliament's prior approval should be required for all expenditure and all revenue proposed by the government';
2. 'parliament's approval should also be required for the allocation of expenditure among items';
3. 'parliament should have the right to approve the accounts of expenditure, in order to check that the government has conformed to what was approved'.[42]

Our task here is to apply these statements to the European Parliament. Initially, it is necessary to distinguish between revenue and expenditure in the Community.[43] Concerning revenue, in 1976 about two-thirds of the EC's expenditure was financed out of the Community's 'own resources' in the form of agricultural levies and customs duties, and the remaining third was financed by direct contributions from the member states. The Council of Ministers had still to agree on a uniform assessment basis for a special value-added tax levy for Community purposes, a percentage of the proceeds of which would cover the third of the EC's budget not financed from own resources. The adoption of such a levy would complete the own-resources system as envisaged by the 1970 Treaty of Luxembourg.[44] In the meantime, however, member states make financial contributions to the budget linked to their share of the Community's total gross national product (see Table 3.2).[45] From this it is apparent that the European Parliament has no influence over the Community's revenue; agricultural levies and customs duties are established by the Commission and the Council, and the member states' financial contributions are determined by the Council. Thus part of Coombes' first statement – the prior approval by parliament of all *revenue* proposed by the government – is not a financial power enjoyed by the European Parliament.

What powers has the European Parliament over Community *expenditure*? How is financial control over this expenditure exercised by the Parliament? The various stages in the budgetary process in the Community are shown in Table 3.3. This reveals that the Parliament's

TABLE 3.2. Revenue of the European Community, 1976 budget
(in millions of units of account)

Country	Total	Own resources	Financial contribution	%
Belgium	481.4	266.9	214.5	6.42
Germany	2070.5	997.2	1073.3	27.58
France	1638.0	640.2	997.8	21.82
Italy	1361.7	637.4	614.3	16.68
Luxembourg	11.7	4.1	7.6	0.15
Netherlands	639.9	409.5	230.5	8.53
Denmark	150.5	74.4	76.0	2.01
Ireland	38.6	38.6	–	0.51
United Kingdom	1223.5	1223.5	–	16.30

Source: European Parliament, *Budgetary Power of the European Parliament*, Press and Information Office of the European Parliament (Luxembourg, 1976).

budgetary powers differ as to compulsory and non-compulsory expenditure. The distinction between these two types of expenditure is made in the Treaty where compulsory expenditure is defined as 'expenditure necessarily resulting from this Treaty or from acts adopted in accordance therewith';[46] this expenditure covers the economic and social objectives of the Community. By contrast, non-compulsory expenditure covers the administrative costs of the Community, and expenditure in policy areas not covered by the Treaty.[47] Furthermore, as Ehlermann has noted, 'Expenditure is compulsory only if the Council has determined the principle *and* amount in a legal act outside the Budget; mixed budgetary items are to be regarded as non-compulsory expenditure'.[48] In 1977 compulsory expenditure comprised about 75 per cent of the Community's budget of which approximately 68 per cent involved agricultural expenditure; the remaining 25 per cent of the budget was non-compulsory.

From Table 3.3 it can be seen that the European Parliament can propose modifications to items of compulsory expenditure to the Council. Different rules apply on whether or not the Parliament's proposals involve an increase in the total expenditure of an institution. If such an increase is involved, it must be adopted by a qualified majority of the Council;[49] if such approval is not forthcoming or the Council takes no decision on it, then it is automatically rejected. In this instance the adoption of a modification proposed by a majority of the Parliament can be thwarted by a minority of the Council.[50] If the modification proposed by Parliament does not, however, involve an increase in the overall expenditure of an institution,[51] it is considered adopted unless it is rejected by a qualified majority of the Council.

It can be seen, then, that the Council of Ministers holds two trump cards in the debate on the budget. Firstly, it accepts the draft budget which is the basis on which Parliament exercises its right of amendment. And secondly, it has the final say on compulsory expenditure, with the reservation that the 1975 Treaty requires it to act by a qualified majority if it wishes to reject proposed modifications which do not have the effect of increasing the total amount of expenditure.

A parallel can be drawn between the Parliament's right to propose modifications to compulsory expenditure which involve increases in the expenditure of institutions and its rights to propose amendments to the Council's legislative views. In both instances the Parliament can do no more than make suggestions, and the final decision on such matters rests with the Council. Thus the Parliament's approval is not sought for some three-quarters of the Community's expenditure.

A further parallel can be drawn between the limitations on the European Parliament's power to amend the compulsory provisions of the budget, and the limitations which exist on the rights of Members of Parliament in budgetary matters in four of the member states.[52] In France, Members can reduce or abolish items of expenditure, but can

TABLE 3.3. The budgetary process in the European Community

1st stage	Commission	Preparation and establishment of preliminary draft: (i) Establishment of maximum rate. Informing the institutions of this rate before 1 May. (ii) Compilation of preliminary draft from budgetary estimates made by institutions, before 1 July; preliminary draft sent to the Council before 1 September.
2nd stage	Council	First reading: establishment of draft by a qualified majority; draft sent to European Parliament before 5 October.
3rd stage	European Parliament	First reading: proposal of modifications and amendments within forty-five days.

	Compulsory expenditure: Modifications proposed by absolute majority	*Non-compulsory* expenditure: Amendments by a majority of members

4th stage	Council	Second reading: decision on proposals and modification of amendments within fifteen days.

	Compulsory expenditure: Decision by qualified majority; proposals that are not accepted are considered to be rejected	*Non-compulsory* expenditure: Modification of amendments by a qualified majority

5th stage	European Parliament	Second reading: decision on the Council's modifications of amendments and formal adoption of the budget within fifteen days.

	Compulsory expenditure: No powers of re-modification	*Non-compulsory* expenditure: Amendments of Council's modifications by a majority of members and three-fifths of votes cast

Formal adoption of the budget if not rejected by a majority of members and two-thirds of votes cast

Source: Adapted from The Budgetary Powers of the European Parliament, Doc. PE 49.730.

only increase them if alternative provisions are made elsewhere; in Italy, Members can propose increases and reductions in taxes and expenditure, but cannot create a new item of taxation or expenditure; in the United Kingdom, Members cannot increase expenditure or taxation without the permission of the Government, but can reduce expenditure and taxation; and in Ireland, Members cannot move amendments to the budget.[53] The European Parliament's position in budgetary matters vis-à-vis the Council of Ministers is, then, similar to that of MPs in the member states vis-à-vis their governments.

Let us now examine what power the Parliament has over the remaining 25 per cent of the budget, that is, over non-compulsory expenditure. Although it is sometimes argued that such expenditure is the most politically significant part of the budget, and although the Parliament has the final say over it, the amount of control it can exercise over it is restricted by various subjective, objective and technical limits on its powers.[54] The 'subjective' limit concerns the majorities that must be achieved at Parliament's first and second readings of the budget. At the first reading, amendments to non-compulsory expenditure can be made by a majority of its members; at the second reading, Parliament can reject the Council's modifications of its amendments by a majority of its members and three-fifths of the votes cast.

Even though the Parliament has the last word on non-compulsory expenditure, and can introduce reductions in it and alter its allocation among different items, a ceiling is placed on any increases that may be made in this expenditure by the 'maximum rate'.[55] Under the Treaty, the Commission is required to establish the maximum rate, which limits increases in expenditure, on the basis of:

'1. the trend, in terms of volume, of the gross national product within the Community;
2. the average variation in the budgets of the Member States; and
3. the cost of living during the preceding financial year.'[56]

The maximum rate is the 'objective' limit to the Parliament's financial powers, and one that severely restricts the exercise of these powers as it limits rates of increased expenditure to the general economic circumstances of the Community. More importantly, however, the rate of increase which limits Parliament's freedom of action over non-compulsory expenditure is determined by the Commission, an executive rather than a legislative body.

In addition to these subjective and objective limits on the non-compulsory items of expenditure in the budget, there are various 'technical' limits which also restrict the Parliament's freedom of action. Most concern administrative expenditure, about which Kapteyn has written that:

The budget constitutes the principal legal basis for Community action involving administrative expenses: the appointment of officials, renting of offices, publishing activities, purchasing of furniture and office appliances, the granting of scholarships, etc. The budgetary authority when making provision for administrative expenditure, is of course bound by financial commitments already authorised under previous budgets. The Community staff appointed by virtue of these previous appropriations are entitled to receive their salaries, remunerations and pensions in accordance with the rules laid down by the Council for that purpose. Trades people and other suppliers of goods must receive payment when they have concluded pluri-annual contracts with the Community for which contracts authorisation has been given in a previous budget.[57]

A further set of technical restrictions concern the Council's authority to determine whether an item of expenditure falls within the compulsory or non-compulsory section of the budget: these became especially apparent in the passage of the 1975 and 1976 budgets and the problems that arose over the classification of the Regional Development Fund.[58]

The third and final parliamentary 'power of the purse' concerns the right to approve the accounts of expenditure, the corollary of budgetary control. On 15 June 1976 the European Parliament established a sub-committee on public accounts as part of its Budgets Committee. This sub-committee works in co-operation with the Community's Audit Board:[59] it checks expenditure for discrepancies and fraud, and has the power to conduct special in-depth inquiries on matters arising from these accounts. Sir Harold Wilson, then British Prime Minister, called for the establishment of such a sub-committee in the Community in 1975 with the words that it 'must be capable of striking terror in the hearts of those who control expenditure'. As the sub-committee has been in existence for less than a year it is somewhat problematical to judge its effectiveness. Palmer has, however, written that 'this sub-committee can only scratch the surface of the many problems involved in the *post hoc* supervision of Community expenditure'. And, looking into the future, he writes:

But a new Community body, the Court of Auditors, should be established during 1977. Following direct elections Parliament's sub-committee, which could usefully be transformed into a full committee, should, working closely with the Court, be able to cut down frauds and abuses in the agricultural sector. Although in the past the Commission has sometimes been reluctant to transmit to Parliament 'confidential' documents relating to expenditure, it will become increasingly difficult for the Commission to refuse to hand over internal documents when so requested by Parliament.[60]

An additional financial power which the European Parliament claims is the right to reject the draft budget in its entirety. Via the 1975 amendment to Article 203 of the EC Treaty, a new paragraph 8 permits the Parliament to reject the draft budget if there are important reasons and ask for the submission of a new draft.[61] The Parliament – with the support of the Commission – was of the opinion that it had this power since the Treaty on the Budget of 22 April 1970 which stated that the President of the Parliament was to declare that the budget had been finally adopted; if he did not do so, the Parliament and the Commission assumed that it had been rejected. In 1971, Parliament gained co-decision powers with the Council on granting a discharge on accounts. Under the new provisions, the draft budget is rejected upon the decision of a majority of the Members of the Parliament, and two-thirds of the votes cast. In the event of it rejecting the draft budget the Parliament has undertaken to give the Council clear and precise reasons for so doing.

On the basis of the four points listed below, we suggest that the European Parliament is *not* a parliament because it neither shares, nor exercises, 'the power of the purse' in an effective manner. Compared to 'the power of the purse' of the national parliaments of the member states:

1. The European Parliament's prior approval for items of revenue is not required.
2. Nor is its approval required for the classification of expenditure between compulsory and non-compulsory items, or for the allocation of compulsory expenditure between different items.
3. Nor is its approval required for some three-quarters of the Community's expenditure (compulsory expenditure) over which it can do little more than express an opinion.
4. And, furthermore, the Parliament's formal powers of decision over the remaining quarter of expenditure (non-compulsory expenditure) is restricted by subjective limits (concerning majorities), objective limits (the maximum rate of expenditure) and technical limits (involving previous and/or contractual obligations).

The Parliament's lack of financial powers is offset neither by its establishment of a Public Accounts Committee nor by its recently acquired power to reject the draft budget in its entirety: the former is not likely to be active enough to be truly effective (so long as the dual mandate divides MEPs' time), the latter is too much of a 'nuclear instrument' for it to be politically viable. This is because rejection of the budget in its entirety would result in expenditure being held at the previous year's levels.[62] It would thus be dysfunctional to integration and to the Community attaining its goals. However, it does have limited use as an ultimate threat since the prospect of the budget being rejected in its entirety by the Parliament may induce the Council of Ministers to seek compromises rather than to risk a confrontation on this issue with the Parliament. Even so, it can be seen that the European Parliament possesses few effective legislative or financial powers. Can the same be said of its control powers?

Notes

1. The Rome Treaty establishing the EEC refers to the Parliament as the 'Assembly'. Its names were Assemblée parlementaire européenne, Assemblea parlamentare Europea, Europäisches Parlament and Europese Parlement until 1962, when the French and Italian titles were changed to Parlement européen and Parlamento Europeo.

2. See the handbook of the Secretariat, Directorate-General for Information and Public Relations, *The European Parliament* (Luxembourg: European Parliament, 1976).

3. *Der Ministerrat im konstitutionellen System der Europäischen Gemeinschaften* (Bruges: de Tempel, 1964) p. 175. Quoted in J. Fitzmaurice, *The Party Groups in the European Parliament* (Farnborough: Saxon House, 1975) p. 40.

4. Fitzmaurice, ibid., p. 39.

5. Sir B. Cocks, *The European Parliament* (London: HMSO, 1973) p. 6.

6. Quoted in Cocks, ibid., pp. 6–7.

7. Lewis Carroll, *Alice through the Looking Glass*, Chap. 6.

8. William Shakespeare, *Romeo and Juliet*, act II, scene ii, lines 42–4.

9. On the functions of parliaments see K. von Beyme, 'Basic Trends in the Developments of the Functions of Parliaments in Western Europe', in Directorate-General for Research and Documentation of the European Parliament (ed.), *Symposium on European Integration and the Future of Parliaments in Europe* (Luxembourg: European Parliament, 1975) pp. 11–22, and K. H. Petersen, 'On the Improvement of the Functions of Parliaments', ibid., pp. 355–63.

10. Directorate-General for Information and Public Relations, *The European Parliament*, pp. 15–19.

11. We must, at this stage, leave open the question as to how much the European Parliament must perform these functions for it to be classified as a parliament.

12. These types of legislation are discussed in Directorate-General for Research and Documentation of the European Parliament, *The Loss of Powers of the Member States as a Result of the Treaty Establishing the European Economic Community* (Doc. PE. 35807, Mar 1974).

13. Article 189, Treaty Establishing the European Economic Community.

14. These data were kindly provided by Dr M. P. C. M. van Schendelen.

15. See D. Coombes, *Politics and Bureaucracy in the European Community* (London: Allen & Unwin, 1970) Chap. 4

16. See P. Allott, 'The Democratic Basis of the European Communities: The European Parliament and the Westminster Parliament', *Common Market Law Review*, XI (1974) 298–326, at p. 315.

17. V. Herman, *Parliaments of the World: A Reference Compendium* (London: Macmillan, 1976) Chap. 53.

18. Article 155, Treaty Establishing the European Economic Community.

19. As one example of this the number of agricultural instruments issued by the Commission can be considered. In 1974 these numbered 2519; in 1975, 2423; and to 1 July 1976, 1005.

20. For a different view see É. Noël, 'The Commission's Power of Initiative', *Common Market Law Review*, X (1973) 123–36 (M. Noël is Secretary-General of the Commission).

21. Adapted from Cocks, *The European Parliament*, Chap. 2, and Directorate-General for Information and Public Relations, *The European Parliament*.

22. Herman, *Parliaments of the World*, p. 571.

23. Fitzmaurice, *The Party Groups in the European Parliament*, p. 3.

24. See Herman, *Parliaments of the World*, part 3, for a general overview of the legislative function of parliaments.

25. Ibid., p. 596.

26. A. Spinelli, *The Eurocrats* (Baltimore: Johns Hopkins Press, 1966).

27. Fitzmaurice, *The Party Groups in the European Parliament*, p. 14.

28. Coombes, *Politics and Bureaucracy in the European Community*, p. 85.

29. Herman, *Parliaments of the World*, p. 675.

30. Allott, op. cit., p. 316.

31. European Parliament Background Note, 'Powers of the European Parliament', 15 Sep 1976 (EPN/8/76).

32. There are twelve committees in the Parliament, as follows: Political Affairs; Legal Affairs; Economic and Monetary Affairs; Budgets; Social Affairs, Employment and Education; Agriculture; Regional Policy, Regional Planning and Transport; the Environment, Public Health and Consumer Protection; Energy and Research; External Economic Relations; Development and Co-operation; and Rules of Procedure and Petitions.

33. Established by Resolution of the European Parliament, 19 Dec 1975.

34. The financial powers of the Parliament are discussed below.

35. In initial exchanges on the establishment of the concertation procedure the Parliament and the Council referred to the 'conciliation committee as, respectively, the 'co-ordination' and 'consultation' committee.

36. *Debates of the European Parliament*, 14 Dec 1976.

37. Herman, *Parliaments of the World*, Chap. 46.

38. Ibid., Chap. 54.

39. Ibid.

40. Ibid., p. 731.

41. D. Coombes, 'The Role of Parliament in Budgetary Decisions', in D. Coombes *et al., The Power of the Purse* (London: Allen & Unwin/PEP, 1976) pp. 264–390, at p. 390.

42. Coombes, 'Introduction', ibid., p. 17.

43. For a discussion of this distinction in the context of national parliaments see Herman, *Parliaments of the World*, p. 732.

44. Article 4, Decision of 21 Apr 1970 on the Replacement of Financial Contributions from Member States by the Community's Own Resources.

45. Article 4, para. 3, ibid.

46. Article 203, para. 4, Treaty Establishing the European Economic Community.

47. In 1975 controversy arose over the first two supplementary budgets concerning the Regional Development and the 'Cheysson' Funds.
48. C.-D. Ehlermann, 'Applying the New Budgetary Procedure for the First Time (Article 203 of the EEC Treaty)', *Common Market Law Review*, XII (1975) 325–43, at p. 343; emphasis in original.
49. Article 48 (2) of the EEC Treaty (as amended by Article 14 of the Act of Accession Treaty and Modified by Article 8 of the Adaptation Treaty) reads: 'Where the Council is required to act by a qualified majority, the votes of its members shall be weighted as follows:

Belgium	5
Denmark	3
Germany	10
France	10
Ireland	3
Italy	10
Luxembourg	2
Netherlands	5
United Kingdom	10

For their adoption, acts of the Council shall require at least:
– forty-one votes in favour where this treaty requires them to be adopted as a proposal from the Commission;
– forty-one votes in favour, cast by at least six members, in other cases.'
50. This is referred to as the 'reversed majority rule'.
51. It may, for example, be offset by other proposals.
52. In the other five countries Members of Parliament can reduce or increase items of expenditure and taxation.
53. Herman, *Parliaments of the World*, Chap. 59.
54. Ehlermann, op. cit., p. 326.
55. The 'maximum rate' applies to all the Community's institutions including the Council and the Commission.
56. Article 203, para. 8.
57. P. J. G. Kapteyn, 'The European Parliament, the Budget, and Legislation in the Community'. *Common Market Law Review*, IX (1972) 386–410, at p. 391.
58. See Ehlermann, op. cit.; also Strasser, 'La nouvelle procédure budgétaire des communautés européennes et son application a l'établissement du budget pour l'exercise 1975', *Revue du Marché Common*, no. 182 (Feb 1975) 74–87.
59. The 22 July 1975 modification to Article 206 replaced the Audit Board by the Court of Auditors. The Council appoints members from the Nine after consulting Parliament. This was ratified in 1977.
60. M. Palmer, 'The Role of a Directly Elected European Parliament', *The World Today*, XXXIII (1977) 122–30, at p. 125.
61. Signed by representatives of the member states on 22 July 1975.
62. For details of how this works see *The Budgetary Powers of the European Parliament* (Doc. PE 49.730, Oct 1977).

4 The Control Powers of the European Parliament

In this chapter we shall evaluate the role of the European Parliament through an examination of the way in which, in its own words, it 'exert(s) some political control over the Council and the Commission'. The centrality of the control powers[1] of parliaments in general can be judged from the following:

> The control that Parliament exercises over the Executive stems from one basic principle: Parliament embodies the will of the people and must therefore be able to supervise the way in which public policy is carried out so as to ensure that it remains consonant with the aspirations of the Nation as a whole. . . . The strength of a Parliament lies in its ability to scrutinise the whole of the political and administrative actions of the Executive, even to the point of arresting it when it no longer corresponds to the movement of public opinion. A variety of procedures are available to enable Parliament to discharge this duty, and to resolve any conflict with the Executive. In a Parliamentary regime the efficacy of these procedures is the key to the power of Parliament.[2]

In the light of this statement our task is twofold: firstly, to examine what procedures are available to the European Parliament to control the executive institutions of the Community, and to make some comparisons between these and the procedures that the national parliaments have in the member states; and secondly, to try and evaluate the efficacy of the European Parliament's control power. Before undertaking these it is, however, necessary to focus attention on a number of control powers that the European Parliament does *not* have; powers that are of central importance to the whole notion of political control; powers that exist in all, or most, of the member states. Three such powers are involved: the power to appoint members of the executive, the power to ensure the collective responsibility of members of both components of the bicephalous executive, and the power to ensure the individual responsibility of members of the executive.

(i) Political Control and the Community

In considering the control powers of the European Parliament it is important to note that it plays no role whatsoever in the appointment of members of either the Council of Ministers or the Commission. Members of the Council are appointed by their national governments,[3] and their membership of the former is conditional upon their membership of the latter. Commissioners are 'appointed by common accord of the Governments of the Member States'[4] for a four-year term of office which is renewable. At no stage during their period in office does the Council or the Commission require a formal vote of investiture by the Parliament – the approval of Parliament to the composition of the Commission and the Council is tacitly assumed, and not explicitly sought, by the national governments.[5] Even if this assumption were false, there is virtually nothing that the Parliament could do to prevent the appointment or the delegation of specific individuals to either the Commission or the Council of Ministers. (Moreover, even if the Parliament were to dismiss the Commission it would have no guarantee that the same Commissioners would not be reappointed by their national governments.) By contrast, in the member states, governments must receive the confidence of parliament – through approval of its programme, an explicit vote of investiture, or some other manifestation of positive support – before they can take office.

Because the European Parliament plays no part in the appointment of members of the Council or the Commission, neither of these bodies can, at any stage of their tenure of office, seek a motion of confidence from the Parliament. Thus the tacit assumption underlying their appointment is continued throughout their period in office. Although, as we have seen, Parliament can pass a motion of censure – the corollary of a motion of confidence – on the Commission, the Treaty gives it no authorisation to pass such a motion on the Council. Hence the control powers of the Parliament do not extend to the appointment of either the Council or the Commission, nor to passing a positive motion of confidence in either of them, but only to passing a negative motion of censure on the Commission. The weakness of the Parliament's control powers is exacerbated by the fact that the chamber's party composition neither closely reflects, nor in any meaningful way determines, the composition of either branch of the executive. Because membership of the Council and the Commission is incompatible with membership of the Parliament,[6] the separation of personnel, roles and attitudes between the executive diarchy and the Parliament is very real.

A second control power that Parliament lacks is its ability to ensure the collective responsibility of the Council of Ministers. Whereas in each of the member states the national government is responsible to at least one – and, in bicameral systems, often two – of the House(s) of Parliament,[7] the Council of Ministers is neither collectively responsible to the European Parliament nor to the national parliaments. The Council can neither be dismissed by, nor does it need the support of, either set of parliaments. 'These facts', as Allott points out, 'make the subjection of the Council as such to political influence unbelievable, because it is not subject to any sanction however formal.'[8] Only in the budgetary area can the Parliament exert effective control over the Council by rejecting the budget. If this were to happen, the Council would have little alternative but to interpret this as a motion of no confidence, but it does not follow that the Council would – or even could – resign from office. This is the only way – and we must admit that in the foreseeable future it is an unlikely possibility – that the Parliament can render the Council impotent; given the existing powers of the Parliament it cannot bring about the resignation or the dismissal of the Council, nor can it ensure its collective responsibility.

The collegiate natures of the Commission and the Council are very different and this has important consequences for the exercise of their responsibilities. The Commission has several characteristics of a collegiate body: its Commissioners are jointly responsible for the Commission's 'legal' acts; the Treaty does not define a notion of individual responsibility for a Commissioner supervising the work of the General Directorate; and all policies and actions of the body are those of the Commission as a whole. However, 'Despite all this, the Commission is not a Cabinet: it lacks both homogeneity and offers no focus for political expectations or power base to its members'.[9] What further distinguishes it from a cabinet is that it has no mandate,[10] no clearly defined policy or ideological orientation (other than its 'Europeanness'), and its members do not belong to the same party(ies). The collegiate nature of the Commission must be compared to that of the Council in which 'Fluctuating membership, the fact that those who attend are delegates rather than representatives, the lack of any concept of collective responsibility, and failure to maintain secrecy about any of the proceedings all militate against collegiality at Council level'.[11] Hence the presence and absence of collective responsibility of the Commission and the Council, respectively, can in part be accounted for by the differing degrees of collegiality inherent in each body.

A third type of control that the Parliament does not possess is the power to ensure individual responsibility of either members of the Council of Ministers or the Commission.[12] At the level of the member state,

> The scope of political accountability is vast; it may apply to any act performed by a Minister in the exercise of his duties or the carrying out of his policies, his actions or failure to act, and even his intentions. A Minister's conduct is not regarded in the light of its legality but simply of its political wisdom in the face of views expressed by Parliament.[13]

The absence of this doctrine in the Community is significant. The idea that individual Commissioners should be made accountable to the Parliament is periodically raised but rejected, in part because the power to force the resignation of individual Commissioners might cause them to become subservient to the wishes of other institutions, and therefore be tantamount to infringement of the terms of their appointment; and in part because such a power, like that to force the resignation of the whole Commission, is a 'nuclear' one. Furthermore, were the Parliament empowered to censure individual Commissioners, the Commission as a whole might run the risk of precipitate cabinet reshuffles,[14] suffer from the resultant policy and personnel instability,[15] and in order to obviate clashes with the Parliament over principles might allow the climate of opinion in the latter to determine the type of initiatives it takes. 'Thus, the Commission would be relegated to the role of a bureaucracy and it would run contrary to traditional parliamentary practice to demand the accountability of bureaucrats to Parliament on the same basis as the democratic accountability of Government Ministers to Parliament.'[16] Although individual Commissioners can be removed from office, the Community institution which has the power to bring this about is the Court of Justice, not the Parliament.[17] Political, as opposed to juridical, notions of individual responsibility are, then, not applicable to either of the Community's executive institutions.

The unique configuration of the Community's institutions affects both the nature and extent of the political control that the Parliament can exercise over the Council and the Commission,[18] and also the way in which it can ensure the responsibility of the latter. The lack of a clear separation of powers between the executive and legislative branches of the Community's institutions contributes in part to this, as does the relationship of these branches to each other which obfuscates key aspects of both presidential and parliamentary models of government.[19]

The mixed presidential/parliamentary nature of the Community's institutions is both a cause and an effect of the Parliament's lack of control over the executive diarchy: one half of the Community's executive (the Council) is completely independent of the Parliament (as, for example, the President is independent of Congress in the United States); the other half (the Commission) is subject to a measure of parliamentary control (as the British Cabinet is to the House of Commons).[20] From the Parliament's point of view these arrangements are not only unique but also inconvenient, for they lead to Parliament being granted control powers over what is widely thought of as the weaker of the two executive bodies, the one that it usually sides with in disputes against the Council,[21] and the one that has, as we have seen, as many characteristics of a bureaucracy as of an executive.

The list of control powers that the European Parliament does *not*

have compared to those that the national parliaments *do* have could be
extended to include things such as:

- the fact that its authorisation is not required for the ratification of
  international treaties and agreements;[22]
- the absence of an independent body such as an ombudsman,
  mediator, or similarly named controlling organisation,[23] to
  exercise control over the executive and which reports to the
  Parliament;
- the lack of the Parliament's power to appoint, or approve the
  appointment of, certain categories of high civil servants and
  judicial officers to the Community's institutions;[24] etc.

It is probably unnecessary to extend this catalogue further. The absence
of such powers is, however, of far less importance than the Parliament's
inability to appoint the executive or to ensure its complete collective or
partial individual responsibility, as these are central to the notion of
political control.

At this stage we must examine the nature and efficacy of the control
powers that the Parliament *does* have. Four such powers exist: the
motion of censure which can be moved against the Commission,
Parliament's debate on the Commission's Annual General Report,
questions which can be put to both the Council and the Commission,
and the work undertaken by the committees of the Parliament. Each of
these will be discussed in turn.

(ii) The Motion of Censure

The principal target of those who criticise the European Community as
an undemocratic organisation is frequently the Commission, which is
seen as an insensitive, impersonal, distant and technocratic body. In the
past the Commission has often been charged with omnipotent – if not
arrogant – behaviour characterised by ignorance of the needs of the
people of the member states. While some parts of these accusations may
contain some elements of truth, the Commission is – alone among the
Community's organs – the only body which is, in any sense at all,
democratically responsible to another body – the European
Parliament. Neither the Council of Ministers, nor either of the
supposedly 'representative' bodies of the Community, the Economic
and Social Committee and the European Parliament – are in any way at
all democratically responsible for their actions.

The responsibility of the Commission to the Parliament is
established in Article 144 of the Treaty of Rome which reads, *inter alia*:

> If a motion of censure on the activities of the Commission is tabled
> before it, the Assembly shall not vote thereon until at least three days
> after the motion has been tabled and only by open vote.

If the motion of censure is carried by a two-thirds majority of the votes cast, representing a majority of the members of the Assembly, the members of the Commission shall resign as a body.

Article 144 was not formally invoked – nor the threat of it even seriously hinted at – in the first fourteen years of the Community's existence. Indeed, although the motion of censure was 'a most revolutionary power for an international assembly to possess',[25] its possession by the Parliament was seen as an 'incongruous prerogative'.[26] In part this incongruity arose because one non-elected body (the Commission) was made responsible to another non-elected body (the Parliament); in part because although the Parliament could dismiss the Commission, it played no role at all in the appointment of its successor; and in part because parliamentary control was established over only one half of the Community's bicephalous executive.

In spite of the lack of recourse to Article 144 in the early years of the Community, four motions of censure against the Commission have been moved in the last five years. The first of these was the censure motion moved by M. Georges Spénale (F. Soc.) which was debated in the last session of the Parliament of the original Six in December 1972.[27] Article 144 remained dormant until three and a half years later when the Parliament debated a censure motion moved by the late Sir Peter Kirk (U.K. Con.) in June 1976.[28] A third motion of censure moved by Herr Heinrich Aigner (G. C-D) was debated in December 1976,[29] and a fourth motion introduced by M. Michel Cointat (F. EPD) was debated in March 1977.[30] It is necessary to examine each of these censure motions in some detail, placing particular emphasis on the nature of the issues which led to the motions being introduced, the replies to them given by the Commission, and the attitudes of Members of the European Parliament to the use of the motion of censure as expressed in debate.

In moving the first censure motion in the Parliament, M. Spénale – who was then Chairman of the Finance and Budgetary Committee – declared that the Commission had failed to meet its commitment of April 1970 to come forward within two years with concrete proposals to strengthen Parliament's powers of control over the Community budget. M. Spénale said that there was no question of condemning the general policy of the Commission – which he thought deserved respect – but the Commission was a political body and could be censured.[31]

Replying, Dr Sicco Mansholt, the President of the Commission, did not deny that in April 1970 the Commission had given an undertaking that the budget should be entirely financed from the Community's own resources by 1 January 1975. However, when this report came out, the ratification of the Accession Treaty enlarging the Community was meeting serious difficulties in the national parliaments of the prospective member states. Furthermore, a summit meeting of the Nine was also a possibility. Thus it would be inappropriate, he argued, for the Commission to submit proposals to the Council of Ministers likely to change the institutional balance of the Community, and requiring amendment to the Treaties. Any such action would have threatened the EC's enlargement and would have seemed 'untimely' to the governments concerned. Finally, Dr Mansholt thought that the enlarged Commission would be in a much better position to make proposals to strengthen the Parliament's budgetary powers.[32]

In the ensuing debate, M. Francis Vals (F. Soc.) said his group reserved the right to use the motion of censure again on the incoming Commission.[33] M. René Ribière (F. Gaullist) said his group was against the censure motion because the Treaties provided for Parliament to censure the Commission for its managerial role, but not for political censure. Additionally, he opposed the Socialists' threat to use the motion again.[34] Mlle. Collette Flesch (Lux. Lib.) said that the censure motion had been a 'warning shot' to the Commission. She disapproved of the compromise motion which was eventually tabled – as did Sig. Fagio Fabrini (I. Com.) – and thought that Parliament should have taken its responsibilities seriously and voted on the motion.[35]

During the debate M. Spénale, recognising the 'extenuating circumstances' which caused the Commission's non-action, withdrew his censure motion in favour of a compromise resolution which, *inter alia*, passed responsibility for the increase in the Parliament's budgetary powers to the enlarged Commission due to take office on 6 January 1973.

At the first meeting of the Parliament of the enlarged Community in January 1973 a memorandum concerning the powers of the Parliament was submitted by the Conservative group then led by Mr Peter Kirk (U.K.). The passages concerning the motion of censure in this memorandum are worth quoting in full in view of the later use of the censure motion made by the Conservatives:

> Although the peculiar institutional provisions of the Treaty do not allow for a Commission deriving its authority directly from Parliament, relations between the two are analogous to those between a national parliament and a national government. In such relations the European Parliament's advantage can only be fully realised by the occasional use of the sanctions it possesses against the Commission.
>
> The power to dismiss the Commission as a body is a negative weapon only and not one which leads itself to the constructive participation of the Parliament in the making of Community policy. But in the absence of the constructive power to build governments, the motion of censure symbolises the dependence of the Commission on the continuing support of the Parliament. In our view the Commission should be reminded of its dependence by a more frequent use of the motion of censure.

No national government, however confident of victory, will lightly ignore a motion of censure tabled in its own Parliament, and much the same applies to the Commission. Moreover, a debate on the policies of the Commission followed by a vote, would do much to clarify in the minds of the Commission, and of the public, the political divisions which exist in the Parliament on major policy issues, and the degree of support which exists for the Commission's overall policies.[36]

The second censure motion on the Commission was moved by Sir Peter Kirk in June 1976. The motion criticised the considerable differences between the Commission's proposals to compel the incorporation of skimmed milk powder in animal feed which had been discussed earlier by Parliament, and the regulation in force at the time. Moving the motion, Sir Peter said that maladministration in the Commission concerning the skimmed milk scheme was so flagrant as to justify its removal from office.[37] In justifying his use of the motion of censure he described it as 'our most potent weapon [which] should be brandished from time to time even if not actually used to clobber the Commission'.[38] He pointed out that there was no other course of action, other than the motion of censure, open to the Parliament:

We have shown the utmost restraint and have now had to bring it out in the open. . . . I suspect that this was forced on the Commission by the Council of Ministers as a compromise of the type we have learned to expect, and the Council are just as much to blame as the Commission. We would have failed in our duty, having tried every means open to us to discover what is going on, if we had not forced the issue out into the open.[39]

M. François-Xavier Ortoli, President of the Commission, replied that the motion of censure was unacceptable as the Commission had not failed in its duty but had done its job 'with the imperfections inherent in all life and action'. This theme was echoed by Heer Jan de Kooning (N. C-D) who said that the motion was premature, materially inaccurate, and aimed at the wrong body – if anybody was to be censured it should be the Council of Ministers. It is, he said, 'an attack on the wrong front, with the wrong weapon, and at the wrong time'.[40] Following an acrimonious debate, the motion was eventually defeated by 109 votes to 18, with 4 abstentions.[41]

The third censure motion, moved by Herr Heinrich Aigner (G. C-D) in December 1976, led to a debate of principle on the extent and practical application of Parliament's right of control in the Community. The motion centred around the payment of excessively high refunds on malt exports in 1975-6, and in particular the Commission's refusal of a request from the Parliamentary Control Sub-committee[42] to be allowed to see a report on the matter prepared by the Commission's Financial Control. Herr Aigner contended that the denial of this information amounted to gross contempt of Parliament's right of control, which Parliament – with direct elections approaching – could not let pass. Although he admitted that it was not really the right time for such a motion – with a new Commission due to be installed in January 1977 – he none the less urged the other party groups to support the motion.[43]

M. François-Xavier Ortoli, replying on behalf of the Commission, said that the latest measures to strengthen Parliament's control power, in regard to discharge and the establishment of a European Court of Auditors, had been proposed by the Commission. This demonstrated that the Commission had, contrary to the sentiment expressed in the motion, been frank with Parliament over its control power. M. Ortoli confirmed that the information in question was contained in an internal Commission document which could not be made public.[44]

Support for the content of the motion came from various parts of the Parliament. Herr Martin Bangemann (G. Lib.) referred to a substitute motion tabled by his party group and by Sig. Vincenzo Vernaschi (I. C-D) whereby Parliament should vote on the censure motion in February 1977 if the new Commission also refused to release the required information.[45] But there was also opposition to the motion. Herr Horst Gerlach (G. Soc.) refused to employ the censure weapon for such a 'trifle', although he agreed in substance with Herr Aigner.[46] Herr Bangemann countered this, saying that the question of how far Parliament's rights of control could go, could be broached only on specific points of detail which often concerned trifling matters.

Finally, Herr Aigner withdrew the motion of censure, and the substitute motion – which the Parliament voted against debating under emergency procedure – was referred to the relevant committee.[47]

The fourth and final censure motion to be debated in the European Parliament was moved by M. Michel Cointat (F. EPD) on 23 March 1977. The motion criticised the Commission for its recent handling of butter sales to Eastern Europe. But it was, M. Cointat said, for essentially political reasons that his group was censuring the Commission. The latter was the Community's executive arm, not its decision-making body, and had no right to act unilaterally, he asserted.[48]

Mr Roy Jenkins (President of the Commission) stoutly defended and forcefully reaffirmed the legality of the Commission's actions. The Commission was confronted with an almost impossible task, he said. Whatever it did in trying to strike a judicious balance between the interests of Community exporters and food consumers, it was bound to come under criticism from one group or another. In this instance, the Commission had acted fully in accordance with its undertakings, and there was no logic in the censure motion.[49]

Herr Ludwig Fellermaier (G. Soc.) pointed out that the Commission had not been in office for one hundred days, the normal period of grace for an incoming executive. Censure motions should not be used to deal with trivialities, he argued, but should be saved for major emergencies, and 'Parliament should not leap to its feet every time it felt that an error had been committed and put down a censure motion'.[50] Also opposing the motion, M. Alfred Bertrand (B. C-D) emphasised that unstable governments were the order of the day throughout Europe, and it would be pointless to add to the confusion by censuring the Commission.[51] Additional opposition was expressed by M. Jean Durieux (F. Lib.) who felt that it was inopportune to censure the Commission on this issue and at that particular moment.[52] The motion was resoundingly defeated by 95 votes to 15, with 1 abstention.

On the basis of this examination of the four instances on which motions of censure have been moved against the Commission, what observations can be made about its effectiveness as an instrument of political control? Although the number of occasions on which the motion has been used are few, and as a consequence any observations that we make must be treated with caution, a number of inferences seem valid.

Firstly, the Spénale and Kirk motions[53] were primarily directed at the Council of Ministers, and the Commission served merely as a convenient target on which Parliament could vent its frustration. This situation arises because, in the words of Fitzmaurice,

> . . . there is no clear delineation of responsibility. The real power of decision-making belongs, formally, to the Council which is not and cannot be held responsible to the European Parliament. The final shape of a policy will depend on the complex interaction between the Commission, the author of the initial proposal, and the Council, which must decide thereon. The Parliament cannot hold the Commission responsible for the end product, only for the initial proposal – but everyone knows that this is only a draft. Inevitably, political responsibility is defused.[54]

Secondly, the Kirk, Aigner and Cointat motions all stemmed from essentially technical issues.[55] It could be argued that those tabling the motions were as concerned with expressing dissatisfaction with various aspects of the Common Agricultural Policy as they were in forcing the dismissal of the Commission. If any of these censure motions had been successful, a new Commission would have faced the same problems that confronted its predecessor.

Thirdly, the timing of the introduction of the majority of the censure motions is of interest.[56] The Spénale and Aigner motions were both moved against immediately outgoing Commissions, the Cointat motion against a Commission supposedly enjoying a 'honeymoon' period in office; only the Kirk motion was moved against a Commission firmly established in office. The compromise motion adopted at the end of the 1972 censure debate, and the substitute resolution proposed in the December 1976 debate, both enabled the Parliament to transfer the responsibility for the matters in question to the Commission-elect. These two motions seem to have been moved as much to influence the incoming Commission as to censure the outgoing one. In addition, as both Commissions were due to resign in a few days, there was no logic in attempting, however futilely, to dismiss them from office.

Fourthly, it is of importance that the Parliament is not empowered to try and ensure the individual responsibility of a particular Commissioner. All the motions moved to date have been directed against the collective decisions of the Commission.

Finally, on the two occasions (Kirk and Cointat) that a motion of censure has been put to the vote it has been heavily defeated, and the Commission has not suffered any danger of being dismissed from office. Only the members of the party groups moving these motions (and then not even all of them) supported each motion. Thus no distinct anti-Commission pattern of voting behaviour has been manifested by the parties on the two occasions when the Parliament has divided on censure motions. Although both the Kirk and Cointat motions were soundly defeated, both of them found a wider measure of support for the substance of the motion than can be measured by the number of votes they received. This is also true of the Spénale and Aigner motions which were eventually withdrawn.

So much for the limited history of the use of the motion of censure. What can be said about its effectiveness as a controlling device? As a means of exerting effective political control over the Commission, the motion of censure has obvious weaknesses. As long as the Parliament does not possess any authority over the nomination and appointment of the Commission, the power to censure it lacks the contextual support that would make it meaningful. If the idea behind the censure motion is to force the resignation of the Commission in order that its personnel – and by that we mean specifically the Commissioners responsible for particular policy areas – be changed with a view to ensuring or promoting more effective policies and decision-making, then the Parliament must be assured that the national governments will heed its recommendations on the appointment of replacement Commissioners, and will not simply reinstate the censured group. Yet the Parliament has no such assurance.

Although the Parliament has made increasing use of the motion of censure in recent months, this has led neither to Commission instability nor to visible alterations or adjustments to its policy. As such, the effectiveness of the censure weapon has been very limited. One reason for this lies with its all-or-nothing 'nuclear' nature. Moreover, MEPs have avoided turning the political responsibility of the Commission into the parliamentary irresponsibility of the Assembly. For the time being, an adequate balance has been struck between responsibility on the one hand, and executive continuity and stability on the other. To date, motions of censure have mainly been moved against the Commission for isolated or relatively unimportant actions, and not for matters of general policy. Yet the sanctions behind the device strongly suggest that it should or might be used for broad political questions, and that it is too serious to invoke for minor administrative matters. It must be emphasised, however, that under the terms of the Treaty the Commission is responsible for administrative matters and not for political questions. Thus the censure device is generally inappropriate given the nature of the Commission's work.

Dissatisfaction with the motion of censure as a controlling device has been expressed by Henig, who has argued that:

On most issues a majority in Parliament supports the Commission line, especially when this meets with national opposition in the Council, and can usually visualise no role other than standing on the sidelines to cheer, usually in the form of a relatively anodyne motion passed virtually unanimously. Any attempt to use the weapon of dismissal would clearly have enormous political implications for the entire Community which would certainly go far beyond any particular issue which occasioned the clash. In effect, Parliament would be making a unilateral attempt to change the entire Community political process by levering itself into the policy-making process. A majority has always felt that this would be far too dangerous a course at this stage in the development of Europe: the resultant institutional crisis would probably weaken the Commission without strengthening Parliament and would only result in further increasing the dominance of the Council.[57]

For all these reasons, and from the experience of its use to date, the motion of censure is not an effective control instrument.

At this stage a brief departure from our main theme is necessary to consider a power of the executive found in all the member states, the power to dissolve one, or occasionally both, Houses of Parliament.[58] Dissolution is 'the counterweapon to ministerial accountability'.[59] At the national level, the existence of the power to dissolve parliament gives the electorate the chance to settle differences between the government and the parliament. Historically,

Dissolution became the counterpart of ministerial accountability from the time when national representation was established on a permanent footing and when the authority of the Cabinet replaced that of the Crown. This established the balance between the

Executive and the Parliament; if the Government was dismissed by the House, the Government could reply by dismissing Parliament. This enabled the Cabinet to avoid total subjugation to Parliament, and as more or less two equal forces were opposed to each other it made collaboration between them possible and necessary.[60]

The power to dissolve the European Parliament does not exist in the Community and to date it has been a body with an unlimited term of office. Following the elections, however, it will have a fixed five-year term, after which it will be automatically dissolved.[61] Given that dissolution is the corollary of responsibility, and given that the Commission can be dismissed by Parliament, it is important to emphasise that neither the Commission nor the Council of Ministers has the reciprocal, and usually granted, constitutional power to dissolve the Parliament. This strengthens, however slightly, Parliament's control position vis-à-vis both of the EC's executive bodies, especially the Commission. Whether the absence in the Treaties of the power to dissolve Parliament will have as much significance in the years to come as Parliament's power to dismiss the Commission remains to be seen.

(iii)   Debates, Questions and Committees

The remaining control powers of the Parliament can be dealt with more briefly. The second of these powers is Parliament's right to debate the Commission's Annual General Report as provided by Article 143.[62] This report is considered by the Parliament's committees prior to being discussed in plenary session. It is difficult to evaluate the effectiveness that such debates have. Cocks, for example, argues that

> . . . the consideration of the report is one of the principal means by which the Parliament exercises its power of supervision over the activities of the Commission. Regular and increasing collaboration between the Commission and the Parliament, however, has made the examination of the Committee's report of less importance than the process of continuing scrutiny of the Communities' activities. Since 1970, moreover, the Commission has presented an annual programme of future Community activity which allows the Parliament to comment on Community policies before, rather than after, they have been implemented.[63]

While it appears to be the case that through the debate Parliament can exert some pressure on the Commission,[64] can change the time-table of its proposals, and can influence its basic policy, it is a very general controlling device, and one that is not backed up by any sanctions.

The third way that the Parliament can exercise its control function is through the use of questions to the Commission, the Council and the Conference of Foreign Ministers. MEPs' right to put questions to the Commission was established in Article 140 of the Treaty which stated, *inter alia*, that 'The Commission shall reply orally or in writing to questions put to it by the Assembly or its Members'. The provisions of Article 140 concerning the Council only stated that 'the Council shall be heard by the Assembly in accordance with the conditions laid down by the Council in its rules of procedure'. However, over the last few years the Council has agreed to answer questions put to it by the Parliament in the same way as the Commission. Since 1975 the Chairman of the Conference of Foreign Ministers has replied to questions tabled by Members of the Parliament on political cooperation.

The controlling device of questions exists in all of the Nine's national parliaments[65] and many salient features of them have been incorporated into the Rules of Procedure of the European Parliament.[66] Three types of questions exist: questions for written answer,[67] questions for oral answer without debate, and questions for oral answer with debate.[68] In January 1973 the Parliament introduced 'Question Time' which takes place on the second or third day of each sitting and lasts for ninety minutes.

How effective has the use of questions been in controlling the activities of the Commission and Council? In answering this it is, first of all, necessary to note that different use has been made of the device by different nationalities.[69] The use made of questions by the Members of the British Parliament – many of whom consider themselves 'grand masters' in the art of asking questions, especially supplementaries – has begun to spread to other national delegations. The Member of Parliament who made 'the written question into his forte'[70] was Heer Henk Vredeling who, between 1958 and 1973, tabled 1650 written questions to the Commission.[71]

As a means of parliamentary control, questions undoubtedly do make the process of government more open, do shed some light on the activities of the Community's institutions, and do provide some form of accountability. As to their effectiveness, we agree with Palmer that 'it is largely through Parliament's question time that some degree of "transparency" has been introduced into the Community. But much of the working of the Community is still opaque.'[72]

However, the efficacy of Question Time is undermined by the fact that the Parliament questions the Commission and the Council on different days, and neither body is formally present to hear the other's replies or to participate in debates to which these replies lead. Furthermore, the attitude of members of the Council has led to the 'parliamentary vacuum' where political responsibility can be located in neither the national nor the European parliamentary bodies. This became evident recently during Question Time in the European Parliament. Following an evasive answer by the President of the Council, the President of the Parliament (M. Georges Spénale) was moved to comment:

> President – Ladies and gentlemen, I should like to tell the President-in-Office of the Council, and I feel I am speaking for the whole House, how much importance we attach to this last question addressed to the Council. It is absolutely essential that the Council should think again about this problem, since the replies which have been given are not satisfactory.
>
> In fact, after replying 'We cannot speak about these matters because they are confidential', you add 'But you can ask your Minister for the answer in your national Parliament'. In other words, the President-in-Office of the Council can reply in the Netherlands Parliament, as the Netherlands Minister for Foreign Affairs, to those of our colleagues who are Members of the Netherlands Parliament, but he cannot reply to them here as President-in-Office of the Council. This means that from the Council, which is a Community institution, we can only obtain fragmentary replies in our national parliaments! Furthermore, by a curious prismatic process, the replies which our Ministers give to our national parliaments do not always coincide exactly, which is not satisfactory either. When we have a Parliament elected by direct universal suffrage, where the dual mandate will not be obligatory, it will become really intolerable if only members of national parliaments are entitled to a reply on Community questions while Members of the European Parliament are not. It is a problem which must be thought about and to which a solution must be found, failing which we shall have conflicts.[73]

The final way in which Parliament exercises control over the executive is through its twelve specialised committees.[74] Each of these deals with a particular area of the Community's activities, and their areas of specialisation broadly correspond to those of the Commission. As we have already seen, they are closely involved in the pre-legislative stages of the decision-making process, and in the consideration of both the budget and the Annual General Report of the Commission, these committees perhaps undertake the most important aspects of Parliament's work. Their reports serve as the basis for debates in the Chamber, and are often adopted as the opinion of the Parliament. Usually these committees meet in Brussels, which makes for easier contact with the Council, the Commission and the relevant interest groups.[75]

It does appear to be the case that the committees of the European Parliament are effective, and that their work is taken seriously by the Council and, especially, the Commission; the latter is obliged to provide information on its plans and its policies to the committees. However, in two crucial aspects the effectiveness of the committees of the European Parliament is weaker than those of the national parliaments:[76] firstly, they do not have the power to summon witnesses to appear before them; and secondly, they do not have the power to call for papers and documents (even though they may undertake fact-finding missions both within the Community and beyond). Nevertheless, the work of these committees is the major way in which Parliament exercises a measure of control over the Commission and the Council.[77]

We can, at this stage, return to our main theme; concerning the existence and effectiveness of its controlling devices over the executive branches of the Community, we would argue that the European Parliament is *not* a parliament for the following reasons:

1. It plays no role whatsoever in the appointment of members of the Commission or the Council of Ministers.[78]
2. It cannot ensure the collective responsibility of the Council.
3. Nor can it ensure the individual responsibility of members of the Commission or the Council.
4. The device which it has to ensure the collective responsibility of the Commission – the motion of censure – is a weapon of very limited effectiveness.
5. Only a minimum amount of control can be exercised by the Parliament over the Commission through its debate on the Annual General Report.
6. More control can be exerted over both executive bodies through oral and written parliamentary questions.
7. And some control – especially in the pre-decisional stages of the legislative process – is exercised through the specialised committees of the Parliament.

Notes

1. On the nature of the ambiguities associated with the phrase 'parliamentary control' see Coombes, 'Introduction', in D. Coombes et al., *The Power of the Purse* (London: Allen & Unwin/PEP, 1976) Chap. 1.
2. V. Herman, *Parliaments of the World: A Reference Compendium* (London: Macmillan, 1976) p. 801.
3. Article 2, Treaty Establishing a Single Council and a Single Commission of the European Communities.
4. Article 11, ibid.
5. 'Non-dismissability has been much less of a bolster to independence, partly because its granting was a little half-hearted. The power of appointment was left in the hands of the member governments, who tacitly agreed that each would appoint its own national Commissioner: there would be no joint selection of a politically homogeneous executive.' S. Henig, 'The Institutional

Structure of the European Communities', *Journal of Common Market Studies*, XII (1973–4) 373–409, at p. 383.

6. Article 10, Treaty Establishing a Single Council and a Single Commission of the European Communities.

7. Herman, *Parliaments of the World*, Chap. 62.

8. P. Allott, 'The Democratic Basis of the European Communities: The European Parliament and the Westminster Parliament', *Common Market Law Review*, XI (1974) 298–326, at p. 317.

9. Henig, op. cit., p. 384.

10. Other than a derivative one from the member states.

11. Henig, op. cit., p. 386.

12. See Herman, *Parliaments of the World*, Chap. 62. Individual responsibility exists in Denmark, Germany, the Netherlands and the United Kingdom.

13. Ibid., pp. 823–4.

14. J. Lodge, 'Parliamentary Reform in the EEC', *The Parliamentarian*, LV (1974) 250–7, at p. 254.

15. See D. Sanders and V. Herman, 'Stability and Survival of Governments in Western Democracies', *Acta Politica*, XII (1977) 346–77; and V. Herman, 'Comparative Perspectives on Ministerial Stability in Britain', in V. Herman and J. E. Alt (eds.), *Cabinet Studies* (London: Macmillan, 1975).

16. Lodge, op. cit., p. 254. See also a statement made by M. René Ribière (F. Gaullist) in the first censure debate: 'This censure, limited under Article 144 by the precision which the authors of the Treaty deliberately introduced, is therefore not a general censure, but an administrative censure.' *Debates of the European Parliament*, no. 156 (Dec 1972) p. 16.

17. Article 13 of the Treaty Establishing a Single Council and a Single Commission of the European Communities reads: 'If any member of the Commission no longer fulfils the conditions required for the performance of his duties or if he has been guilty of serious misconduct, the Court of Justice may, on application by the Council or the Commission, compulsorily retire him.'

18. See J. Fitzmaurice, *The Party Groups in the European Parliament* (Farnborough: Saxon House, 1975) p. 3; Allott, op. cit., p. 316; and D. Coombes, *Politics and Bureaucracy in the European Community* (London: Allen & Unwin, 1970) p. 85.

19. See D. V. Verney, *Analysis of Political Systems* (London: Routledge & Kegan Paul, 1959).

20. Cf. President Pompidou on the Constitution of the Fifth French Republic: 'I think that our Constitution is half-way between a properly presidential regime and a properly parliamentary regime. The balance between the two – which is moreover difficult – has the advantage of making our political system capable of firmness, stability, and at the same time of flexibility.' Quoted in D. Pickles, *Government and Politics of France* (London: Methuen, 1972) vol. I, p. 13.

21. This was emphasised by Herr Ludwig Fellermaier in the debate on the Kirk censure motion: 'The history of this House has taught us that the Commission and the European Parliament very often find themselves in the same boat while the helmsman – the Council of Ministers – is pulling the boat in a totally different direction.' *Debates of the European Parliament* (hereinafter *DEP*), no. 204 (June 1976) p. 14.

22. One of the decisions taken by the Council of Ministers on 15 October 1973 to improve relations between it and the Parliament was to allow the latter the right to debate Community trade agreements with third countries after their signature but before ratification.

23. Which exists in Denmark, France, the United Kingdom and Germany (Defence Commissioner).

24. The power to make such appointments generally belongs in the hands of the national governments.

25. Fitzmaurice, *The Party Groups in the European Parliament*, p. 14.

26. A. Spinelli, *The Eurocrats* (Baltimore: Johns Hopkins Press, 1966) p. 153.

27. *DEP*, no. 156 (Dec 1972) pp. 1–26.

28. *DEP*, no. 204 (June 1976) pp. 18–42.

29. *DEP*, no. 210 (Dec 1976) pp. 115–33.

30. *DEP*, no. 215 (Mar 1977) pp. 39–48.

31. *DEP*, no. 156 (Dec 1972) pp. 7–10.

32. Ibid., pp. 21–2.

33. Ibid., p. 12.

34. Ibid., pp. 14–17.

35. Ibid., pp. 17–20.

36. Reported in *The Times*, 7 Jan 1973.

37. *DEP*, no. 204 (June 1976) pp. 25–7.

38. Reported in *The Times*, 16 June 1976.

39. Ibid., 14 June 1976.

40. *DEP*, no. 204 (June 1976) pp. 25–7.

41. Ibid., p. 106.

42. Herr Aigner was the chairman of this sub-committee.

43. *DEP*, no. 210 (Dec 1976) pp. 115–17.

44. Ibid, pp. 118–20. M. Ortoli also challenged Parliament's right to censure the Commission: 'The institutional structure of the Communities is based on four autonomous and independent institutions of which the Commission is one. It is true that by voting a motion of censure, Parliament can force the members of the Commission to resign as a body.' However, the Commission is not an offshoot of Parliament: it works according to its own rules and is not subject to the guardianship of another institution.' Ibid., p. 119.

45. Ibid., pp. 122–4.

46. Ibid., pp. 120–2.

47. The document in question was eventually made available to the Parliament at the end of April 1977.

48. *DEP*, no. 215 (Mar 1977) pp. 40–2.

49. Ibid., pp. 42–5.

50. Ibid., p. 45.

51. Ibid., pp. 45–6.

52. Ibid., p. 46.

53. For the sake of convenience we refer to the four motions by the names of the Members of the European Parliament who moved them.

54. Fitzmaurice, *The Party Groups in the European Parliament*, p. 14.

55. The wording of Article 144 in the different languages of the Community is of interest here. The French text of Article 144 refers to the 'gestion' or administration of the Commission, the German to the 'Tätigkeit', the Italian to

62 The European Parliament and the European Community

'operaio', while the English text refers to its 'activities'. On the implications of this see the statement made by M. Ribière, *DEP*, no. 156 (Dec 1972) p. 15.
56. See the comments on the timing of censure motions made by M. Spénale, ibid., p. 2.
57. Ibid., pp. 392–3.
58. See Herman, *Parliaments of the World*, Chap. 63, for details.
59. Ibid., p. 841.
60. Ibid.
61. Act Concerning the Election of Representatives of the Assembly by Direct Universal Suffrage, Article 3, para. 1.
62. Article 143 reads: 'The Assembly shall discuss in open session the annual general report submitted to it by the Commission.'
63. Sir B. Cocks, *The European Parliament* (London: HMSO, 1973) p. 110.
64. Commissioners take part in the meetings of the committees which consider the report, and in the debates in plenary sessions.
65. See Herman, *Parliaments of the World*, Chap. 64.
66. See Rules of Procedure of the European Parliament, Articles 55–7, for details.
67. See J. J. Schwed, 'Les Questions écrites du Parlement Européen à la Commission', *Revue du Marché Common*, no. 135 (1970) 365–8.
68. The procedure for these is similar to the 'Interpellation' procedure used in many of the national parliaments.
69. In 1973 the number of columns, by national delegation, to the *Official Journal* reporting questions was as follows:

United Kingdom	28.5
Germany	15.5
France	8.75
Italy	8.15
Netherlands	6.5
Belgium	3.5
Denmark	2.0
Luxembourg	0.9
Ireland	0.7

These data were kindly supplied to us by Dr M. P. C. M. van Schendelen.
70. Fitzmaurice, *The Party Groups in the European Parliament*, pp. 185–6.
71. Heer Vredeling is now a Commissioner. His reputation for asking questions while he was a Member of the European Parliament was such that he earned the nickname Henk Vrageling, from the Dutch 'vragen', to ask. *European Parliament Report*, no. 32 (Feb 1977) p. 4.
72. M. Palmer, 'The Role of a Directly Elected European Parliament', *The World Today*, XXXIII (1977) 122–30, at p. 125.
73. *DEP*, no. 209 (Nov 1976) p. 87.
74. Each committee has 35 members, with the exception of the Committee on Rules of Procedure and Petitions which has 18 members.
75. R. Bieber and M. Palmer, 'A Community without a Capital', *Journal of Common Market Studies*, XV (1976) 1–8.
76. For details see Herman, *Parliaments of the World*, Chaps. 37–40.

77. D. Sidjanski, 'Auditions au Parlement Européen: Expérience et Avenir', *Res Publica*, XVIII (1976) 5–32.

78. The European Parliament called on 11 July 1975 for its effective participation in the appointment of Commission and Court of Justice members. See European Parliament Doc. 166/167/75.

5 The Powers and Functions of the European Parliament

(i) The Powers of the European Parliament

In the last two chapters we have attempted to evaluate the European Parliament's claim to be a parliament by examining the performance of its legislative, financial and control powers and by comparing these with the powers of the national parliaments. Our findings are summarised in the following sets of statements:

A. Concerning the performance of the *legislative* power, the European Parliament is *not* a parliament because:

1. There is no clear-cut separation of powers between the legislative and executive branches of the Community's institutions.
2. The legislative power is not exercised wholly or even partly by the European Parliament, which has neither the power to initiate nor to amend legislation.
3. The European Parliament is not involved in the passage of all of the Community's legislative items.
4. The Parliament's legislative role is largely consultative and is limited to the pre-legislative stages of the decision-making process.

B. Concerning the performance of the *financial* power, the European Parliament is *not* a parliament because:

1. Its prior approval for items of revenue is not required.
2. Nor is its approval required for the classification of expenditure between compulsory and non-compulsory items, or for the allocation of compulsory expenditure between different items.
3. Nor is its approval required for some three-quarters of the Community's expenditure (compulsory expenditure) over which it can do little more than express an opinion.
4. And the Parliament's formal powers of decision over the remaining quarter of expenditure (non-compulsory expenditure) is restricted by subjective limits (concerning majorities), objective limits (the maximum rate of expenditure) and

technical limits (involving previous and/or contractual obligations).

C. Concerning the performance of the *control* power, the European Parliament is *not* a parliament because:

1. It plays no role whatsoever in the appointment of members of the Commission or the Council of Ministers.
2. It cannot ensure the collective responsibility of the Council.
3. Nor can it ensure the individual responsibility of members of the Commission or the Council.
4. The device it has to ensure the collective responsibility of the Commission – the motion of censure – is a nuclear weapon of very limited effectiveness.
5. Only a minimum amount of control can be exercised by the Parliament over the Commission through its debate on the Annual General Report.
6. More control can be exercised over both executive bodies through oral and written parliamentary questions.
7. And some control – especially in the pre-decisional stages of the decision-making process – is exercised through the specialised committees of the Parliament.

Our argument, then, is that the European Parliament is *not* a parliament (or, more accurately *not much* of a parliament) because it fails to meet a series of basic political, constitutional and decision-making requirements concerning the performance of legislative, financial and control powers. When further comparisons are made with the national parliaments, a constellation of other reasons could be advanced for suggesting that the European Parliament is not a parliament. These would include:

- the absence of a government drawn from the Parliament;
- the absence of an opposition within the Parliament which opposes this government;[1]
- the fact that the various party groups in the Parliament lack electoral mandates;
- the fact that Members of the European Parliament do not represent specific constituencies.

(ii) The Functions of the European Parliament

At this stage it is therefore necessary to pose two questions. First, if the European Parliament is not a parliament, what then is it? Second, in what ways, if any, does it matter that the European Parliament is something other than a parliament?

What is it? Vedel suggests that the European Parliament's position within the institutional framework of the Community 'is reminiscent of certain obsolete political structures'.[2] A similar theme is emphasised by Fitzmaurice who, after comparing the Parliament with the House of Commons in the eighteenth century, describes it as 'a developing parliament, an embryonic parliament, in an emergent political unit. It faces all the difficulties inherent in that situation.'[3] Such descriptions of the Parliament are apposite.

The evolution of the Parliament within the Community's institutional framework has been confused and confusing. What is most noticeable about the development of the European Parliament to date has been the absence of an institutional blueprint for it.[4] Quite simply, towards which parliamentary model the European Parliament has been developing is unclear. For reasons discussed below, we believe that any developments towards the blue-print of the Nine's national parliaments in the member states – especially their performance of the legislative, financial and control powers – are unrealistic. Given this, what then is the Parliament? Although it might have been regarded as little more than an institutionalised pressure group within the EC until recently, it is potentially much more.

The second question raised earlier was in what ways, if any, does it matter that the European Parliament is something other than a parliament? It is necessary to ask this because of two distinct sets of forces – direct elections, and the likely development of the Parliament's powers in the future.

The holding of European elections will be one of the most significant events in the short history of the Community.[5] The present emphasis on elections to the Parliament highlights a manifest concern that the Community as a whole should be democratised and a latent concern that the institutions of the Community should be reformed.[6] As we saw in Chapter 1, a series of assumptions concerning the future scope, development and functioning of the Parliament and the other main Community institutions are dependent on these elections.[7] Firstly, it is assumed that the authority of Members of the European Parliament will be considerably strengthened if they can claim legitimacy from the electorate.[8] A second assumption is that an increase in the democratic legitimacy of the European Parliament will increase the legitimacy of other EC institutions, namely the Commission, in that the Treaty gives the Parliament the power to dismiss the Commission. A final set of assumptions posit that the attainment of democratic legitimacy is dependent upon increases in the representativeness and effectiveness of the Parliament.

Underlying all these assumptions is a widespread feeling that reforms in the exercise and distribution of authority among the Community's institutions are inevitable;[9] that such reforms should be centred around a directly elected Parliament; and that an elected Parliament has – or should have – a major role to play in the future governing of the EC.[10]

However, the holding of European elections is a necessary but not sufficient condition for either the evolution of the Parliament, or reform of the Community's institutions. In addition, the Parliament's future also depends upon the exercise and development of its powers.

Since its inception the Parliament has been trying to expand its legislative, financial and control powers vis-à-vis the Commission and the Council. In an incremental and essentially pragmatic way the Parliament has undoubtedly increased its powers. The introduction of the concertation procedure, the agreement of the Council to have questions put to it, the increasingly large share of the budget classified as non-compulsory, and so on, attest to this. Both the advocates of European elections and parliamentary reformers at the Community level argue that it is essential, if not inevitable, for the powers of the Parliament to be further increased after it becomes a directly elected body: as one part of the 'chicken–egg' dilemma will have been resolved by the holding of elections, the other part must follow through institutional and parliamentary reform. However, while the European Parliament has been trying to increase and align its legislative, financial and control powers with those that the national parliaments are thought to have, the latter's powers over their respective governments in those very same areas have declined considerably as we saw in Chapter 2. In other words, the Parliament has perhaps been trying to 'fly in the face of history' in seeking to develop powers that national parliaments have either consciously or unconsciously, avoidably or unavoidably, lost or conceded to national governments. The European Parliament's quest for greater powers is predicated on the belief that in the *sui generis* supranational system, not only should there be democratic parliamentary controls, but that a supranational parliament should exercise such controls in any area where national parliaments are no longer able, for whatever reasons, to do so.

At this stage we must return to the absence of an institutional blueprint for the Parliament. The lack of a widely shared and coherent vision as to what Parliament's role is, partly accounts for the limited impact it has had so far on EC decision-making and on the lives of the Community's citizens. It is usually taken for granted that if the European Parliament is to influence EC decision-making to a greater extent, it should develop along the lines of the Nine's national parliaments. However, it is questionable whether the national parliaments effectively play a greater role in these processes than the European Parliament does in the Community, and this notwithstanding the fact that the national parliaments are the beneficiaries of (sometimes considerable) constitutional grants of power whereas the European Parliament is not.

Questions rarely asked are, should the European Parliament develop along the lines of the national parliaments? Should it try to acquire 'traditional' legislative, financial and control powers and perform 'the established parliamentary role'?[11] Is it possible, or desirable, for the European Parliament to gain these powers given the unenthusiastic attitudes of (some of) the EC's member governments?

If the European Parliament cannot as yet exercise these traditional legislative, financial and control powers, what should it do and, in doing it, how could it become a parliament? We believe that the European Parliament should perform certain *functions* in respect of the *public*, namely communication, education and information functions. The prospect of European elections heightens the significance of these functions and of the European Parliament's capacity to fulfil them. Moreover, if these are effectively executed, changes to the EC's institutional balance and the constitutional powers of the European Parliament are likely to be advanced. The physical and psychological remoteness of the Community to date, the intangibility of its decisions and actions to the people of Europe, and the lack of intelligibility and visibility of its institutions, have together contributed to the failure of the European Parliament to emerge as a salient reference-point, or as a political cue-giver, for the mass public. Quite simply, the public does not think of the European Parliament as a parliament because of what it is (or, more accurately, what it is not, that is, a 'parliament' in the sense that a national parliament is) and because of what it does (or rather what it has so far failed to do, that is, have any impact on their lives). European elections are a means by which the European Parliament can become something *to*, and eventually provide a platform from which something can be done *for*, the people of Europe.

Notes

1. See R. A. Dahl, 'Introduction', in Dahl (ed.), *Political Opposition in Western Democracies* (New Haven: Yale Univ. Press, 1966).
2. G. Vedel, 'The Role of the Parliamentary Institution in European Integration', in Directorate-General for Research and Documentation of the European Parliament (ed.), *Symposium on European Integration and the Future of Parliaments in Europe* (Luxembourg: European Parliament, 1975) pp. 236—41.
3. J. Fitzmaurice, *The Party Groups in the European Parliament* (Farnborough: Saxon House, 1975) pp. 205–6.
4. On 'blue-prints' see E. Damgaard, 'Structural Adjustments of the Danish Parliament in the Twentieth Century', in F. Heapley and A. Baaklini (eds.), *Comparative Legislative Reforms and Innovations* (State University of New York Press, 1977).
5. This is emphasised by statements made by the President of the European Parliament (M. Georges Spénale) on the occasion of the signing of the Council Decision concerning direct elections, by the President of the Council (Mr Max van der Stoel) at the signing of the texts, and by the President of the Commission (M. François-Xavier Ortoli) at the signing of the documents con-

cerning the election. These speeches can be found in Directorate-General for Information of the European Parliament, *European Elections, May–June, 1978.*

6. See C.-A. Morard, 'Le Contrôle Démocratique dans les Communautés Européennes', presented at the 8th Colloquium on the European Communities, Liège, Mar 1976; and P. Pescatore, 'Les exigences de la démocratie et al légitimité de la Communauté Européene', *Cahiers de Droit Européen*, X (1974) 499–514.

7. See M. Stewart, 'Direct Elections to the European Parliament', *Common Market Law Review*, XIII (1976) 283–301.

8. See P. Allott, 'The Democratic Basis of the European Communities: The European Parliament and the Westminster Parliament', *Common Market Law Review*, XI (1974) 298–326.

9. D. Norrenberg, 'Un modèle institutionnel déficient: la communauté européenne', *Res Republica*, XVIII (1976) 203–14.

10. See Leo Tindemans, 'Report on European Union', *Bulletin of the European Communities*, Supplement 1/76. For a comment on the Tindemans Report see J. D. B. Mitchell, 'The Tindemans Report: Retrospect and Prospect', *Common Market Law Review*, XIII (1976) 455–84.

11. Fitzmaurice, *The Party Groups in the European Parliament*, p. 13.

Part Two

6 Democratic Legitimacy and Direct Elections

For the first time a Parliament is coming into existence that has been legitimised in the European sense.

Hans-Dietrich Genscher (1977)

Direct elections to the Parliament will give this Assembly a new political authority. At the same time it will reinforce the democratic legitimacy of the whole European institutional apparatus.

Tindemans Report (1976)

On 20 September 1976 the Nine signed the 'Act concerning the Election of the Representatives of the Assembly by Direct Universal Suffrage'. This Act represented not only the culmination of a process that began over twenty years ago,[1] but also the start of a process designed to facilitate European elections by June 1978. The elections pose numerous problems. Although a common electoral system is supposed to be adopted for subsequent elections, the politically sensitive nature of this issue resulted in each member state adopting the electoral procedure it deemed appropriate for the first elections. Even so, the decision to elect the European Parliament by direct universal suffrage remains contentious.

A number of arguments are commonly advanced against European elections. Opposition is usually justified in terms of emotive arguments imputing losses of sovereignty by national parliaments as a result of the direct election of the European chamber. It is often asserted that European elections will be a waste of time and serve no useful purpose given the limited nature of the European Parliament's powers, the ostensible 'irrelevance' of its affairs, the logistical problems of conducting a supranational campaign, the remoteness of the European Parliament from most citizens, and the dispersal of political talent between national parliaments and the European Assembly.[2]

By contrast, supporters of European elections usually justify the elections in terms of the impact they believe they will have on the distribution of authority among European institutions; on increasing democracy in the Community by giving citizens the right to elect representatives to a chamber accountable to them; on legitimising the European Parliament's claims for greater decision-making powers, especially in areas where national parliaments are unable to exert effective control; and finally, on the nature of the EC's legitimacy.[3] In addition, advocates of European elections suggest that, following the elections, EC institutions will become more democratic, representative and legitimate.

A large measure of conceptual confusion exists over the term 'democracy' in the debate on European elections. On the one hand, European elections and 'democracy' in the EC are considered synonymous. On the other hand, it is argued that the elections will increase the elements of democracy at the supranational level in the Community. Confusion inheres, firstly, in the failure to disaggregate the concept of democracy, and secondly, in an inclination to confuse one aspect of the conduct of democratic politics (the periodic holding of elections in which citizens elect candidates from various parties to represent them in a parliament) with democracy itself. This confusion is further aggravated by the fact that the notions of representativeness and accountability are also associated with the conduct of democratic politics in the member states, and that these notions are implicitly subsumed in the ways in which the term 'democracy' has been applied to European elections and the EC. In particular, the ideas of 'direct' and 'derivative' legitimacy[4] are predicated on assumptions concerning the way in which European elections will make Members of the European Parliament (MEPs) *directly accountable* to the people who elected them and whom they represent. While it is easy to see why the notions of accountability, representativeness and democracy should have become intertwined where European elections are concerned, it must be remembered that European elections *per se* will not enhance the democratic element in EC decision-making in the sense that the elections will not cause the EC's supreme decision-making body, the Council of Ministers, to become accountable on a collective basis to any other EC body. This observation is important since it not only highlights the European Parliament's lack of control powers vis-à-vis a quasi-governing body, but alerts us to the fact that it is inappropriate to regard European elections as something that will 'democratise' EC decision-making itself. At most, European elections will lead to a reappraisal of aspects of the distribution of authority among EC institutions because of the changed basis of the Parliament's legitimacy.

The theme of 'democratic legitimacy', and the way it affects the institutions and the development of the Community, is a recurrent one both in the literature on Western European integration and, especially, in debates among European politicians and parliamentarians.[5] Some idea of the centrality of the theme and its relationship to direct elections can be obtained from the following quotations:

Direct elections to the European Parliament are essential to enable the peoples to play an immediate part in the unification of Europe. They would thus lend to the exercise of power by the Communities a *legitimacy* which has hitherto been lacking. The Treaties establishing the European Communities specifically provide for this direct link between the peoples and the European Parliament, but it has not yet proved possible to convince the responsible politicians of the need to take this step which is so fundamental to integration.[6]

... there are sectors of opinion to which the *democratic legitimacy* of the Community and of its structures and machinery seems inadequate. The transfer of national powers to the Community, generally regarded as a limitation of state sovereignty, *also* constitutes the transfer of powers belonging to the national Parliaments or under their control, to organisations (the Council, the Commission) whose *democratic legitimacy* is very indirect. The development of the European parliamentary institution would facilitate the transfer of national powers to the Community and remove the above objections.[7]

Direct elections to the Parliament will give this Assembly a new political authority. At the same time it will reinforce the *democratic legitimacy* of the whole European institutional apparatus.[8]

In other words, consensus is that European elections *per se* will increase the 'democratic legitimacy' of both the European Parliament and the Community. We shall argue that, to the contrary, European elections may exacerbate rather than mitigate legitimacy problems. They may augment elements associated with democratic practices in the EC and the Parliament but they may not lead to concomitant increases in legitimacy.

This possibility has, by and large, been overlooked by both supporters and opponents of European elections. In some respects it is, however, a restatement of a familiar theme in the voluminous literature on political development – a move towards one intrinsically valid and much sought-after goal (for example, participation) may involve a move away from another equally valid and equally sought-after goal (for example, stability).[9] The similarity between institutional aspects of political development faced by the Community on the one hand, and newly independent countries on the other hand, is striking.

Although it is outside the scope of this essay to develop the theme of the last paragraph, it can be substantiated by drawing parallels between the Community and newly independent countries with regard to six 'crises' which are inextricably linked to the multifaceted process of political development.[10] The first of these is the 'identity crisis', that is, 'the tension between the culturally and psychologically determined sense of personal-group identity and the political definition of the community'. The second involves the 'participation crisis' that is, 'an increase in the number of people involved in the political process . . . manifested in the growth of parties and mass movements'. The third involves the 'distribution crisis', that is, 'the rapid increase in the popular demand for material benefits from the government and with the contemporary belief that governments are responsible for the level of living'. The fourth involves the 'penetration crisis', that is, 'the depth and extent of central political control including areas of activity and parts of the geo-polity'. The fifth concerns the 'institutionalisation crisis', that is, the process by which the adaptability, complexity, autonomy and coherence of the political system's organisations and procedures acquire value and stability.[11] The final crisis concerns political legitimacy. Given that political legitimacy is of critical importance in any democratic system of government (or, in the EC's case, in a system comprising democratic polities), and as European elections appear to be central to the notion of political legitimacy in the Community, a more detailed consideration of firstly the concept of legitimacy, and secondly its relationship to European elections, is warranted.

The Concept of Legitimacy

There is little agreement in the literature about the concept of 'political legitimacy'. Although a study synthesising existing writings is needed, our task here will be far more limited. We shall attempt to bring some theoretical and analytical clarity to the concept not as it is used in a wide sense but as it is particularly applied in writings on the Community. We shall do this firstly by discussing the general concept of legitimacy; secondly, by examining its relationship to European elections; and thirdly, by reference to four recent works which have focused on the problem of legitimacy. Through our examination of these, we shall hope to enhance understanding of the relationship between European elections and legitimacy in the Community.

The Problem of Legitimacy in the European Community

The terms 'legitimacy' and 'democratic legitimacy' are used ambiguously, indiscriminately, and largely without qualification or explanation in much of the literature on European integration and the EC's institutions. It is usually assumed that the EC's basis of legitimacy is wanting but that it can be remedied through the holding of direct elections to the European Parliament. Such elections are expected to fulfil a dual function: firstly, to alter the basis of the EC's legitimacy so that it changes from being 'derivative' to 'direct'; and secondly, to augment the democratic nature of the EC by providing for public participation in decision-making. The questions of democracy and legitimacy are inextricably linked since by participating in European elections it is assumed that citizens will give expression to their assent to the EC's authority structures and so confer 'direct' legitimacy on the Community – its legitimacy to date having been 'derivative' because its authority derived from the member states.

Why was the derivative form of legitimacy deemed inferior to the direct form, and why has the acquisition of the latter assumed particular importance for the EC? The acquisition of direct legitimacy by a political system is normally deemed important since legitimacy is believed to confer authority on a system of domination, making its decisions regarding policies, priorities or the allocation of resources just. 'Legitimating rationales, necessary to any system of domination,' according to Mueller, 'are effective only if their underlying principles have been internalised by the public, that is, collectively accepted as normative and thus as binding.'[12] For Mueller, 'legitimacy, once established, serves as the most effective justification for the manner in which political power is exercised. It is the most effective argument against change to the structure of the political system.'[13]

This latter qualification is important for the EC. So long as its legitimacy has been derivative, it has been faced with the theoretical possibility of being dissolved by the very states that constituted it simply through a withdrawal of their assent to its authority structures. It has been argued that were the basis of the EC's legitimacy to be changed, specifically by way of direct elections to the European Parliament, the EC would acquire an existence independent of the member governments.[14] This argument derives from advocates of democracy, and hence of direct elections, evoking the principles of the people's sovereignty as the base for legitimacy.[15] By implication, as member governments opposed to such elections clearly realised, this view challenged the existing basis of authority in the EC. Legitimacy based on the people's sovereignty rather than on member governments' assent was viewed as preferable and superior. Since the people's sovereignty was supposed to find expression in and through Parliament, the holding of direct elections assumed particular importance. They were to fulfil three distinct functions: firstly, to legitimise the Parliament and the EC; secondly, to confer autonomy of existence on the EC; and thirdly, to realise democracy. But if direct elections confer direct legitimacy on the EC, this need not, as is often assumed, serve as justification for the manner in which political power in the EC is exercised. It may, and most probably will, have the contrary effect because, as we shall argue below, MEPs will seek to effect a redistribution of power and to enhance the role of the Parliament in EC decision-making. This, in turn, will affect the EC's institutional balance

– that is, the distribution of political authority among its institutions – and also, therefore, the manner in which political power is exercised. Unlike other EC bodies, however, the European Parliament's claims to political power will be advanced as legitimate by reference to its having been popularly elected. MEPs will therefore be able to evoke some source of authority beyond the European Parliament itself – the EC electors. Such a source of authority is, according to Schaar, an essential facet of traditional conceptions of legitimacy[16] since it is vital to establish claims or entitlement to rule. Thus, in the past, when the rights of kings were challenged, advocates of democracy, according to Mueller, could convincingly evoke the principles of a social contract or the people's sovereignty as bases for legitimacy in opposition to monarchic principles of dynastic lineage and divine right.[17] The traditional concept of legitimacy was based on custom, divine law, the law of nature, or a constitution.

The European Parliament can have recourse neither to the Rome Treaty nor to other 'higher principles' in order to justify its claims for greater decision-making powers. Even so, Article 138 can be invoked to support claims for direct elections. Claims for greater powers can then be based on the notion of Parliament as the embodiment of the people's sovereignty.

However, claims to right or entitlement to rule are not, as we shall see, sufficient conditions for legitimacy to exist. Instead, as Mueller argues, 'a congruence between the citizen's perception of what is right and proper and the actual performance of the government buttresses a system's claim to legitimacy'.[18]

Basing their concepts of legitimacy on the notions of efficient task performance and citizen compliance, contemporary social scientists, according to Schaar, have tended to view legitimacy as no more than 'acceptance or acquiescence.'[19] Indeed, these views underline Lindberg and Scheingold's view of the relationship between 'permissive consensus' in the EC and the legitimacy of the EC's authority structures[20] – the latter being deemed legitimate because they are acquiesced to. They appear to subscribe to the view that political institutions can exert normative power by their mere existence over a long period of time, and that this induces citizens to accept a system, and that its continued efficient operation induces compliance. But as Schaar and Friedrich point out, legitimacy and acquiescence, and legitimacy and consensus, are not identical.[21] Nevertheless, Easton maintains that it is essential that citizens perceive a system's authority structure as legitimate if the system is to persist (and the EC has faced problems in this respect) and if citizens are to submit voluntarily to its outputs even if they oppose specific policies.

Whereas a belief in democratic legitimacy can be instilled in people via socialisation and education processes, the EC lacks both the institutionalised mechanisms through which it could perpetuate a belief among EC citizens in the Community's democratic legitimacy, and any legitimating rationales or ideologies. However, European elections are often seen as a kind of legitimating rationale, and the European Parliament has, not unsurprisingly, been regarded as potentially the one institution that could engender popular belief in its own and the EC's democratic legitimacy. This is important since, on the one hand, 'democratic consent' is supposed to afford authority legitimacy,[22] and since, on the other hand, legitimacy can be generally understood as 'the capacity of the system to engender and maintain the belief that the existing political institutions are the most appropriate ones for the society'.[23]

Let us now consider a general analysis of legitimacy before scrutinising those works that focus on the problem of legitimacy in the EC.

(a) Stillman's general analysis of legitimacy   According to Stillman, all definitions of legitimacy can be subsumed in the following outline:[24]

A rulership is legitimate if and only if:
1. It is based on the beliefs of one or more of the following groups;
   (a) (all or some) other nations, states or persons
   (b) the people unanimous
   (c) a majority of the people
   (d) a majority of some portion of the people
   (e) the king, dictator, etc.
   (f) tradition, ancestors, prescription, etc.
   (g) God
   (h) other
   (i) none or irrelevant.

2. It has any one or more of the following classes of norms:
   (a) possession of a certain quality (or qualities)
   (b) pursuit of a certain value (or set of values)
   (c) none or irrelevant.[25]

On the bases of the first criteria, the EC's legitimacy appears to be founded on the Nine member states (1a), a majority of the people in some of these states (1c), and (1d). Where the second criteria are concerned, the EC's legitimacy seems to rest on the possession of certain qualities (2a) such as democracy and representative government, and the pursuit of certain values (2b) such as integration. Within the parameters of this broad framework, three other works which specifically relate the concept of legitimacy to the Community can be examined.

(b) Pryce and the 'invisible' Community   In a paper stressing the importance of the role of information in promoting European integration, Pryce described the Community as 'invisible.'[26] He argued

that the legitimacy of a political system is conditioned by formal constitutional constraints and, more importantly, by 'the ability of a system to make itself visible, tangible and intelligible to its citizens. In other words, if citizens are unable to perceive the existence of a political system, they are unable to accept its legitimacy.'[27] He argues that whereas all national political systems have a real and direct impact on the lives of their citizens, the Community

> ... is virtually invisible to the great mass of its citizens. It makes hardly any demands on, and it offers very few services to, the individual .... At the same time, the Community is almost totally bereft of any of its own symbols. It has no flag, and no anthem, and is still locked in earnest discussion about the possibility of a symbol to be put on the proposed common passport for its citizens. One can travel the length and breadth of the Community without being made aware of its existence.[28]

So, apart from farmers who experience a 'direct and tangible relationship' between their incomes and decisions taken in Brussels, for almost all EC citizens the Community remains 'remote and mysterious'. Emphasising the role of European elections in making the Community more visible, Pryce argues that they will 'create a direct and active link between the citizens of the Community and the European Parliament.'[29]

(c) Henig and the institutional structure of the Community   In a report based on the work of a Federal Trust Group examining the institutional structure of the Community, Stanley Henig (the Group's rapporteur) analysed the capabilities and weaknesses of the existing institutions.[30] He advanced two 'general yardsticks' by which the performance of the institutions could be measured – efficiency and legitimacy:

> Europe's institutions will be legitimate insofar as individual citizens are prepared to accept decisions made by them even when their own lives and livelihoods are affected and insofar as there is (consequently) a transfer of loyalties and expectations to those institutions. Without this acceptance of the institutions and some associated transfer of loyalty, integration – the peaceful merger of decision-making processes and the creation of joint policies to the point of effective political union – will be unable to proceed beyond a certain point. It is desirable, of course, that the European institutions receive the accolade of legitimacy only if they are organised in accordance with certain democratic principles, but the critical operating condition for integration is legitimacy rather than democracy. One might posit three criteria for legitimation – tradition, democracy

and success in performance. It is arguable that at least two of these criteria will be needed for the Community to receive the accolade of legitimacy. In the absence of any tradition and lacking any very credible democratic structure, the Community has usually been forced to rely on performance for its own legitimation.'[31]

Elsewhere Henig has stressed the importance of European elections to the legitimation process: 'Ultimately, though, [the European] Parliament must have legislative and budgetary powers and be directly elected if the European institutions as a whole are going to acquire the degree of legitimacy necessary for the transfer of loyalties and expectations.'[32]

(d) Allott and the psychological dimension of legitimacy Allott, comparing the democratic bases of the European and Westminster parliaments, advances a different approach to the problem of political legitimacy.[33] He argues that two critical psychological factors which undermine the legitimacy of the European Parliament are, firstly, the secretive nature of EC decision-making, and secondly, the remoteness of the decision-making process from the peoples of Europe. These two factors take on special importance with regard to sovereignty and taxation. On the subject of sovereignty, Allott writes:

> ... Beyond the question of the actual influence of Parliament is the underlying conviction that there should be some place where the *ultimate* power to make the law of the land is exercised openly and in front of the representatives of the people.... At the end of the day, the law as adopted in Parliament becomes a legal order and a legal authority to those whose role is to enforce that law, and so far as the people are concerned, it is the law behind which, they know and (in all normal circumstances) accept, lies the sanction of public force. In short, it is the cornerstone of the system because if the authority of law made in Parliament is accepted, then all else in the system follows, all other legal authority is then tolerated on the understanding that it could be revoked or modified at any time by means of a law made in Parliament.[34]

On the subject of taxation, a similar argument is advanced:

> And yet, once again, it must be said that the *idea* that Parliament, and particularly the House of Commons is the *place* where taxation is imposed remains an idea of great political importance, one of the familiar psychological pillars on which public loyalty to our system of government rests.[35]

In short, and irrespective of its powers, parliament is the 'grand forum' of the whole political system: the place where the legislative and financial actions of the government are legitimised. For this reason, European elections have often been justified in terms of the 'no taxation without representation' argument.

Drawing on the above concepts of legitimacy, we shall argue that if the Community and the European Parliament are to be perceived as legitimate, the following eight criteria must be satisfied:[36]

1. Democracy.
2. Tradition.
3. Transfer of loyalties.
4. Acceptance of decisions.
5. Tangibility.
6. Intelligibility.
7. Visibility.
8. 'Grand forum'.

Let us first ascertain how applicable each criterion is to the Community as a whole, and to the European Parliament in particular; and secondly, consider what contribution European elections may make to public perceptions of the EC's legitimacy.

Diagnosis: The Legitimacy Problems of the Community and Parliament

Our first criterion, *democracy*, is inextricably linked to the legitimacy problem. None of the Community's institutions is democratic and legitimate in the sense of having been directly elected by the peoples of the Community. None of the institutions is therefore able to evoke claims to a *direct* authority base beyond itself. None possesses direct legitimacy. European elections are, however, supposed to give expression *at the supranational level* to some of the basic liberal-democratic norms and practices of the Nine, and to be accomplished by making the EC a participatory democracy. The European Parliament made this clear as early as 27 June 1963, when it adopted a resolution seeking enlargement of its competence and powers. In so doing it 'insisted on the fact that the election of representatives ... by direct universal suffrage constitutes an indispensable element for conferring a more democratic character on the Community'.[37] Via European elections, voters are to accord the EC's authority structures democratic consent.

Our second criterion, *tradition*, is hardly applicable to the Community. Although it possesses a few traditions, these are not prominent. Instead, the fact that it has persisted is often taken to mean that its authority has been accepted. However, the notion of acceptance should be dichotomised into, on the one hand, active acceptance of the EC's authority structures and outputs by aware and participating elites and publics, and, on the other hand, into passive acquiescence by either publics aware of the EC but ignorant of, or uninterested in, ways in which they can influence outputs, or by publics largely unaware of the EC. Moreover, although interest groups largely accept EC outputs, dissatisfied groups, such as farmers, sometimes contest even the EC's derivative legitimacy through their occasionally violent demonstrations against Commission and Council decisions (or lack of them). Demonstrations indicative of dissatisfaction with the degree of efficiency shown in the performance of tasks by a political system can undermine claims to legitimacy. This highlights a dilemma associated with European elections, and partly accounts for our suggestion that they could lead to decreased legitimacy. The transition from a tradition of passive compliance to active participation and active expression of an acceptance or rejection of the EC could, therefore, be problematic.

Our third, fourth and fifth criteria – *transfer of loyalties, acceptance of decisions* and *tangibility* – apply to the EC as a whole and not solely to any one institution. It is, moreover, almost impossible to determine, on the basis of existing survey data, whether or not mass loyalties are being transferred from national to European institutions, or whether or not the latter's decisions are perceived as tangible by EC publics. For the present, it appears that although acceptance of the EC is not internalised by EC publics, either through ignorance or habituation, they appear to acquiesce to the EC. They accept its legality (a prerequisite of legitimate authority) but do not necessarily regard it as legitimate. Although it is difficult to evaluate these criteria with any certainty, it appears that they are at best only partially, and generally inadequately, satisfied by the EC.

Our sixth and seventh criteria, *intelligibility* and *visibility*, are equally applicable to the EC and its individual institutions. None is sufficiently intelligible or visible to EC citizens. After European elections, the intelligibility and visibility of the Parliament will (or, as advocates of the elections would argue, should) become much greater than that of the Community as a whole. Our final criterion, the '*grand forum*', is especially applicable to the Parliament, and is absent for reasons closely associated with its lack of intelligibility and visibility.

The legitimacy of the EC can then be distinguished from that of its individual institutions. The Parliament's legitimacy problems stem from the nature of its authority, its intelligibility, visibility, and the way in which it acts as the EC's 'grand forum'. We shall argue that European elections *per se* will not result in increasing the internalised and active acceptance of the European Parliament by EC citizens unless it first becomes more visible and intelligible to them. If publics are unaware of its existence, powers, functions and performance, they may perhaps be expected to continue to accept the *legality* of its role in the EC but not necessarily to regard it as *legitimate*. In other words, the traditional notion of efficient performance eliciting compliance and legitimacy will not obtain unless publics are aware of the tasks performed by Parliament. Unless the Parliament serves as the EC's 'grand forum', legitimacy will be wanting. What we are therefore suggesting is that the concept of legitimacy needs to be disaggregated. On the one hand, we have legitimacy expressed in terms of direct consent via European elections. On the other hand, we have legitimacy expressed in terms of visibility and the associated aspects of efficient task performance, the intelligibility of Parliament's powers and functions, and the tangibility of its outputs.

(a) The problem of intelligibility The fundamental intelligibility problem lies in defining what the European Parliament is, and in giving a straightforward explanation of such basic things as what its powers are, how these powers compare with those of national parliaments, where the Parliament meets, how its members are chosen, and who its members are. Consider, for instance, the following hypothetical dialogue:

Q. Where is the Parliament located?
A. Half of its sessions are held in Luxembourg where its Secretariat is located, the other half in Strasbourg. Almost all the work done by the parliamentary committees takes place in Brussels. So it is really located in three separate places in three different countries.

Q. What powers does Parliament have?
A. Briefly, a few legislative powers, a few more budgetary powers, and hardly any effective oversight powers. Its major powers, such as the power to reject the EC's budget, and the power to dismiss the Commission, have rarely been used.

Q. How do these powers compare with those of national parliaments?
A. Not very favourably. The Parliament is a rather toothless creature at the moment, even though it is trying to acquire greater influence in the decision-making process.

Q. Is it really a Parliament?
A. Yes and no. It calls itself a Parliament, and in some senses it is one. But the Rome Treaty refers to it as an Assembly – and its name has never formally been changed.

It would be easy to continue along these lines and to refer to other unique features of the European Parliament that handicap its intelligibility when it is compared to national parliaments. While it can be argued that because the European Parliament, by adopting the nomenclature 'Parliament' in place of 'Assembly', increased its intelligibility, changes in nomenclature do not compensate for the lack of certain other features common to most of the Nine's parliaments. These would include: the absence of a government drawn from the Parliament; the absence of an opposition in Parliament; and the absence of a programme or policies specifically advanced by Parliament's party groups as alternatives to those put forward by the Commission. Clearly, the European Parliament differs so widely from any other parliament that it is difficult for non-specialists either to make sense of these differences or to conceive of it as a 'parliament' in the familiar sense. The Nine's national parliaments share a number of common features (a fixed location, a government, an opposition, etc.) which are understood at the national level, but which are absent at the European level.

The problem of Parliament's lack of intelligibility is part of the larger problem of the low level of intelligibility of the EC institutions. Even by attempting to locate the Parliament within the overall institutional context of the Community, an understanding of it is not appreciably advanced. The EC's institutions are not modelled on the arrangements of any system of government in any one of the member states, or elsewhere. The EC's institutional set-up is *sui generis*.[38] This exacerbates the intelligibility problem since it militates against a ready transfer of knowledge, symbols and understanding of governmental processes from the national to the supranational level. Equally important, in this respect, is the complexity of the EC's institutional arrangements. There is a Parliament; a bicephalous executive but no government; and various institutional appendages, some of which (such as the Economic and Social Committee and European Investment Bank, for example) are provided for in the Rome Treaty, others of which (for example, COREPER and the European Council) developed in response to specific contingencies and to the requirements of effective decision-making.[39] Only a few of these, notably the Economic and Social Committee, have parallels in either one or more of the member states. The uniqueness of the EC's institutional set-up complicates matters when it comes to explaining to EC citizens exactly what the various institutions are and how they relate to each other.

The main reference points for the people of the EC's member states are the legislative and executive branches of their own governments. The EC's intelligibility problems, by contrast, are highlighted if comparable reference points are sought among its institutions. Allott argues that 'certain basic types of political activity which characterise political systems within states are exceptionally confused in the Community system.' One of these, central to our argument, is that 'Community legislation is not formally adopted by the Community Parliament: it is adopted by two bodies (Council and Commission) which are more executive than legislative in style and composition.'[40] If there can be no easy understanding of the nature, composition and sources of legislative and executive authority in the Community, the problem of the intelligibility of the Parliament cannot be solved simply by the introduction of European elections.

(b) The problem of visibility The period prior to European elections gives supporters and opponents of a united Europe a unique opportunity to put their arguments to a wide audience and to make EC publics aware of the Parliament's existence and functions. In doing so its visibility will be increased, and this is a prerequisite to people being made aware of their European franchise.

A major reason for the Parliament's lack of legitimacy lies in its low level of visibility: in part this is connected with its lack of intelligibility, but visibility is a wider, and different, phenomenon from that outlined earlier. There are a number of reasons for Parliament's visibility problem: a major one derives from the nature of its role in EC decision-making. Fitzmaurice notes that 'the position of the European Parliament in the decision-making process of the Community has not been logically considered.'[41] Allott maintains that the Parliament faces three main obstacles in the legislative process, none of which is experienced by any of the national parliaments. The first of these is that the Council is not collectively responsible either to the European Parliament or to the national parliaments and thus is not subject to any sanctions: as such it cannot be controlled by the European Parliament in the same way that a national government can be controlled by a national parliament. The second is that the 'process of legislation is not conducted in the presence of representatives of the people or even of indirect representatives of the people of the Community. It is a half-secret process attended by ministers, diplomats and civil servants on the margins of which journalists eavesdrop on behalf of the public. It has neither the secrecy of a Cabinet nor the publicity of a Parliament.' And the final obstacle is that legislation is a result of negotiations to find a common basis of agreement among the specific national interests of the Nine member states. Allott concludes that:

> These obstacles are sufficient to brand the present situation as an essentially Executive-legislation situation of abnormally low susceptibility to political influence, particularly by representatives of the people. Such a situation carries a serious risk that the legislation which it produces will not be regarded as legitimate and that the system will not attract the habitual loyalty without which government is a fragile operation.[42]

Not only are Parliament's outputs and EC legislation likely to lack legitimacy in the sense that Allott uses the term, but also, because of their volume and content, they are likely to escape the attention of the public and hence lack tangibility.[43] Parliament's visibility problem is aggravated by the fact that EC publics are, by and large, ignorant of what work it does, even though they may be aware of the EC's existence. One reason for this is that the mass media pay little attention to it.[44] The more newsworthy items of the Community can be found in the work of the Commission and the Council, and, from the point of view of the media, can be more easily covered from Brussels than from Luxembourg or Strasbourg. The lack of attention paid by the media to the Parliament is understandable. Much of Parliament's work is of a detailed, routine and non-spectacular nature which is hardly newsworthy. In addition, most of the work is carried out in the secrecy of parliamentary committees, and the extent of these activities makes coverage of their work problematic. The media occasionally focus on Parliament when it discusses major issues or has confrontations – which contain an element of political drama, however slight – with the Council or Commission; but these are rare. A careful reader of even a quality newspaper, or fervent watcher of television news or documentaries, in almost any of the member states could be easily excused for knowing very little, if anything, about the work of the Parliament.

Other features contribute to the low visibility of the Parliament. One of these is the failure of MEPs to establish their 'Europeanness' at the national level. It is undoubtedly the case that almost all of the work done by an MEP is politically unrewarding and unglamorous. Although he may be a conscientious and hard-working member, he is, for the most part, unlikely to be rewarded for his efforts by either his national electorate in the short run or even by his political party in the long run. (There are, of course, exceptions to the general pattern, especially where the smaller states are concerned.)[45] Moreover, MEPs can neither perform analogous tasks to those of MPs in the national parliaments, nor can their efficiency be equated with and measured against national criteria. An MEP who becomes engrossed in his duties and work in the European Parliament runs the risk of becoming electorally unpopular at home either because he becomes less visible there, or because his work at the European level is not perceived as being sufficiently salient to home electors and, hence, is not regarded by them as indicative of an efficient pursuit of their interests. Contrariwise, an MEP who is insufficiently visible at either the supranational or national level may fail to promote adequately the work and activities of the European Parliament and fail to bring it to the attention of the public in a meaningful way. By and large, MEPs have both failed to increase the Parliament's visibility and to make a significant impact on the conduct and discussion of EC matters within national contexts. Shortcomings exist both in respect of their work in national parliaments, and in respect of the provision of links between EC publics and the EC's institutions. These can be accounted for by the constraints imposed by the dual mandate and by the fact that the European

Parliament is not, with few notable exceptions, particularly attractive to those seeking national governmental office. As Vedel has noted, 'If it is acknowledged that politics are a by-product of personal ambition – as seems obvious – it is disturbing that the European Parliament has little attraction for the ambitious. In the Six, and now the Nine, the political careers are forged in the national Parliaments and not in the European Parliament.'[46] One very obvious reason for this is that no European government is drawn from the European Parliament – in the same way that national governments are drawn from national parliaments in the member states. This perhaps accounts in part for the reluctance of British Labour MPs to apply for places in the European Parliament in 1975. According to Michael Stewart, only 48 applicants contested the 18 Labour places.[47] The Parliament's lack of power, therefore, acted as a deterrent – especially before the 1970s.[48]

If these factors account in part for the low visibility of the European Parliament, they also contribute to the low visibility of the chamber's party groups for whom there was, until European elections, little incentive to become more cohesive and prominent, and no need for them to make electoral or other appeals to a wide public.

Thus, it can be seen that a number of features contribute to the Parliament's low visibility. The European Parliament's retiring profile and the low salience of its activities resulted in little media coverage of its affairs. The absence of any government–opposition schism between the parties already referred to, and Members' underlying commitment to integration as evinced by broad support for the Commission, also meant that the Parliament's image was that of a forum oriented towards consensus politics. In spite of censure motions, and resolutions against the Council of Ministers, the European Parliament seemed to be uncritical of the executive, and its affairs seemed to be devoid of political interest for want of highly visible political controversies. This is not to suggest that nothing controversial occurred, for, on the contrary, contentious issues were (and are) raised. However, it is to suggest that the absence both of party-political controversies and competing policy alternatives contributed to the generally low level of media interest in the European Parliament.

The lack of party-political controversies is, however, also partly due to the absence of either an incentive, or need, to form majorities. In the Parliament, parties coalesce on an *ad hoc* basis depending on the nature of an issue since it does not much matter which groups constitute the majority because neither consistency of attitude nor support for each Commission proposal is politically rewarding, or even politically necessary. Majorities are not important since they neither determine whether or not a Commission proposal is passed and becomes part of EC law, nor whether or not a Commission more in tune with the political predilections of the majority would be nominated following any successful motion of censure. The Parliament's committee system also tends to obfuscate and attenuate party differences, thereby reducing MEPs' visibility and attractiveness to the media.

(c) The problem of Parliament as the 'grand forum' We have already suggested that the European Parliament fails to play the 'grand forum' role familiar in national political systems. It is neither the place where the legislative actions of the Commission and Council are legitimised, nor the focus of public attention even though it is the place where the latter's representatives scrutinise Commission proposals. There are a number of reasons for the European Parliament's failure to act as the EC's 'grand forum'.

Firstly, the decision-making process relegates it to an unimportant role in all but budgetary matters. Consequently, it matters very little how effectively Parliament's committees scrutinise Commission proposals since Parliament's opinions on the proposals do not determine whether or not the proposal should either be passed to or by the Council of Ministers. Parliament thus exercises the scrutiny role common to other parliamentary bodies but cannot, as a matter of course, ensure that account is taken of its views. The first Commission President publicly to attach much importance to Parliament's views was Roy Jenkins, and this was partly attributable to the imminence of European elections and to his appreciation of their significance for the Parliament's legitimacy and the consequential importance of taking cognisance of its views. However, no such recognition emanated from the Council of Ministers.

Secondly, Parliament has no real control power vis-à-vis the Council. Although it might cause the Commission to resign, increase expenditure on non-compulsory budgetary items, reject the budget, or air in debates matters raised during the conciliation procedure held *in camera*, none of these gives Parliament the power its national counterparts possess vis-à-vis national governments. It cannot force the Council of Ministers to resign, or exercise any other form of effective control over it. The Council's membership depends on the political composition of national governments and it is neither determined nor altered by anything done by the Parliament.

Thirdly, the technical and complex nature of many Commission proposals militates against their being the subject of interesting debate in the chamber. Moreover, since parliamentary activities are partly governed by the type and content of Commission proposals (which in turn are governed in respect of their content by the parameters of the Rome Treaty, and the climate of governmental opinion towards measures furthering 'in-depth' integration),[49] it is not entirely surprising that Parliament's affairs have been perceived as low on topicality. This has, however, been unfortunate for Parliament in that it has reduced its opportunities for attracting media attention, and has created the impression of its engaging in activities of but marginal importance to the EC's publics.

Again, this may well have been the case until recently. However, as MEPs have begun to make better use of their right to question the Commission – largely at the instigation and on the example of British Members – a greater element of political topicality and salience has emerged. As the salience and newsworthiness of the Parliament's activities have increased, so has the media's attention to it. However, the extent of media coverage varies from state to state, and depends in part on government and public opinion in the member states.

Finally, both the physical and psychological remoteness of the Parliament, and the lack of a compelling need for it to act as the EC's 'grand forum', have militated against it becoming one. The limited nature of its legislative, financial and oversight powers and its 'distance' from EC citizens have meant that there has been little incentive for it to develop as the EC's 'grand forum'. However, such a development would increase the Parliament's visibility and intelligibility, would create the impression that the Parliament was performing some useful role in the EC, and would contribute to increasing its political legitimacy.

The Nature of the Election Campaign

European elections are also likely (and are intended) to affect Parliament's legitimacy. However, additional institutional and non-institutional conditions must be fulfilled if Parliament's legitimacy is to be increased by way of such elections. Prior to considering these and how they may be fulfilled, it will be useful to consider briefly what functions elections in general, and European elections in particular, serve. Focusing on these will facilitate appreciation of the similarities and differences between European and national elections.

According to Hogan, elections serve a number of purposes in the representational function of a political system.[50] A government based upon democratic principles, he argues, is distinguished from other types by a wide diffusion of political power, a sense of participation, and an accountability to the electorate for at least the main lines of public policy. For him, the functions of elections are to facilitate participation, representation, accountability, the expression of interests and opinions, the recruitment of personnel for the tasks of government, and the legitimisation of the agents of the people by establishing the bond of consent.

European elections will fulfil but some of these functions. They will facilitate participation, representation and legitimisation; they will also mean that MEPs become accountable to publics in that 'consent is maintained by the necessity for frequent renewal of mandate'.[51] They will also facilitate the expression of interests and opinions, but they will neither determine the recruitment of personnel for the tasks of government, nor enforce government accountability to the electorate for policy outputs. The EC's government will neither emanate from among those elected to the European Parliament, nor will it be accountable to them. The nature of executive–legislative relations in the EC proscribes this.

If European elections establish a bond of consent between MEPs and EC publics, it could be argued that the European Parliament's legitimacy might be expected to increase. It does not follow, however, that the legitimacy of the Parliament or of the Community will automatically or concomitantly increase as a result of European elections. Before the first elections are held not only must the various mechanical and logistical difficulties concerning the nature of the various national electoral systems be overcome, but a number of additional problems must be faced.[52] These stem from the purpose of the European elections, the conduct of the campaign, and from the need to motivate people to vote. If turn-out, for example, were low, it could be argued that the elected Parliament would be only marginally more directly representative and legitimate than its predecessor. European elections would then have failed to achieve one of their main purposes. It is to these problems that we now turn.

Notes

1. Article 21 of the Treaty of Paris (which established the European Coal and Steel Community) stipulates that 'the [Common] Assembly shall consist of delegates who shall be designated by the respective Parliaments once a year from among their members, or who shall be elected by direct universal suffrage'. Article 138 of the European Economic Community reads: 'The Assembly [the European Parliament] shall draw up proposals for elections by direct universal suffrage in accordance with a uniform procedure in all Member States. The Council [of Ministers] shall, acting unanimously, lay down the appropriate provisions, which it shall recommend to Member States for adoption in accordance with their respective constitutional requirements.'
2. See, for example, M. Steed, 'The European Parliament: The Significance of Direct Election', *Government and Opposition*, VI (1971) 462–76; and M. Stewart, 'Direct Elections to the European Parliament', *Common Market Law Review*, XIII (1976) 283–301.
3. P. Allott, 'The Democratic Basis of the European Communities: The European Parliament and the Westminster Parliament', *Common Market Law Review*, XI (1974) 298–326.
4. R. Pryce, 'Legitimacy and European Integration: The Role of Information', *International Political Science Association Paper* (Edinburgh, 1976); and see Bulletin, EC-2, 1977.
5. See, for example, A. J. R. Groom and P. Taylor, *Functionalism* (London:

Univ. of London Press, 1975) pp. 122, 265 ff.; also J. Galtung, *The European Community: A Superpower in the Making* (London: Allen & Unwin, 1973).

6. *Report of the Political Affairs Committee on the Adoption of a Draft Convention Introducing Elections to the European Parliament by Direct Universal Suffrage* (Patijn Report), PE 37.881/fin, p. 11; emphasis added.

7. G. Vedel, 'The Role of the Parliamentary Institution in European Integration', in Directorate-General for Research and Documentation of the European Parliament (ed.), *Symposium on European Integration and the Future of Parliaments in Europe* (Luxembourg: European Parliament, 1975) pp. 236-44, at p. 238; emphasis added.

8. European Union: Report by M. Leo Tindemans, Prime Minister of Belgium, to the European Council, *Bulletin of the European Communities*, Supplement 1/76; emphasis added.

9. See, for example, S. P. Huntington, *Political Order in Changing Societies* (New Haven: Yale Univ. Press, 1968) chap. 1.

10. L. Binder *et al.*, *Crises and Sequences in Political Development* (Princeton: Princeton Univ. Press, 1971) chap. 1.

11. Huntington, *Political Order in Changing Societies*, pp. 12-24; see also G. Ben-Dor, 'Institutionalisation and Political Development: A Conceptual and Theoretical Analysis', *Comparative Studies in Society and History*, XVII (1975) 309-25.

12. C. Mueller, *The Politics of Communication* (New York: Oxford Univ. Press, 1973) p. 129.

13. Ibid.

14. J. Lodge, 'Towards a Human Union: EEC Social Policy and European Integration', *British Journal of International Studies*, IV (1978) 47-74.

15. This is explained by P. Trudeau, 'Federalism, Nationalism and Reason', in P. A. Crepeau and C. B. Macpherson, *The Future of Canadian Federalism* (Toronto: Toronto Univ. Press, 1965) pp. 17-19.

16. J. H. Schaar, 'Legitimacy in the Modern State', in P. Green and S. Levinson (eds.), *Power and Community: Dissenting Essays in Political Science* (New York: Random House, 1970) p. 283.

17. Mueller, *The Politics of Communication*, p. 129.

18. Ibid., p. 131.

19. Schaar, in *Power and Community*, p. 284.

20. L. N. Lindberg and S. A. Scheingold, *Europe's Would-Be Polity* (Englewood Cliffs, N.J.: Prentice-Hall, 1970).

21. Schaar, in *Power and Community*, p. 284; and C. F. Friedrich, *Man and His Government: An Empirical Theory of Politics* (New York: McGraw-Hill, 1963) p. 233.

22. Schaar, in *Power and Community*, p. 288.

23. S. M. Lipset, *Political Man* (New York: Doubleday, 1960) p. 177.

24. P. G. Stillman, 'The Concept of Legitimacy', *Polity*, VII (1974) 32-56.

25. Ibid., p. 37.

26. Pryce, op. cit.

27. Ibid., p. 1.

28. Ibid., pp. 3-4.

29. Ibid., p. 4.

30. S. Henig, 'The Institutional Structure of the European Communities', *Journal of Common Market Studies*, XII (1974) 373-409.

31. Ibid., p. 397.
32. S. Henig, 'New Institutions for European Integration', *Journal of Common Market Studies*, XII (1973) 130–7, at p. 137.
33. Allott, op. cit.
34. Ibid., p. 305; emphasis in original.
35. Ibid., p. 306; emphasis in original.
36. 'Democracy' is common to the three works cited. 'Tradition', the 'transfer of loyalties' and the 'acceptance of decisions' all come from Henig. 'Tangibility', 'visibility' and 'intelligibility are all concepts central to Pryce's argument, and the idea of the 'grand forum' comes from Allott.
37. Cited from European Parliament, *Annuaire II* (1963–4) pp. 40–42, by W. N. Hogan, *Representative Government and European Integration* (Lincoln: Nebraska Univ. Press, 1967) p. 227.
38. R. Mayne, *The Institutions of the European Community* (London: PEP/Chatham House, 1968).
39. See J. Lodge, 'Towards the European Political Community: EEC Summits and European Integration', *Orbis*, XIX (1975) 626–51.
40. Allott, op. cit., pp. 301–2.
41. J. Fitzmaurice, *The Party Groups in the European Parliament* (Farnborough: Saxon House, 1975) p. 14.
42. Allott, op. cit., p. 317.
43. Lodge, 'Towards a Human Union: EEC Social Policy and European Integration', op. cit.
44. Of the major European newspapers only *The Times* regularly carries reports of the plenary sessions of the European Parliament.
45. Members drawn from Communist parties have tended to include more prominent national figures, too.
46. Vedel, in *Symposium*, p. 237; also Fitzmaurice, *The Party Groups in the European Parliament*, part 3.
47. *The Economist*, 12 July 1975, p. 31.
48. H. Vredeling, 'The Common Market of Political Parties', *Government and Opposition*, VI (1971) 448–61.
49. A. Etzioni, *Political Unification* (New York: Holt, Rinehart & Winston, 1965).
50. Hogan, *Representative Government and European Integration*, p. 93.
51. Ibid., p. 94.
52. J. Lodge, 'Citizens and the EEC: The Role of the European Parliament', *The Parliamentarian*, LVIII (1977) 176–81; and V. Herman and J. Lodge, 'Is the European Parliament a Parliament?', *European Journal of Political Research*, VI (1978) (forthcoming).

7 Citizens and the Elections

> European Union must be experienced by the citizen in his daily life. It must make itself felt in education and culture, news and communications, it must be manifest in the youth of our countries, and in leisure time activities. It must protect the rights of the individual and strengthen democracy through a set of institutions which have legitimacy conferred upon them by the will of our peoples.
>
> Tindemans Report (1976) p. 12

The extension of the franchise to.EC publics will not necessarily by itself augment the representativeness and legitimacy of the European Parliament. It will, however, represent a step towards increasing the element of democracy in the Community. It will also ensure that citizens are represented in the Parliament by those whom they have elected. By contrast, the extent to which the representativeness of the Parliament is increased will depend on the electoral systems adopted by the member states for, and on the level of turn-out at, the European elections. If turn-out were low, it could be argued that the directly elected Parliament were hardly more representative than its predecessor and that, therefore, its claims to greater decision-making powers were no more legitimate. From this it is apparent that the European Parliament has a particular interest in stimulating high turn-out. To do this, however, it must perform a number of parliamentary functions it has thus far inadequately fulfilled. These functions are ones normally associated with parliamentary fora in the member states. According to Zellentin:

> If one were to base an analysis of the European Parliament on a somewhat simplified form of Bagehot's classic definition of the functions of a parliament, one would find the following similarities and differences. The *elective* function (with regard to the executive) is lacking: the European Parliament is not an electoral chamber. The *expressive* function ('to express the mind of the ... people on all matters which come before it') would be more effective if there were direct elections. This is also true of the *teaching* function ('a great and open council of considerable men cannot be placed in the middle of a society without altering that society'). The *informing* function is zealously carried on by the European Parliament in order to familia-

rise the public with the administrative discussions and measures on integration. But it takes part in the *legislative* function only consultatively. As regards Bagehot's sixth function, namely the *financial* one, the European Parliament must be consulted during the preparation of the budget, but it is the Council . . . which has the last word in this matter. Finally, a seventh function should be added, *pace* Bagehot, which is most important for all developing parliaments of the continental type, namely the control of the executive. For this particular purpose, the motion of censure is in theory the strongest instrument in the European Parliament.[1]

The European Parliament has failed to perform expressive, teaching and informing functions adequately. Its members and parties have not developed their links with EC publics in a useful manner. They have failed to communicate with them. Yet the ability to communicate effectively is basic both to their exercising their expressive, informing and teaching functions, and to their stimulating public awareness of the EC and fostering a sense of 'we-ness'[2] among them. However, we intend to argue that European elections are likely to have ancillary effects on the Parliament. Not only will elections give citizens the opportunity to participate in EC activities, but they will prompt reconsideration of Parliament's performance of – and ability to perform – communicative, informative and educative roles, all of which are essential to ensuring a high level of public participation in the elections. Prior to considering how these roles can be carried out, and how a high level of participation can be ensured, it will be useful to examine obstacles to the performance of such functions in general, and to the communicative function in particular.

Performance of the communicative, educative and informative functions by the Parliament presupposes that it and its members can communicate with their target audiences. However, it is here that one of the Parliament's basic problems lies. This derives not so much from the nature and composition of Parliament and its parties, as from the linguistic diversity of the Community.

Linguistic diversity has often been regarded as one of the chief impediments to horizontal integration. Clearly, if people are to understand one another they must comprehend each other's language. The lack of a common language in the EC aggravates the communication process. Experience shows that difficulties encountered are not insurmountable. But language has a number of additional functions. Over and above facilitating the transmission of information, language acts as a socialising agent and is part of an individual's means of self and group identification. Brief comments on these functions of language are in order since they shed some light on the reasons why the problem of creating a common European identity among citizens cannot be resolved simply by affording them common political rights (such as the franchise), obligations or symbols of identity; and cannot, therefore, be overcome simply through the holding of European elections.

The Functions of Language

Generally speaking, language, or the language spoken as a mother-tongue by a person, serves to differentiate people from each other, and helps to distinguish 'in-groups' from 'out-groups'.[3] Although nationality and linguistic demarcations do not necessarily coincide, particular languages spoken in the EC tend to be associated with particular member states. Language is, therefore, a symbol of identity. It is, moreover, a repository of cultural tradition; it 'provides the group or individual the means to identify with a given culture or political entity'.[4] The absence of a single EC language and EC cultural norms means that language in the EC cannot serve this end. Instead, linguistic and cultural diversity emphasise differences between and within the member states. They make it difficult, therefore, for groups and nations, accustomed to viewing those who speak different languages as members of out-groups, to view them as members of their own in-group. Language also acts here as a deterrent to different groups communicating with or exhibiting interest in each other except under threatening circumstances. Thus, in the EC, language has not had a socialising function. Linguistic diversity militates against citizens in the member states perceiving themselves as part of a wider community.

A second important function of language lies in its use as a vehicle of socialisation. Through it jointly shared symbolic expressions, roles, social relationships and political images[5] are transmitted and internalised.[6] Language (along with education, family background, and social and economic status) is basic to socialisation.[7] In the EC the absence of a common language and tradition means that political socialisation (the process by which the citizen becomes aware of the political system, its traditions and institutions, and how he is expected to behave toward it)[8] has to be accomplished by other means. We shall suggest that the European Parliament and its parties have contributions to make in this respect, and that these are important since successful political socialisation is regarded as a basic prerequisite for the effective functioning of a polity,[9] and as contributing to the creation of a common identity among members of a community.[10] The Commission and European Councils want to achieve this and have sought to promote it through the introduction of common symbols of identity such as Euro-passports and a Citizens' Charter. In other words, there has been widespread failure to appreciate the way in which the Parliament could contribute to political socialisation in the EC.

A third function of language lies in its importance to communication between individuals and groups. Interests have to be articulated before they can be acted upon and institutionalised. The expression of interests presupposes that a group or class shares a language through which its interests can be articulated.[11] While it is true that some of the EC's elites are multilingual, this is not the case where EC publics are concerned. Transnational communication, by being problematic, renders effective political action and communication of demands and interests difficult, although not impossible. Conversely, the absence of a common language or code makes it difficult for MEPs to communicate uniformly and simultaneously through a television broadcast, for example, with potential EC voters throughout the EC.

What we are saying, then, is that the linguistic diversity of the EC has hampered political communication. This was not considered important until the holding of European elections became likely, and until the member governments accepted that the EC had entered a new phase in its development. This phase is associated with its growth towards 'political maturity' and emergence as a political rather than simply socio-economic entity.[12] The holding of European elections has highlighted the problem of political communication for the Parliament and parties who have an interest in the effective communication of political images and messages. The problems they face derive, however, not simply from the EC's linguistic diversity but from the European Parliament's low visibility, intelligibility and tangibility.

However, it is felt that the franchise will be both a means of increasing the Parliament's tangibility and intelligibility, and a means of instilling a sense of 'we-ness' among voters since it will be the first concrete expression of their membership of a community extending beyond single nation-states. The European franchise is seen, then, as a way of making the EC a reality to citizens. This was stressed by Commission President Roy Jenkins in his address to the European Parliament on 11 January 1977. Attaching the highest political importance to European elections, he said: 'We must graft the idea of Europe onto the lives of its citizens.'[13] This will not be possible unless (among other things) there is effective communication with citizens. Given that citizens normally associate large-scale elections with voting governments in or out of office, and given that elections to the European Parliament are not about electing governments, the distinct purposes of the elections and the Parliament will have to be explained to citizens. Since candidates for the Parliament have a stake in ensuring that citizens do indeed vote, they have an interest in promoting effective communication with them. Consequently, they can be expected to perform educative, informative and expressive functions more assiduously than hitherto. Their own awareness of a need to become involved in the process of generating awareness among citizens of their common European identity has increased.

The question we now have to ask is whether or not the absence of a common language will matter. Is effective political communication between citizens and MEPs impossible unless they all speak the same language? Candidates are obviously only going to stand for election in countries whose language(s) they speak. However, transnational communication would be difficult not least because of language barriers. But the way in which the first European elections are to be contested, with candidates from national parties standing in their own member states, means that the communications problems associated with linguistic diversity will be minimised.

By contrast, the communications problem for those concerned with drafting European manifestoes for the Parliament's main party groups has proved more problematic since different languages attach different nuances to specific words and furnish a potential source of misunderstanding. Even so, there are few grounds for believing that such problems will prove insurmountable given the experience in the Commission, Council, ECOSOC, Parliament and Court of Justice. This leads us to two conclusions: firstly, that the problems associated with linguistic diversity have been overstated in the past; secondly, that while language cannot perform the socialising function in the EC that it does in the member states, alternative socialising agents exist in the shape of the European Parliament and its members. European elections provide MEPs with an incentive to develop and effectively perform their communicative function, and for increasing the educative, informative and communicative capabilities of the Parliament. The implication of this is that the European Parliament's importance lies not so much in its formal legislative, financial or control powers, nor in any medium- or long-term development of these powers, but rather in its short-term potential for playing educative, informative and communicative functions vis-à-vis EC citizens and, in so doing, in furthering integration.

In the EC, political communication is usually seen as facilitating four things. It is supposed to (i) increase the visibility, intelligibility and tangibility of the European Parliament and EC; (ii) inform citizens of opportunities for participating in the political affairs of the EC; (iii) enable competing candidates and parties to transmit their messages to voters with a view to securing their support; and (iv) to enable MEPs, after the elections, to perform an expressive function by communicating voters' interests to other MEPs and EC decision-makers, and to enable the European Parliament to perform a 'voice of the people' role. The first three are of particular importance in view of the elections. But why is it important to the European Parliament that citizens should be made more aware of the EC and Parliament, and that they should be encouraged to vote?

The European Parliament's interest in promoting citizen awareness of the EC derives largely from a belief that only if there is a high turn-out on the occasion of European elections will it be able to claim that it is either the only legitimate source of authority in the EC or the only body representative of Community opinion and politics.[14] Since this is related to the Parliament's quest for greater decision-making powers and is the basis upon which claims for such powers are advanced, there is a sense in which the Parliament's interest in encouraging a high turn-out would be motivated by self-interest.

It is generally thought, as we have argued, that interest in turning out will have to be actively stimulated. A corollary of this has been a fear that turn-out would otherwise be low. However, we doubt that this will be so. If one examines turn-out patterns in elections in the Nine on the one hand, and attitudes towards the Community and European elections on the other, there appear to be grounds for cautious optimism.

Average turn-out at general elections in the Nine is 85 per cent, with the original Six having turn-out levels some 9 per cent higher than the new members (88 per cent as against 79 per cent) (see Table 7.1). The average turn-out in local elections for the Nine is 72 per cent, with a 20 per cent difference between the Six and the new members (77 per cent as against 57 per cent). This suggests that voters by and large are disposed towards voting. This predisposition must not be overstated, however, since voting is obligatory in some member states, and in others heavy social pressures exist for citizens to do their 'civic duty' and vote. A uniform turn-out throughout the Nine cannot be expected for European elections for reasons associated with political cultures and electoral laws *inter alia*. However, one might expect turn-out to fall, on average, between the mean for general and local elections, and therefore to be over 70 per cent. Indeed, the *Eurobarometer* survey of July 1977 found that in the EC 74 per cent of respondents were certainly or probably going to vote in European elections (see Table 7.2).

Turning now to the question of attitudes towards the EC, will unfavourable attitudes mean low turn-out? Greater favourability towards the EC among the original Six is indicative of greater acceptance of the EC on their part, and this may be reflected in a greater readiness to vote in European elections. The region a voter resides in, along with his nationality, are the most reliable predictors of attitudes towards the elections.[15] An implication of the nationality variable is that countries whose publics are on average less favourably disposed towards the EC may either have lower than average turn-outs (thereby leaving those whom they have elected open to the charge of being only partially representative of public opinion) or greater propensities to elect parties believed on balance to be committed to protecting national interests rather than to advancing integration. While a positive corre-lation between support for the EC – between those considering the EC a 'good' thing – and support for a directly elected European Parliament exists, it is significant that more than three-quarters of those who gave a neutral reply to the question as to whether the EC was a 'good' or 'bad' thing supported European elections in November 1976, as did almost half of those most critical of the EC.[16] Similarly, the original Six tend to

TABLE 7.1. Turn-out at general and local elections and at referenda

	General election (lower/only house)		Local election			Referendum		
	Year	%	Level	Year	%	Issue	Year	%
Belgium	1977	82.3	Municipal	1976	90.0	–	–	–
Denmark	1977	88.7	Municipal	1974	62.9	Entry into EEC	1972	90.1
France	1973 (1st round)	80.9	Departmental (1st round)	1976	65.3	Enlargement of EEC	1972	60.5
Germany	1976	90.7	Länder	1973–6	81.8	–	–	–
Ireland	1977	76.3	Borough, county and district councils	1974	62.0	Entry into EEC	1972	71.0
Italy	1976	97.0	Provincial and municipal	1975	91.8	Abrogation of divorce legislation	1974	88.1
Luxembourg	1974	85.2	Commune	1975	70.0	–	–	–
Netherlands	1977	87.5	Provincial	1974	74.3	–	–	–
UK	1974 (Oct)	72.8	Metropolitan and non-metropolitan district councils	1975–6	40.0	Continued EEC membership	1975	64.0

Source: Data supplied by embassies.

TABLE 7.2. Intention to vote in European elections

There are going to be elections to the European Parliament in the spring of 1978. How likely is it that you will go and vote? Certainly, probably, probably not or certainly not?

%	B	DK	D	F	IRL	I	L	NL	UK	EC*
Certainly	37	42	28	51	52	64	44	60	47	47
Probably	21	18	36	26	26	20	35	22	26	27
Probably not	11	7	11	5	7	5	8	5	11	8
Certainly not	19	12	7	5	8	5	3	5	10	7
It depends	6	9	4	6	3	3	7	5	3	4
No reply	6	12	14	7	4	3	3	3	3	7

*Weighted average

Source: *Eurobarometer*, no. 7 (July 1977)

attach greater significance to the European elections for the EC's political development (see Table 7.3).

Our argument that visibility would affect attitudes seems to be supported by recent data. There has been a more marked increase in positive attitudes among non-leaders than among leaders. It was concluded in the January 1977 *Eurobarometer*, which compared 1975 and 1976 opinion poll results, that 'the idea of electing the European Parliament is becoming more popular as plans take shape'.[17] The July 1977 *Eurobarometer* noted that while in all the member states opinion leaders were much more in favour of European elections than the general public, 'the idea of an elected European Parliament is becoming increasingly popular as election day approaches and the debate livens up' (see Table 7.4). Since this has been accompanied by increased media attention to and coverage of the question of European elections (as we shall see in the next chapter), it is likely that the increases in public awareness of the elections and in the visibility of the European Parliament affected the level of public support for the holding of such elections. Thus, it can be tentatively hypothesised that as awareness of and favourability towards European elections rise, the likelihood of a low turn-out decreases.

Turn-out will be affected by a number of factors including the role played by the information services of the Commission, Parliament, member governments, national and transnational parties, the conduct of the campaign, and the novelty value of the elections and voting in them. The main variables, however, will be public awareness of the election and motivation to vote. Reflecting on this in the European Parliament in 1976, M. Boano (It. C-D) noted that the Chamber's first task vis-à-vis European elections should be to educate EC publics and to inform

TABLE 7.3. The importance attached to direct elections to the
European Parliament*

Which of these opinions comes closest to your own views on
the future elections to the European Parliament:
 — it is an event of important consequences which is certain
   to make Europe more politically unified?
 — it is an insignificant event because the Heads of State
   will not be bound by votes in the European Parliament?

%	Important consequences	Insignificant event	Don't know
Italy	56	19	25
Belgium	53	19	28
Luxembourg	53	25	22
Netherlands	48	29	23
Germany	47	35	18
France	46	28	26
UK	41	31	28
Ireland	38	27	35
Denmark	35	33	32
Community	47	28	24

*November 1976. The countries are listed in descending order
according to the number of positive replies ('important
consequence').
†Weighted average.

Source: *Eurobarometer*, no. 6 (Jan 1977).

them about the EC's dimensions, and opportunities for participating in
its political life.[18] This view was reiterated by Mr Jenkins on 8 February
1977:

> In less than two years time, an electorate of 180 million will be called
> upon to determine the composition of this House. We have two clear
> objectives: to ensure that each voter is aware of the ways in which his
> own life is affected by decisions taken at Community level and of the
> way in which he can affect the direction of those decisions by casting
> his vote and, at the same time, to ensure that we are aware of the
> attitudes and aspirations of the voters whose interest we seek to
> serve.[19]

What attributes, then, does the European Parliament possess that
would enable it to perform such educative and informative tasks, and
what conditions must be met to ensure that its efforts will be successful?

TABLE 7.4. Attitudes towards the election of the European Parliament by direct universal suffrage, Jan–Feb 1970, Sep 1973, Nov 1976, Apr–May 1977

	% For				% Against			
	1970	1973	1976	1977	1970	1973	1976	1977
Belgium	56	52	69	64	12	14	9	13
France	59	51	69	74	16	18	13	12
Germany	63	69	76	69	11	12	10	8
Italy	71	64	77	81	8	12	8	10
Luxembourg	70	67	77	85	11	12	9	7
Netherlands	60	62	74	82	21	16	11	9
Denmark	–	36	42	44	–	43	37	27
Ireland	–	45	63	76	–	31	14	12
UK	–	33	57	67	–	49	22	22
Community		54	69	72		23	14	13

Source: Adapted from *Eurobarometer*.

The Party System

That political parties play specific educative and informative roles in promoting political awareness and knowledge, and in establishing new bases of legitimacy, has been well documented.[20] Parties can be regarded as both foci of political attention and as loci of political loyalty. Within their confines other divisions might be transcended so that a sense of identity, cohesion and common purpose is instilled among groups of people. Byars suggests that parties 'function in the affective-integrative sphere, while formal government structures perform in the instrumental-adaptive areas'. Parties are 'one type of institutional device for performing the social-emotional and integrative functions of affective leadership on the level of society, and for mediating the symbolic, normative or instrumental involvement of citizens'.[21] Thus, provided citizens are aware of parties, the latter will be able to contribute to citizens' internalisation of a society's norms, their identification with that society, and their awareness of opportunities for participating in it. By and large these conditions are met at the national level.

The European Parliament's party groups might be expected, if appropriately organised, to perform similar functions to those of national parties in acclimatising EC citizens to the Community dimension of their lives; in heightening their awareness of the EC; in acting as a link between the government and governed; and in stimulating participation in the EC's political activities. As Patijn

suggests, 'Not until the parties succeed, within the Community framework, in establishing close links between themselves, developing joint
programmes and creating supranational party structures, can direct
elections ... become a key factor in the process of political
integration'.[22]

The participatory aspect is of particular importance in view of
European elections and, given the interest in ensuring a high turn-out,
the party groups might be expected to develop their educative,
informative and communicative roles. Whatever communicative links
they establish between themselves and EC citizens during the
preparations for European elections will be useful and will need to be
cultivated thereafter, since the parties' simultaneous accessibility to
government and to citizens means that they will be in a position to
encourage a two-way communication process in the transmission of
information and demands. In the interim, however, the party groups'
educative and informative functions will be decisive since there is considerable evidence to suggest that the level of citizens' participation in a
given political process depends upon their knowledge of it, their sense
of personal political efficacy, their ability to articulate their interests
effectively, and their awareness of and access to means affording
participation.[23]

If the party groups are to generate public interest in European
elections, and if they are to assist citizens in distinguishing European
elections from other elections held within the member states, it will be
crucial that MEPs possess and project clear images of themselves as
European, not national, politicians even though they may also be members of, and have strong identification with, familiar national parties. In
the past, MEPs' perceptions of themselves, in Lord O'Hagan's terms, as
ambassadors of their national political parties first, and MEPs second,
coupled with their inability – for a variety of reasons – to constitute
genuine transnational parties with distinct European profiles, has
limited the European Parliament's ability both to offer the public a
European focus of political interest and to play an effective role in
promoting integration.

Unless citizens are made aware of the EC's activities and
opportunities for communicating with its decision-makers, disaffection
from politics at the national level may spill over to the European level.[24]
Thus, those with a low sense of political efficacy, and/or those who feel
that their vote does not affect outcomes in national elections, may see
no point or value in participating in European elections and abstain.
Feeling among disaffected citizens that by voting they cannot influence
policy outcomes[25] (partly because they lack clear images of the different
parties and regard their policies as alike, or as likely to be so irrespective
of which major party gains election) may not only dissuade them from
considering the European Parliament as an alternative body to which
representations can be made, but deter them from paying much

attention to EC affairs. Careful distinctions must, however, be made between non-voting occasioned by active rejection of the EC, and non-voting resulting from a communications failure. By contrast, voters with a higher sense of personal political efficacy may exhibit greater readiness to vote in European elections.

Recent psephological findings indicate that the more knowledgeable, more highly educated and more politically aware people feel more efficacious, and exhibit higher degrees of sensitivity to ideological and political facets of questions, than do the less knowledgeable, less educated and less aware.[26] However, participation in politics is one way for the latter to acquire political awareness and a sense of efficacy. Although, in the member states, the European Parliament's party groups lack a distinct identity and separate party organisations, and although they can only involve citizens indirectly in European-level politics via the medium of their national constituent parties, this need not mean that their ability to perform educative, informative and communicative roles is thereby severely curtailed. Neither need the EC's polyglot nature preclude effective communication between EC citizens, parties[27] and supranational elites provided the parties and MEPs project clear self-images, programmes and objectives. This does, however, demand that the constituent parties of the transnational party groups are able to communicate effectively among themselves.

So long as MEPs constituted party *groups* as opposed to united political *parties*, and so long as there was little need for these groups to clarify their basic persuasions with a view to putting them before EC electors, discrepancies arising from linguistic diversity and nuances were not particularly important. But the need to discern, agree upon, develop and project clear party images and programmes not only underscored intra-party communication difficulties, but also highlighted those relating to the transmission of information to EC publics.

The prospect of European elections stimulated the development of new transnational political *parties*. However, it is unlikely that these will increase significantly their existing autonomy from national constituent parties until either full-time MEPs are clear about their roles and those of a supranational Parliament, or the Parliament acquires the kind of decision-making authority, and deliberates upon the kind of contentious and politically salient issues that are the stuff of politics at the national level. This is to suggest that the higher the political salience of issues before the Parliament, the greater will be the incentive for the party groups to cohere and to seek to determine outcomes according to political/ideological preferences. This in turn presupposes that the parties possess clear views as to their preferences and that they have the will and the ability to constitute majorities – the ability to muster a sufficient number of votes being contingent both on the persuasiveness of their case and, more especially, upon the cohesiveness of the group and its numerical strength in the chamber. Recognition of opportunities offered by performing communicative, educative and informative roles has heightened party competition among the parliament's party groups. This is exemplified by the creation of the European Peoples' Party and the recent development and activities of the other two main parties, the Liberal Party Federation and the Association for a Democratic and Socialist Europe.

Origins of the EC's Party System

The European Parliament had its origins in the ECSC's Common Assembly which first met in Strasbourg on 10 September 1952. There were then 78 'representatives of the peoples of the Member States'. The membership of this Assembly has been increased twice: firstly, when the Rome Treaties were under negotiation, upon acceptance of the Assembly's proposal that it be dissolved, enlarged and reconstituted as the 'single Assembly' of the EEC, ECSC and EURATOM; and secondly, upon the EC's enlargement in 1973. In the first instance its membership was increased to 142 and in the second instance to 198. Following European elections, the number of seats will have been increased to 410. The practice of allotting seat quotas on a national basis (roughly proportional to population) will be retained for the time being (see Table 7.5).

From the outset it has been the practice for members to sit in groups according to political conviction rather than nationality. The decision to sit as political groups was taken in order to distinguish the Parliament from other international bodies in which parliamentarians

TABLE 7.5. The distribution of seats in the European Parliament

	1952	1958	1973	1978
Belgium	10	14	14	24
France	18	36	36	81
Germany	18	36	36	81
Italy	18	36	36	81
Luxembourg	4	6	6	6
Netherlands	10	14	14	25
Denmark	–	–	10	16
Ireland	–	–	10	15
UK	–	–	36	81
Total	78	142	198	410

TABLE 7.6. Political groups in the European Parliament
(at 1 February 1977)

Political group	Number of seats	Number of parties in group	Number of member states in group
Socialists	64	13	9
Christian Democrats	52	13	7
Liberals	26	13	8
Euro-Progressive Democrats	17	4	3
Communists	17	4	3
Euro-Conservatives	17	2	2
Independents	5	3	3

Source: Adapted from material supplied by the European Parliament.

were represented, to give expression to federalist ideals, and to promote integration. Membership of a political group is not compulsory, but *'non-inscrits'* (non-affiliated) members lack the weight of the affiliated. The Rules of Procedure stipulate that for a group to be officially recognised it shall comprise at least 14 members (or 10 if drawn from three or more countries). Since it is the party groups that select chairmen of Parliament's committees; since, moreover, group spokesmen have priority in debates; since the organisation of Parliament's business –including the setting of the agenda for plenary sessions – is determined by the 'enlarged Bureau' of Parliament (that is, the President, the eleven Vice-Presidents – appointed on the basis of party balance – and the political groups' leaders); and since Parliament allocates funds from its own budget to pay for the political groups' secretariats (which assist in the preparation of policies and political research), there are advantages in being affiliated.

Prior to European elections, the main groups were the Socialists (the largest group), Christian Democrats, European Conservatives, European Progressive Democrats, Liberals and allies, and Communists and allies (see Table 7.6). Members could also choose to remain *non-inscrit*. The prospect of European elections, and the concomitant need for the groups both to project their distinctive images and to formulate election manifestoes, gave impetus to the formation of supranational political *parties*. It stimulated greater group cohesion. It would, however, be erroneous to assume that the internal cohesiveness of the groups was minimal before then. While it is true that it varied from group to group, the two largest groups – the Socialists and Christian Democrats – were more than a loose coalition of national parties. Their party organisations, policy-making machinery and rules governing voting and dissent from the majority opinion of the group attest to this.[28] The Socialists, for example, alone among the groups, had a tradition of supranational party discipline and decided when, and if, free votes should be allowed.[29] This is not to suggest the absence of dissent, but to stress that party rules governed its expression, and that these were intended to assist in the projection of a cohesive party image in the chamber. Similarly, the Conservatives had a whip, and three-line whips were issued on major issues.[30] It has also been found that on average party groups have been more cohesive than national delegations.[31]

However, the groups have found difficulty in, and have in the past been reticent about, projecting their European profiles to EC publics. They have not been effective in communicating with them. Again, both the nature of EC business and the lack of needs or incentives for such communication probably accounted for this. However, the prospect of European elections changed this. While campaigns in the member states will be conducted by national parties, the political groups in the European Parliament have become more polarised and alert to the importance of establishing their identities and roles in the eyes of the EC's publics as they, not national party members *per se*, are expected to embody and represent voters' interests in the Parliament.

It is not surprising that the election campaigns will be dominated by national parties rather than by European parties *per se*. This is because, on the one hand, MEPs are to stand as members of national parties which may, or may not, express support for a given European party. On the other hand, the European parties, although well organised administratively at Luxembourg, as yet lack the grass-roots organisations, infrastructures and policy-development machinery associated with established national parties. They also lack highly visible, well-known leaders or members capable of regularly attracting media attention to the European Parliament. Even the pro-European unity groups (such as the European Federalists) have chosen to avoid drawing great attention to themselves and their aims for fear of jeopardising the holding of European elections. In other words, both European parties and member governments perpetuate the myth that European elections signify neither important steps towards political integration nor to qualitative changes in the EC's institutional balance.

The elections must also be dominated by national parties, given that none of the European parties yet possesses supranational organisations capable of recruiting party members. Such duties fall to constituent parties seeking their own recruits. The support-seeking activities of the European Parliament, therefore, centre on mobilising voters to turn out in the elections. This means that the parties seek to contribute to the inculcation of a sense of European identity among voters by making them aware of a European party to which they can owe allegiance via the medium of constitutent national party candidates whom they elect to the European chamber. Imperfect and rudimentary as this is for instilling a sense of belonging among citizens, the right to vote for party candidates in the elections will be a symbol of citizenship, and it should not be forgotten that the elections will have this symbolic function.

As we have indicated, a major problem confronting candidates and parties will be how to stimulate a sufficiently high turn-out to justify the European Parliament's claim to being representative of public opinion and to having legitimate claims to greater decision-making powers.

Two factors that will affect the extent to which the elected Parliament will be able to claim to be representative of the voters are: firstly, the impact of different electoral procedures in the Nine on the representation of electoral opinion in the European Parliament; and secondly, the level of turn-out in each of the member states. A low turn-out (and/or a sizeable percentage of votes cast for anti-EC parties or candidates) may well undermine both the Parliament's claims to representativeness and legitimacy, and its claim for greater decision-making authority based on these. Thus, in performing educative and informative functions, the Parliament, MEPs and parties must counteract dominant, negative images of the EC in these states if it is supposed that turn-out will be low in countries whose publics negatively evaluate the EC, and that this in turn may be used by member governments to vindicate decelerating the Parliament's formal development as the EC's legislature.

Let us now examine problems associated with the existence of differing electoral procedures, and comment on their relevance for the European Parliament's claims to being representative of EC public opinion.

Electoral Procedures

For the first European elections, member states were permitted to adopt whatever electoral procedures they deemed appropriate in selecting their quota of MEPs. For subsequent elections, however, a uniform procedure is to be elaborated and adopted. Whereas it was thought that the right to hold elections to the Parliament in accordance with national preferences would both minimise controversy and expedite the introduction of any enabling legislation in the member states, this proved not to be the case. By permitting member states to choose their own electoral procedures, it had been hoped to avert protracted debates over the political and constitutional significance of European elections for the sovereignty of member states and national parliaments vis-à-vis the European Parliament. But these materialised none the less. Not only did some member states find themselves divided over the choice of electoral procedure, but some governing parties were split by internal rifts which jeopardised the elections themselves. The problem was particularly acute in Britain where the government was so divided that the Prime Minister (faced with renewed secessionist and renegotiation calls by members disputing the fact that Britain had pledged itself to European elections when it signed the Rome Treaty) allowed a free vote on the issue. In France, acceptance of European elections was conditional upon the understanding that the European Parliament's powers were to remain strictly limited.[32] In Denmark, retention of an obligatory dual mandate was considered essential; and in Germany, the SPD/FDP government's proposal for elections through federal lists on the basis of proportional representation was opposed by the CDU/CSU who favoured a system closer to that used in federal elections.[33]

What the disputes over appropriate electoral procedures revealed was not so much discrepancies as to the desirability of European elections, or opposition intentions to exploit governmental disunity with a view to ousting the government,[34] but recognition of the apparent increase in the stature and importance that national parties attached to the extent of their representation in the European Parliament. This is instructive because it suggested that they recognised both the potential role of the European Parliament (and therefore attached importance to securing as high a proportion of their member state's seat quota as possible) and that they suspected that the amount of support they secured in European elections would have repercussions for them at national-level elections and vice versa. This was evident in Germany where the CDU/CSU felt they would fare better under their preferred electoral system, whereas the SPD's small coalition partner, the FDP, feared it would not only have difficulty in surmounting the 5 per cent clause (which requires parties to poll a minimum of 5 per cent of votes cast in order to gain representation) but would lose votes to the CDU/CSU, and suffer similarly in subsequent *Land* elections. This, in turn, would have had serious repercussions for the viability of the federal government. In Britain, cognisance of its declining popularity, coupled with its 'pact' with the Liberals, led the Labour Government initially to intimate support for a system of proportional representation over the simple majority system favoured by, and deemed favourable to, the Conservatives. Calculations concerning the impact of either system on the electoral advantage to one or other of the major parties indicated that European elections were a good deal more significant to governments than many of them were prepared to admit. Particularly in some countries where government majorities were slender, it was thought that 'defeat' in European elections would increase governments' vulnerability in the national arena.

By the middle of 1977 most member governments had expressed a preference for a form of proportional representation, although commitment to it by all of them remained tenuous. However, such a system recommended itself because, firstly, it was believed that it would produce a more accurate reflection of political opinion than would a simple majority system; and secondly, it was thought that it would facilitate agreement on a common electoral system to be considered by members of the directly elected Parliament and to be based on some form of proportional representation for subsequent elections. Indeed, in Britain it was felt that if MEPs were elected on the same basis as Westminster members, serious discrepancies would arise. In September 1976 Lord Gladwyn pointed out that an unbalanced representation of British parties in the European Parliament would result.[35] Others suggested that under the simple majority system Liberals would fail to gain election, the SNP would be over-represented, Catholics from Northern Ireland would fail to win any seats, and variations in the popularity of the government of the day would be reflected in the European Parliament.[36]

The Nine's different provisions regarding voter eligibility are a potential source of discrepant representation.[37] Commenting on their electoral practices, M. Bertrand (B, C-D) advocated the national parliaments taking action to facilitate the introduction of a 'European' provision into national electoral laws so that EC citizens, no matter what member state they happened to be in at the time of the elections, would not be deprived of the right to vote.[38] The various proxy and postal provisions for voters absent from either their constituency or their country on the day of a national election vary from state to state. A House of Commons Select Committee has considered the possibility of allowing United Kingdom citizens resident in other EC countries to vote by proxy in the consituency in which they last resided.[39] The adoption of a provision along these lines will be necessary when a common electoral system is adopted by the EC for subsequent elections to the European Parliament.

Similar differences exist in respect of the age of majority.[40] Again, harmonisation on this and on electoral disqualifications[41] will be necessary.

Problematic though the elaboration and adoption of a common electoral system and procedures may be, they would have certain advantages. A common electoral system would, for example, help to establish the uniqueness of European elections in the minds of EC citizens. For the first European elections, the provisions adopted by the member states will be transitional only. Subsequently, the elimination of differences and the adoption of a common electoral system can be justified on the grounds of the need to ensure 'equality' and comparability in the representation of the member states. The electoral system will, however, be neither the sole nor the primary determinant of the representativeness of each member state's delegation to the European Parliament. Instead, this will be influenced by, firstly, the general level of turn-out; and secondly, the relative success of different parties in mobilising support. The Parliament's interest in promoting a generally high turn-out has already been alluded to, as has the instrumental role of the parties in increasing the chamber's visibility, intelligibility and tangibility. While the election campaign may be dominated by national party candidates, the European parties will provide the backcloth against which the campaigns will be conducted, and the political organisations through which those elected will work at the European level.

The Campaign

Inevitably, the campaign will differ from those conducted in the member states for usual national, regional or local elections. However, European parties will face two major problems: firstly, the ways in which their electoral programmes are distinguished from those of national parties; and secondly, the ways in which the campaign can be best conducted to ensure voting.

The Liberal-Democratic Federation indicated in 1976 that it favoured the adoption of a mixed campaign strategy whereby the party's European manifesto would be combined with those of the component parties. The former was therefore seen as a kind of 'umbrella' manifesto, and allowances were to be made for circumstances peculiar to individual member states and parties. In effect, this meant that national parties were to retain a high degree of autonomy in determining both the content of their electoral appeals and campaign styles. At the same time, however, the linking of national and European campaigns was deemed desirable. While a mixed strategy appeared advantageous in terms of underlining the special nature of European elections, it posed logistical problems. Although these need not make a mixed strategy impracticable, special efforts are needed to accommodate national peculiarities in order to ensure that a successful campaign is conducted.

The manner in which parties seek to mobilise support is also problematic. The parties will not be able to encourage electors to vote on the basis of policy-oriented undertakings or appeals to traditional aspects of voter self-interest given the European Parliament's limited legislative power, and the EC's limited authority, resources and power to commit funds to expenditure on traditional vote-catching issues like employment, health, housing and social welfare. The parties will therefore have to concentrate on awareness-building rather than policy-oriented activities. The more visible MEPs are, the more likely it is that such activities will be successfully accomplished.

While, at times of elections, parties can provide some link between the institutional workings of a political system and the public, and simplify the former for the latter, at other times the public needs other points of reference.[42] Individual politicians and MEPs are especially important in this respect for they must establish themselves as the links between the public and the EC's authority structure if the EC is to be constantly visible to its citizens, and if it is to make sense to them. In the first instance, it will be necessary to impress upon voters that the objectives of European elections are quite different from those of general elections. They are neither about the election of a government nor about the election of representatives to perform tasks strictly analogous to those carried out by national MPs. For example, while an MP might normally perform 'errand' functions for a constituent[43] (for example, by intervening, perhaps, on his/her behalf with a local or central authority), an MEP is unable to perform similar functions to the same extent not least because of the nature of EC decision-making. The MEP is unable to deliver the same amount or type of 'goods' that an MP might deliver in the national arena. An MEP in unable to exert effective sanctions over EC authorities in order to further voters' interests. How, then, is a candidate contesting European elections to persuade voters to elect him? What are the advantages and disadvantages of candidates being members of national parties and European parties?

An MEP's simultaneous membership of a national and European party will be advantageous during the election campaign to the extent that voters are able to select the candidate of their choice by simply isolating familiar party preferences. Attitudes towards European integration have been found to be affected by existing party loyalties and class.[44] Therefore, an individual's commitment to a given national party may determine both his/her attitude towards the EC, the selection of particular candidates and his/her readiness to vote.

Identification with familiar parties and candidates will enable voters to minimise expenditures of time and energy on informing themselves about various issues and candidates.[45] Disadvantages accrue, however, from voters screening out or distorting unfamiliar or contrary information.[46] In other words, while voters' knowledge about the EC remains low, there might be a greater tendency to adhere to existing preconceptions and myths about the EC[47] and to reject contrary views.

Further disadvantages arise from European elections being contested on national party tickets. Were voters to select their normally preferred parties without first investing time in perusing European party programmes presented by candidates, they might fail to associate the elections clearly with EC activities. Moreover, if voters having little awareness of, or knowledge about, EC affairs were to be faced by a selection of programmes distributed by both European and national parties, confusion might again follow if they regarded European elections as merely a form of, or variant on, national elections. To minimise this, national and especially European parties will, on the one hand, have to rely heavily on political broadcasts prior to the elections to inform electors of manifesto content and candidates contesting the elections; and, on the other hand, they will need to educate and advise voters of the separate nature of European elections, and also of the possibility of making representations to MEPs in addition to any made to national

MPs. National and European parties and candidates will therefore have to capitalise on the Commission's Information Programme and launch educative campaigns to explain basic points about the EC; to portray the European Parliament as an alternative body to which representations can usefully be made; and to convince voters of the advantages to them of voting. A number of problems confront them in this respect.

If national and European parties and candidates are to act as links between voters and decision-makers, as channels through which voter and interest-group demands can be articulated and presented, as foci of citizen attention and identity, and as a means of stimulating and facilitating participation, then to be effective they must possess some knowledge about the interests and aspirations of those whom they seek to represent. This may pose an acute problem for candidates standing for election in newly drafted electoral constituencies since they may face a lack of precise information about the electoral composition of the area. To conduct an effective campaign, candidates require information about voters' preferences, the distribution of support for rival parties in national-level elections, the impact of EC policies on different social groups and, assuming the latter's awareness of them, their evaluation of and attitudes towards such policies. Candidates must also possess an appreciation of which and how many voters can be mobilised, how, when and to what purpose.

Retention of normal national electoral practices for European elections might make it slightly easier for parties and candidates to organise campaigns and predict outcomes. In some instances candidates might be expected to have an accurate view of electoral opinion and preferences, and of voters' responsiveness and susceptibility to certain kinds of appeals. On the one hand, this might tempt candidates to campaign on local issues thereby reinforcing parochial identifications and preoccupations. On the other hand, it could be the case that appeals to strictly parochial concerns might, especially on the occasion of the first European elections, be one of the more effective ways of mobilising support. This is because such issues would be more easily recognised and comprehended by electors, and would have a higher degree of salience to them, than would vague, remote and intangible European appeals. Moreover, the less a national party identifies or aligns itself with a European party, the greater will be the tendency to emphasise local, regional or national issues. This tendency will also be higher, the more hostile public opinion is to the EC or to specific EC policies, and the more a candidate or party attempts to capitalise on them.

Candidates will face two problems where there appears to be both greater public awareness of aspects of EC policies – such as agricultural surpluses and the cost of storing them or subsidising their export – and a tendency to extrapolate dissatisfaction with one EC policy to the whole Community. On the one hand they could support public opinion in condemning the policy and/or Community, partly with a view to making it more difficult for candidates projecting contrary images to win votes and, hence, election. Additionally, it could lead to candidates from the same national or European party adapting their campaigns to match prevailing opinion in different regions with the result that they may gain election on the basis of incompatible views of the EC. (Even though this happens to some extent in national elections, the results may prove more confusing at the European level.)

On the other hand, candidates facing publics hostile to the EC or to its policies may be tempted to seek election on the basis of undertakings to defend parochial interests. This might win them support and/or ensure a high turn-out. But a candidate would be ill-advised to so commit himself given his own, and the Parliament's, limited ability to influence EC legislation. Although a candidate may choose to conduct such a campaign, he may face a more hostile, disillusioned or disaffected electorate upon subsequently seeking re-election.

By contrast, assuming that a candidate stresses a European identity and policies, and that he has adequate knowledge of the region he contests, he will still have to conduct a skilful campaign to interest voters in turning out. Because prospective MEPs cannot campaign on the basis of policy-oriented undertakings or traditional appeals to voters' self-interest, they cannot offer tangible rewards in exchange for voters' support. Voters will not only face an absence of specific appeals usually associated with national elections, they will also lack easily recognisable yardsticks by which to measure, compare and evaluate incumbent MEPs and their opponents. However, it must be emphasised that MEPs and national MPs do not, and will not, perform strictly analogous roles. Indeed, it may be suggested that apart from acting as representatives of EC citizens, the most immediate functions of MEPs and those contesting the elections will be in arousing public interest in the EC and in promoting a direct expression of public consent to it.

The major tasks of present MEPs, parties and candidates differ in crucial respects from those of national MPs. Of necessity, they will initially have to be directed more towards awareness-building rather than to policy-oriented activities. Public participation will have to be encouraged without the simultaneous generation of excessive and unsatisfiable expectations of MEPs' and EC bodies' performance. The elections will also afford candidates and parties the opportunity of not simply reacting to public opinion but of stimulating its formation and expression. Elections do not simply uncover existing opinions. They help to create and modify them through the processes of party debate and confrontation. The campaigns will provide the electorate with information. This, if accurate and reliable, should improve public understanding of issues and contribute towards an intelligent expression of opinion.[48] The need for candidates to inform and persuade is, moreover, central to ensuring their accountability since they will, at subsequent elections, be obliged to defend their records against those of their rivals.

Conclusion

Related to concern with awareness-building activities is the belief that electoral turn-out will depend on the Parliament's and EC's visibility; on the public's perceptions of the salience of EC activities; on voters' sense of their personal political efficacy; on their awareness of opportunities for participating in decision-making and access to decision-makers; and on the role that the media and parties play in the election campaign. The Commission's Information Programme and attempts at impressing the EC's salience on citizens rest on the assumption that the higher this is perceived to be, the more likely it will be that citizens will participate in the EC's political processes. Preparations for European elections are themselves seen as a way of increasing citizen awareness and as a chance for MEPs to underline the EC's relevance to the public. This is of considerable importance given that *Eurobarometer* surveys have found that interest in EC problems has remained 'remarkably stable'. A poll conducted in November 1976, a few weeks after the Nine had agreed in principle to European elections in 1978, found that on average more than two in ten interviewed claimed that they were 'very interested' in EC problems, five in ten were 'a little interested', and three in ten were 'not at all interested' or gave no reply. However, for every two claiming to be 'very interested' only one discussed EC affairs 'often' with family or friends. This led to the conclusion that interest was passive rather than active. Interest in the EC also correlated positively with income, level of education and leadership rating.[49] In all member states except Britain (where interest in the EC has been above the EC average since the June 1975 referendum campaign) personal interest in the Community has not been consistently high. What is interesting from the point of view of European elections is that politicisation of EC issues tends to increase awareness of and interest in the Community. Thus, we should expect interest in the EC to rise as European elections gain more momentum and salience for EC publics. Clearly, the Parliament has a role to play here.

Although the Parliament's limited ability to influence legislative proposals and outputs restricts the making of commitments by MEPs to citizens and interest groups in exchange for their support,[50] links with them should be expanded in view of Mr Jenkins' undertaking to afford the present Parliament (and the future directly elected one) greater scope for influencing decisions. He said that the Commission would consider whether its proposals were ones likely to gain the support of a majority in the Parliament.[51] There can be little doubt that were the Parliament to develop its own expertise, the Commission's and Council's interest in consulting it and heeding its views would increase.[52] Similarly, it can be expected that, irrespective of the Parliament's formal powers, directly elected MEPs accountable to citizens will become more active in scrutinising and seeking to influence EC decision-making given their interest, when seeking re-election, in being able to demonstrate the success with which they have advanced their supporters' interests.

Following European elections the EC's institutional balance is likely to be modified, not simply because of the changed basis of the EC's legitimacy, but also because MEPs will have more time and incentives to scrutinise, follow up and express their views on Commission proposals and questions affecting the EC. MEPs will come to play a greater role in decision-making and can, ultimately, be expected to seek formal endorsement of an extension of the European Parliament's powers, possibly through amendments to the Rome Treaty and a redefinition of the EC's institutions' roles. In the immediate future a high turn-out in the elections will boost MEPs' self-confidence and encourage them to emphasise the Parliament's special roles in the EC. Its potential for influence is already greater than its powers, and provided its members and parties effectively perform awareness-building, information, education and communication functions, it will help to advance integration.

Notes

1. G. Zellentin, 'Forms and Function of the Opposition in the European Communities', *Government and Opposition*, II (1967) 416–35, at p. 418.

2. J. N. Rosenau, *Domestic Sources of Foreign Policy* (New York: Free Press, 1967) p. 414.

3. Ibid.

4. C. Mueller, *The Politics of Communication* (New York: Oxford Univ. Press, 1973) p. 18.

5. D. Nimmo, *Popular Images of Politics*, (Englewood Cliffs, N.J.: Prentice-Hall, 1974).

6. G. Granai, 'Communication, Language et Société. *Cahiers Internationaux de Sociologie*, XXIII (1957) 57–110, cited ibid.

7. See F. I. Greenstein, *Children and Politics* (New Haven: Yale Univ. Press, 1965); R. E. Dawson and K. Prewitt, *Political Socialisation* (Boston: Little, Brown, 1969); and D. Easton and J. Dennis, *Children in the Political System* (New York: McGraw-Hill, 1969).

8. H. van Dalen and L. H. Zeigler, *Introduction to Political Science: People, Politics and Perceptions* (Englewood Cliffs, N.J.: Prentice-Hall, 1977) p. 180.

9. Ibid., pp. 180–1.

10. Ibid., p. 182.

11. Mueller, *The Politics of Communication*, pp. 70–71; G. A. Almond and

118   *The European Parliament and the European Community*

J. S. Coleman (eds.), *The Politics of the Developing Areas* (Princeton: Princeton Univ. Press, 1960) p. 17.

12. R. Dahrendorf, 'The Foreign Policy of the EEC', *The World Today*, XXIX (1973) 47–57.

13. *Debates of the European Parliament* (hereinafter *DEP*), Jan 1977.

14. M. Stewart, 'Direct Elections to the European Parliament', *Common Market Law Review*, XIII (1976) 283–301.

15. At six-monthly intervals *Eurobarometer* reports on 'public opinion concerning the Community, its institutions, their performance and general questions of interest to the public at large. The surveys are made by specialised institutions using strictly harmonised methods and interviewing about 9000 people (throughout the EC) aged 15 or over.' J. J. Rabier, 'European Surveys and Social Research', *European Journal of Political Research*, V (1977) 103–114, at p. 113. See also R. Inglehart, 'Changing Value Priorities and European Integration', *Journal of Common Market Studies*, X (1971) 1–36, and his 'Public Opinion and Regional Integration', *International Organisation*, XXIV (1970) 764–95.

16. *Eurobarometer*, Jan 1977, pp. 53 ff.

17. Ibid.

18. *DEP*, Sep 1976, p. 89.

19. *European Report*, 9 Feb 1977.

20. See N. H. Nie and S. Verba, 'Political Participation', in F. I. Greenstein and N. W. Polsby (eds.), *Handbook of Political Science*, vol. IV (Reading, Mass.: Addison-Wesley, 1975). See also S. H. Barnes, 'Participation, Education and Political Competence', *American Political Science Review*, LX (1966) 348–53, and A. Kornberg et al., 'Legislatures and the Modernisation of Societies', *Comparative Political Studies*, V (1973) 471–91.

21. R. S. Byars, 'Small Group Theory and Shifting Styles of Political Leadership', *Comparative Political Studies*, V (1973) 451.

22. *Report of the Political Affairs Committee on the Adoption of a Draft Convention Introducing Direct Elections to the European Parliament by Direct Universal Suffrage* (Patijn Report) (PE.37.881/fin) p. 22.

23. B. Hedges and R. Jowell, *Britain and the EEC: Report on a Survey of Attitudes Towards the European Economic Community* (London, Social and Community Planning Research, 1971), and J. J. Rabier, *L'Europe vue par les Européens* (Brussels, EC Commission, 1974).

24. J. Lodge, 'Towards a Human Union: EEC Social Policy and European Integration', *British Journal of International Studies*, IV (1978) 47–74.

25. See on this S. Verba and N. H. Nie, *Participation in America: Political Democracy and Social Equality* (New York: Harper & Row, 1972), and A. Campbell, 'The Passive Citizen', *Acta Sociologica*, VI (1962) 9–21.

26. Barnes, op. cit.

27. See on linguistic diversity G. Smith, *Politics in Western Europe* (London: Heinemann, 1972) chap. 1.

28. See J. Fitzmaurice, *The Party Groups in the European Parliament* (Farnborough: Saxon House, 1975) pp. 163–74.

29. Ibid., p. 165.

30. Ibid., p. 169.

31. Zellentin, op. cit.

32. *European Report*, 11 June 1977.

33. *The Times*, 22 June 1977.

34. *The Times*, 25 June 1977. Following an RPR initiative, the French National Assembly's Foreign Affairs Committee passed a motion on 9 June seeking to adjourn the debate on the ratification of the convention of direct elections. Left-wing parties abstained from the affair which seemed linked to rivalry between RPR leader Chirac and President Giscard d'Estaing. Yet it had been Chirac who had signed the Convention as Prime Minister in September 1976. Some EC circles accused him of breaking his word. See *European Report*, 11 June 1977.

35. *DEP*, September, 1976, p. 99.

36. *Sunday Times*, 28 Nov 1976.

37. *Direct Elections to the European Assembly*, Cmnd 6768 (London: HMSO, 1977).

38. *DEP*, Sept 1976, p. 86.

39. See the *Third Report of the House of Commons Select Committee on Direct Elections to the European Assembly*, Cmnd 6623 (London: HMSO, 1976).

40. During the last decade the minimum voting age has been reduced to 18 in France, Germany, the Netherlands and Britain. Debate on reducing the age to 18 took place in Denmark in 1977.

41. See Stewart, op. cit. The importance of the second set of elections is stressed by J. D. B. Mitchell, 'The Tindemans Report: Retrospect and Prospect', *Common Market Law Review*, XIII (1976) 455–84.

42. The role of leaders and charisma in integration is well documented. See L. N. Lindberg and S. A. Scheingold, *Regional Integration: Theory and Research* (Cambridge, Mass.: Harvard Univ. Press, 1971), and C. Ake, *A Theory of Political Integration* (Homewood: Dorsey, 1967).

43. See, for example, J. C. Wahlke *et al.*, *The Legislative System: Explorations in Legislative Behaviour* (New York: Wiley, 1962) chap. 13.

44. R. J. Shepherd, *Public Opinion and European Integration* (Farnborough: Saxon House, 1975) chap. 9.

45. A. Downs, *An Economic Theory of Democracy* (New York: Harper & Row, 1957).

46. L. Festinger, *A Theory of Cognitive Dissonance* (New York: Harper & Row, 1957).

47. *Direct Elections to the EEC Assembly or 'European Parliament'* (London: Safeguard Britain Campaign, 1977).

48. W. N. Hogan, *Representative Government and European Integration* (Lincoln: Univ. of Nebraska Press, 1967) p. 95.

49. *Eurobarometer*, no. 6 (Jan 1977).

50. W. Averyt, 'Europroups, Clientèla and the European Community', *International Organisation*, XXIX (1975) 949–72.

51. *DEP*, Jan 1977.

52. This was emphasised by the late Anthony Crosland in his first speech to the European Parliament on 14 January 1977 when he stated: '. . . my crucial aim will be the closest possible cooperation with the Parliament and the Commission in the interests of Community cohesion'. *DEP*, Jan 1977.

8 The European Parliament and the Media

Rule 1: Maximise publicity.

Jeremy Bentham, *Constitutional Code*, vol. I (1830)

If the visibility and intelligibility of the Community and European Parliament are to increase, greater media coverage of their affairs must be gained. This will be important both before and after the elections.

While press coverage of Parliament's debates has increased since 1973, we intend to suggest that it has been inadequate, and has failed to reach mass audiences. A number of factors account for this. Firstly, it is usually the quality press that reports parliamentary activities. Secondly, if reports on the European Parliament are carried at all, the extent of their comprehensiveness is determined by competing claims on column space, by the nature of the reporting staff's interests and duties, and by the location of the Parliament's sessions. Thus, for example, the relative remoteness of Luxembourg, and the interrupted and peripatetic nature of the Parliament's plenary sessions (coupled with the often uninspiring content of its debates), has meant that there has been little incentive for the media to station a permanent press corps in Luxembourg. There has therefore been limited press coverage of the Parliament's activities by even the quality press. The lack of coverage given by the popular press to either national or European parliamentary affairs has meant that it has not contributed to increasing the European Parliament's visibility and that MEPs, for their part, have not really perceived the popular press as a useful medium through which to gain publicity for their activities. This is not surprising given the low salience of much of the Parliament's business in the past.

While it would be inaccurate to suggest that the popular press never covers the European Parliament's proceedings, it must be recognised that items that have been regarded as 'good copy' have often dealt with the more ludicrous aspects of EC legislative proposals, such as 'Euro-beer', or with items likely to raise public indignation either because of their 'triviality' or their 'effects on the shopping basket'. Moreover, attention has focused on the Commission and the Council rather than on the European Parliament. It appears that the press has generally disregarded the latter's affairs, and that the coverage it has afforded EC

TABLE 8.1. Perceptions of bias in reporting of European affairs

European problems are reported in a biased manner in (this country)

%	F	UK	D	I	NL	DK	B	L	IRL	EC	(N)
Agree	48	44	26	54	39	37	34	49	44	42	3780
Disagree	22	27	41	18	31	26	25	20	40	28	2558
Don't know	30	29	33	28	30	37	41	31	16	30	2793

Source: *Eurobarometer*, no. 2 (1974).

matters in general has been regarded as often biased by EC publics (see Table 8.1). Without underplaying the role the press could play in increasing the European Parliament's visibility – especially in view of the elections – we would suggest that the impact of the audio-visual media would be greater in this respect.

As yet, there are no regular radio or television broadcasts of the European Parliament's debates either in full or in summary form. Instead, only the most salient or controversial items are covered and, as with press coverage, radio and television coverage are subject to subjective and technical constraints. Contributory factors include the general images of the European Parliament and its members as not newsworthy – in part because of the latter's low status and influence relative to more eminent members of national parliaments. More importantly, perhaps, the EC lacks supranational television and broadcasting channels independent of those of the member states. The programmes produced by the EC have to be inserted into slots in the news and documentary programmes of the member states, and the latter determine the amount of time to be given to EC matters. Programmes produced either by the European Parliament's information and media office, or by the European Broadcasting Union (whose members include non-EC states), have to be transmitted via member states' television and radio networks. Technical constraints have also limited the extent of coverage given to EC and European parliamentary affairs. The recently perfected link-up system with Brussels should improve matters. Once in use, the system will facilitate simultaneous exchanges and discussions between Commissioners, politicians and interviewers in different EC centres. Since this will create the illusion of the participants all being in the same studio, and all in direct and immediate contact with one another, the impact – in terms of immediacy for television viewers – should be greater than it has been in the case of teletapes. The more immediate and the less distant Commissioners and European Parliamentarians are perceived to be, the more tangible and salient their activities will appear to be to viewers. Since *Eurobarometer* surveys indicate that the public tends to have difficulty in following Community affairs (see Table 8.2) this will be important.

TABLE 8.2. Perceptions of difficulties in understanding involvement in EC affairs

The newspapers, radio and television give only simple summaries of European problems, so it is difficult for people like myself to see how we are involved in what is being discussed.

%	F	UK	D	I	NL	DK	B	L	IRL	EC	(N)
Agree	56	72	47	67	48	44	48	58	70	59	5070
Disagree	30	17	33	20	37	37	27	23	28	26	2586
Don't know	14	11	20	13	15	19	25	19	2	15	1404

Source: *Eurobarometer*, no. 2 (1974).

Skilful exploitation of the audio-visual media could increase the visibility, intelligibility, immediacy and tangibility of the EC, thereby reducing its remoteness and increasing public awareness of the Community and of the salience of its outputs. That this has been recognised by the European Parliament is attested by the increased activity of its information and media services in preparation for the elections. The use made by the member states of the facilities offered by this service shed additional light on the extent to which different member states perceive the European Parliament's affairs to be newsworthy. Prior to examining this in greater detail, we shall briefly consider why the media are important and what contribution they might be expected to make to the elections and to promoting integration.

As already intimated, greater media attention to the European Parliament would increase its visibility to EC publics. This is deemed important to stimulating public awareness of the EC, Parliament and elections. In other words, greater media coverage of Parliament would facilitate the transmission of images, ideals and information, and thereby help the Parliament to fulfil its communicative, educative and informative functions in respect of EC citizens. At the same time, it would be likely to stimulate public awareness of the elections and voting opportunities. In other words, the media have a part to play in not only familiarising EC citizens with, and acclimatising them to, the EC's dimensions, but also in the electoral campaign itself. This is because candidates might not only use the media in the way in which they are accustomed to doing in local and national elections, but the European parties might also use the media to conduct skilful campaigns with a view to influencing voters' choices, to publicising their own and the Parliament's activities, and to persuading people of the usefulness of voting and encouraging them to turn out. In other words, skilful use of the media made by the European Parliament and parties in preparation for the elections could foster integration by helping citizens to become aware of their European identities. As Commission President Roy Jenkins pointed out in the President's traditional beginning-of-the-year programme speech which accompanies presentation of the Commission's Annual Report, European elections will in themselves help to foster a sense of common identity among electors.

How can this be achieved? We have already hinted at the potential role of the media, and noted why its role has hitherto been inadequately exploited. Let us now scrutinise media attention to the Parliament during a twenty-eight-month period beginning January 1975 with a view to isolating any general trends and similarities in the time accorded to the European Parliament by each of the member states.

A rough guide to media interest in the Parliament can be obtained by studying the attendance of television film crews at, and the use of radio studios during, Parliament's sittings. For two main reasons, the figures reported below must be interpreted cautiously. Firstly, the figures for television coverage include only film reports known to have been made by correspondents during sessions in Luxembourg and Strasbourg. They do not include news agency reports or studio discussions carried by TV stations in their own country. For example, the Italian programme *Giorni d'Europa* frequently features the work of the Parliament and MEPs, but only when film had been shot in the Parliament would it be included in the data here. Secondly, figures for radio coverage represent only the number of studio circuits booked during sessions in Luxembourg and Strasbourg. Radio correspondents also use telephone and telex circuits for their daily reports and make local recordings for transmission on return to their stations.

The Audio-Visual Section of the European Parliament has no regular means of monitoring all local, regional or even national radio and television transmissions. As a result, the data presented here, which were provided by this Section, do not encompass all member states' media coverage of the Parliament and MEPs. They do, however, represent the universe of radio and television reporting of the Parliament during its Strasbourg and Luxembourg sessions.

Our analysis begins with an examination of media coverage during 1975 and 1976; in part these years have been selected because of the availability of data, in part because this represents a recent and important period in the Parliament's development. We shall then examine in some detail television coverage during the January to April 1977 period.

Television Coverage, 1975—6

As can be seen from Table 8.3, television coverage of the 1976 sessions was lower than in 1975. In 1976, 33 films were shot, compared to 48 in

TABLE 8.3. Television films, 1975–6*

	Number		Duration (min)	
	1975	1976	1975	1976
Belgium	2	2	28 (5.8%)	48 (11.8%)
Denmark	6	4	49 (10.2)	18 (4.4)
France	6	6	22 (4.6)	53 (13.0)
Germany	7	4	33 (6.9)	14 (3.4)
Ireland	1	0	2 (0.4)	0 (0)
Italy	6	3	68 (14.2)	42 (10.3)
Luxembourg	2	3	5 (1.0)	8 (2.0)
Netherlands	4	2	65 (13.5)	47 (11.5)
United Kingdom	14	9	208 (43.3)	178 (43.6)
Total	48	33	480 (99.9)	408 (100.0)
Average/session	4	2.75	40	34

*Data in this and all other tables refer only to coverage of the Parliament by radio and television reporters from the member states of the Community. Programmes made on the Parliament by non-Community countries are excluded.

1975 – a reduction of 33 per cent. Whereas the average number of films shot was 4 per session in 1975, this fell to 2.75 per session in 1976. The total length of film was also down from 480 minutes (40 per session) in 1975, to 408 minutes (34 per session) in 1976 – a 15 per cent drop. Several reasons can be advanced for this: some relate to the Parliament's work; others to political events elsewhere in the EC; and yet others to the vagaries of the Nine's TV companies.

The British referendum of June 1975 and the eventual arrival of the British Labour delegation to the Parliament stimulated extra media interest both in Britain (where TV companies were responsible for over two-fifths of the total film shot during 1975 at the Parliament) and elsewhere. In 1976, however, the major news concerning the Parliament – the Council's spasmodic progress on reaching a decision on European elections – occurred outside Parliament's sessions. The non-coincidence of the Council's and Parliament's sessions was not peculiar to this event. Rather, it is a general pattern which exacerbates problems arising from the Parliament's low visibility. Because of the timing of its sessions, the Parliament is too divorced from both the Council–Commission dialogue and, more importantly, from decisional output sessions of the Council and European Council. Moreover, the Parliament rarely gets the opportunity to involve Council and Commission representatives in the same debate. This, in turn, minimises its chances of establishing a three-way debate and of creating the type of government–parliament rapport found in the member states.

Comparisons of media coverage on a country-by-country basis also reveal the extent to which coverage was determined by national criteria. Danish coverage fell in 1976 partly because its chief European correspondent was recalled to Copenhagen in the midsummer, and a replacement was not made until the end of the year. Moreover, much Danish coverage during 1975 can be accounted for by the British referendum: once the British Government accepted continued EC membership, the possibility of Danish secession receded, and so did media attention to the EC. Federal elections in Germany in October 1976 reduced ARD and ZDF film coverage of the Parliament, even though interest among German radio correspondents generally remained high throughout the year.

The amount of coverage afforded the Parliament from its sessions by the French and Luxembourg media depended on where the sessions were held: all 8 minutes of film shown on Luxembourg TV in 1976 were shot while sessions were held in Luxembourg, whereas all 53 minutes of French TV film were shot during Strasbourg sessions. British radio and TV coverage is higher than in many other member states, and regional companies give the Parliament greater attention than do national companies. Of 178 minutes of film shot in 1976, less than 30 minutes (16 per cent) was for national news; and in 1975 regional companies were responsible for over 75 per cent of the film shot for British TV. Indeed, British television coverage figures are somewhat inflated because they include film profiles made by regional TV companies of local politicians appointed to the European Parliament. However, such programmes are of regional significance given that they help to create public awareness directly of their local MP's European parliamentary activities, and indirectly of the European Parliament. The regional companies will indubitably perform similarly useful roles during the European electoral campaign. With the exception of a single 2-minute film made on the occasion of President O'Dalaigh's visit to the Parliament's June 1975 Strasbourg session, no Irish TV crews filmed the Parliament in 1975 or 1976.

TV coverage of Parliament's activities was not uniform throughout the period. Of twelve sessions held in 1976 (one monthly except in August when there were no sessions, and two in October), two were filmed by Dutch and Belgian television, three by German, Luxembourg and Italian TV, and four by various French TV companies. Danish radio also covered four. British TV companies, which filmed in seven of the twelve sessions, were the only ones to cover more than half of the sessions.

No film was shot during the second (and short) October session when Parliament was preoccupied with the EC's budget. Film coverage of the June, July, September and November sessions was all less than 10 minutes. This represented a marked decrease over 1975 when TV coverage only dropped below 10 minutes in one session. The decline in coverage can be attributed partly to national political developments - such as German federal elections in October 1976, for example - and partly to the technical nature of EC budgetary proceedings. However, since the latter were significant for Parliament, given its recent acquisition of extended budgetary powers, MEPs might have been expected to have sought greater media coverage of their activities.

A monthly analysis of TV films made in Luxembourg and Strasbourg reveals some interesting patterns. Looking at 1976 sessions, once again the importance of national considerations becomes apparent. Of 8 minutes film made for Luxembourg TV, 4 minutes was concerned with Gaston Thorn's assumption of the Presidency of the Council of Ministers in January 1976. In February, 125 minutes of film were shot, mainly in the form of lengthy documentaries by Tyne-Tees TV (30 minutes), BRT (Belgium, 30 minutes), Italian TV (28 minutes), and FR3/TF1 (France, 26 minutes). The debate over European elections in March resulted in the BBC's *Tonight* team making a 13-minute feature, and coverage by French and Danish TV. The longest film shot during 1975–6 was made in March 1976 for the Dutch *Panoramiek* programme. Apart from a 2-minute feature on the Parliament in 1976, that was the only other piece on it in the Netherlands in two years.

In April 1976 Anglia TV made two 26-minute features. The only other film shot that month was made by ZDF. In May the debate on multinational corporations attracted the attention of FR3 correspondents from the Toulouse and Alsace regions, who shot 13- and 2-minute films respectively. Granada also made a 30-minute documentary in May. Only one programme was shot during the June Strasbourg session when the main item of business on Parliament's agenda was the motion of censure moved by the late Sir Peter Kirk (UK Con.): the 5-minute film made by the BBC included an interview with him.

Film shot during the second half of 1976 dropped from the 336 minutes of the first half to 72 minutes. In July the Council Presidency was assumed by the Dutch. Only TV crews from Luxembourg and the Netherlands recorded this. During September, Danish and Italian crews covered the Luxembourg session. During the first October session a 17-minute film was made for the BBC's *Westminster* programme, and a 2-minute one for FR3. None was shot during the second short session and only Luxembourg shot a 2-minute item in November. 1976 ended with British and Italian TV shooting 23- and 10-minute features respectively.

Radio Coverage of the Parliament, 1975–6

Given the incompleteness of data for two of the Parliament's twelve sessions in 1976, it is difficult to compare 1975 and 1976 radio circuits. However, as is clear from Table 8.4, the average number of circuits booked rose from 16.5 in 1975 to 20.4 in 1976: this is a different trend from that noted earlier in respect of TV, when 1976 saw a reduction both in the number and duration of films shot. On a technical level the opening in July 1976 of the Parliament's radio studios in the Bâtiment Schuman boosted radio coverage of the Luxembourg sessions. During 1976 an average of 26 circuits was booked for each Strasbourg session, compared to 19 for each Luxembourg session.

Noticeable about the country-by-country breakdown of radio circuits is the large number booked by German correspondents: over half in 1975, almost three-fifths in 1976. The reduction in German TV coverage of Parliament during 1976 was partially compensated for by a significant increase in radio coverage. In the first quarter of 1977, there was a marked increase in both the duration and number of the radio circuits booked, as can be seen from Table 8.5. This was probably due to the greater attention accorded EC matters in the wake of the new Commission taking up its duties under the Presidency of Roy Jenkins who was regarded, in some quarters, as a former MP who had experienced a not uncontroversial time at Westminster, and who was, moreover, expected to help to moderate the attitude of the British Labour Government towards the Community. In addition, contentious

TABLE 8.4. Radio circuits, 1975–6

	1975	1976
Belgium	13 (6.6%)	14 (6.9%)
Denmark	3 (1.5)	7 (3.4)
France	9 (4.5)	11 (5.4)
Germany	101 (51.0)	122 (59.8)
Ireland	3 (1.5)	9 (4.4)
Italy	13 (6.6)	0 (0)
Luxembourg	0 (0)	0 (0)
Netherlands	46 (23.2)	31 (15.2)
United Kingdom	10 (5.1)	10 (4.9)
Total	198 (100.0)	204* (100.0)
Average/session	16.5	20.4

*Excludes January and April sessions in Luxembourg for which no figures are available.

TABLE 8.5. Radio circuits, January–April 1977

	Number	Duration (min)
Belgium	9 (6%)	98
Denmark	4 (2.7)	72
France	8 (5.3)	203
Germany	73 (48.7)	876
Ireland	9 (6.0)	131
Italy	7 (4.7)	98
Luxembourg	0 (0)	0
Netherlands	19 (12.6)	264
United Kingdom	21 (14.0)	332
Total	150 (100.0)	2074
Average/session	37.5	518.5

issues – over and above matters relating to direct elections – were being discussed and presented to the Council of Ministers at the time of the British Presidency. The question of how Community-minded the British Government would prove to be while it occupied the chair of the Council of Ministers was itself something to focus media attention on EC activities. (German-language coverage during 1976 was, in fact, higher than that shown in Table 8.4, as the booking of Belgian radio circuits shown therein was mostly for regional German-language services.) A reverse pattern exists in respect of Britain where relatively high TV coverage contrasts with low radio coverage in both 1975 and 1976. Once again, national news coverage was minimal.

The number of radio circuits booked in the Parliament and shown for France and Luxembourg in Table 8.4 is artificially low owing to the proximity of national broadcasting studios in Strasbourg and Luxembourg which are preferred and used by local correspondents. Thus, the number of radio broadcasts was higher than shown. Although Dutch TV coverage tended to be sporadic in 1976, radio coverage was more regular throughout the year. While Italian TV coverage was quite high in both 1975 and 1976, the number of radio circuits fell from 13 in 1975 to none in 1976. Whereas, with one exception, no TV film was made by Irish correspondents, the RTE correspondent attended all of Parliament's sittings and sent regular reports to his company by both radio circuit and telephone.

A detailed examination of the use made of radio circuits in two sessions – July 1975 and June 1976 – gives some impression of the work of radio reporters. The main items of interest during the July 1975 Strasbourg sessions were the arrival of the British Labour delegation, and the Bertrand Report on European Union. On the first day of the session four radio programmes were transmitted – two for Dutch, and one each for German and Belgian radio – on the arrival of the British Labour delegation. Fifteen programmes were broadcast on the second day by German, Danish and Belgian radio: one on European Union, four on the Labour delegation, and five each on energy problems and the Parliament's general work. The third day of the session saw 18 programmes made – 7 on Parliament's work, and 11 on European Union – for Belgian, French, Irish, German and British radio. Eight programmes were made on the fourth day of the session, and six of these dealt with the Parliament's general work. Six programmes were transmitted on the final day of the session; five of these summarised Parliament's activities during the week.

Of 51 programmes broadcast during the session, 25 were for German radio, 11 for Dutch, 7 for Belgian, 4 for British, 2 for Irish, and one each for Danish and French radio. No circuits were booked by Luxembourg or Italian radio. The average length of programmes was 9½ minutes: 41 programmes consisted of short items – lasting between 3 and 12 minutes – primarily made for news programmes, 10 consisted of documentaries lasting upwards of 15 minutes.

A similar pattern can be seen from an examination of the June 1976 session, in which the main items on Parliament's agenda were the Kirk censure motion and a debate on European elections. On the first day of the session 10 radio programmes were made by German (8), British (1) and Irish (1) reporters – half on the censure motion, while the British and Irish focused on the elections. The second day, six programmes were made for German (4), Dutch (1) and French (1) radio: five were on the elections and one on the motion of censure. The third day, Parliament debated the textile industry, the subject of two Dutch and one German programmes. The last day, only one programme was made – by the Irish on elections.

Television Coverage, 1977

Let us now examine media coverage of Parliament during the first four months (five sessions) of 1977. A detailed breakdown of TV films made is given in Table 8.6. Summary statistics facilitating comparisons with 1975 and 1976 are given in Table 8.7, from which it is apparent that there was a marked increase in TV coverage. In each of the four whole sessions and one part-session an average of just over 12 films were shot, compared to the 1975 and 1976 averages of 4 and 2.75 respectively. The average duration of films also rose from 40 minutes in 1975 and 34 in 1976 to 134 in 1977. With the exception of Luxembourg, each country produced as many or more films on the Parliament during the first four months of 1977 than it did during the whole of 1976. More TV film was

TABLE 8.6. Television broadcasts, January–April 1977

Country	January	February	March[a]	April	No. of programmes	Length of programmes
Belgium		RTB/BRT Jenkins speech 4'		RTB/BRT Human rights 10'	2	14
Denmark	DR Jenkins declaration	DR Fishing policy 1' DR Portrait of Mr Jakobsen 40'		Greenland TV, European Parliament 25'	4	70
France[1]		TDF Jenkins speech	FR3 Election of President Colombo 4' 2' FR3 Mario Soares President Colombo 3'	Antenne 2 Direct elections 4' FR3 Human rights 3'	6	16
Germany[2]	ZDF Jenkins declaration 35' ZDF — 2' ARD — 2'	ZDF Jenkins speech 4' ARD — 8' SR — 6' SR Direct elections 20'	ZDF Election of President Colombo 4' 2' ZDF Euro-Communism 20'		12	119

Country					
Ireland	RTE Jenkins declaration 2' RTE — 13' RTE Jenkins press conference 3'	RTE Jenkins speech	RTE Direct elections 25' 4'	5	47
Italy[3]		RAI Jenkins speech	RAI Election of President Colombo 15' RAI — 2' RAI Interview with Pres. Colombo 2' RAI European passport, European transport 25' 4'	6	48
Luxembourg		RTL Jenkins speech	3'	1	3
Netherlands	NOS Jenkins press conference 25' VARA Portrait of Mr Vredeling 15'	NOS Jenkins speech	4' NOS Human rights 2' NOS Unemployment 2'	5	48

TABLE 8.6 (*continued*)

Country	January	February	March[a]	April	No. of programmes	Length of programmes
United Kingdom	BBC Jenkins declaration 5' ITN — 2' BBC — 3' BBC Jenkins press conference 12' ITN Crosland declaration 3' BBC *Newsday*, interviews 6' BBC *Westminster*, interviews 2'	BBC Jenkins speech 4' ITN — 4' BBC *Tonight*, Jenkins speech 7' BBC *Newsday*, Jenkins speech 9' BBC *Westminster*, Direct elections 20' BBC *Nationwide*, portrait of Mr Dykes 10' BBC *Tonight*, general report 20'	BBC Dual mandate 10'	BBC Scotland Direct elections 30' ITV Anglia — 30' ITV London Weekend, Direct elections 20' ITN London Owen speech 2' BBC *Newsday*, dual mandate 6'	20	205
Total programmes	17	21	11	12	61	
Total length (min)	131	199	106	134	570	

[a] Combines the part-session with the regular monthly session.

[1] Excludes full details of one programme in February made by Antenne 2, a portrait of M. Faure, for which the length of transmission is not known.

[2] Excludes full details of three programmes – one made in February by ZDF Wiesbaden on Euro-Communism, a ZDF programme in March on the new Palais de l'Europe, and a third made in April by Südwestfunk Deutschland on the European Parliament at work – for which the lengths of transmission are not known.

[3] Excludes full details of one programme made in January by RAI Rome for which the length of transmission is not known.

TABLE 8.7. Television coverage, 1975–7

	1975	1976	1977*
Average number of programmes/session	4.0	2.75	12.2
Minutes of film/session	40	34	134

*January–April. Excludes the five programmes mentioned in notes 1, 2 and 3 to Table 8.6.

shot during these months than during the whole of 1975 or 1976; and more minutes of broadcasting time were devoted to the Parliament during this period by Danish, German and Irish TV than in 1975 and 1976 combined. An analysis of the subject-matter of these programmes sheds some light on the significance of these increases.

The declaration of Commission President Jenkins to Parliament attracted 65 minutes coverage by German, British, Irish and Danish companies. An additional 40 minutes of film were shot during Jenkins' press conference by Irish, Danish and British stations. The other longest programme made in January was a 15-minute feature by Dutch TV about Commissioner Vredeling. Two reasons account for the high media coverage secured by Mr Jenkins. On the one hand, he was the Commission's new President, and incoming presidents tend to gain media attention during their first months in office and in respect of their initial public statements. On the other hand, the fact that Mr Jenkins was a renowned British pro-Marketeer occupying one of the most prestigious *supranational* offices in the Community was especially newsworthy given division in the British Government over the EC and the continued vociferousness of anti-Marketeers. Indeed, these facts alone provided plenty of copy for those who wanted to speculate on whether or not Mr Jenkins' assumption of the Commission Presidency would encourage a favourable change of attitude on the part of the British towards the EC. Thus, in some respects, the attention Mr Jenkins secured was related to general concern over the attitude of what was perceived as a recalcitrant British Labour Government. It is instructive that the Dutch programme on Mr Vredeling, by contrast, had a distinct national appeal and bias. Similarly, in February, with the exception of coverage of Mr Jenkins, most programmes had national slants.

Mr Jenkins' February speech to the Parliament was filmed for Eurovision by RTL (Luxembourg) and 4-minute highlights of it were broadcast by all the EC members bar Denmark. Four quite lengthy programmes were made during February. Danish TV made a 40-minute film featuring Mr Erhard Jakobsen, Chairman of the Centrum Democrats and MEP. Saarländischer Rundfunk produced a 20-minute programme on European elections which incorporated material from Luxembourg, Strasbourg and Brussels. BBC *Tonight* shot a 20-minute film which included an interview with the new Commissioner from Britain, Mr Christopher Tugendhat, and interviews with two MEPs, Mrs Gwyneth Dunwoody and Mr Erik Blumenfeld. BBC *Nationwide* produced a 10-minute portrait of Mr Hugh Dykes showing him during Question Time in the Parliament, at a meeting of the Conservative Group, addressing a party of German visitors to the Parliament and in discussion with Commissioner Ortoli.

The full and part-sessions in March were much quieter. The main item on Parliament's agenda then was the election of Signor Emilio Colombo (C-D) to the Presidency of the Parliament. This was the subject of five films shot by French, German and Italian TV. RAI (Italy) made a 25-minute feature on the European passport and on European transport, a programme that incorporated interviews with the chairmen of the political groups. German television produced a 20-minute piece on Euro-Communism.

In April, three regional British companies made films on European elections. These accounted for 80 of the 134 minutes of film broadcast during the month. Human rights were the subject of films featuring Andrei Amalrik made for Belgian, French and Dutch television, and a 25-minute general programme on the Parliament was filmed by Greenland TV.

MEPs and the Media

Media interest in the Parliament has been of two main kinds: on the one hand, interest in topical events especially suitable for news programmes; and on the other hand, interest in general, although not immediate, events suitable for documentaries. Media coverage tends to vary with the newsworthiness of events taking place in the Parliament. When Parliament debates matters of public interest, or when it comes into political contact, or more especially political conflict, with the Commission or Council, then it gains media attention. But by and large the Parliament is remote – both physically and in a decision-making sense – from newsworthy Community items. The Parliament's separation from the Brussels-based Commission and Council makes it difficult to attract more than a handful of the specialised press and media corps to Luxembourg or Strasbourg. Moreover, the Parliament does not exert significant control or influence over the EC's executive, and MEPs have often maintained a low profile and failed to project European (as opposed to national) images to either national, or the broader European, publics.

European elections are likely to change this, not least because a different type of MEP is likely to be returned to the Parliament. MEPs are likely to be more dynamic and committed to advancing the EC, especially if they lack the additional time constraints imposed by the dual mandate. They are likely to be more active in seeking extensions to the Parliament's legislative, financial and control powers than their predecessors.

Public opinion of the EC is, on balance, sympathetic. But the EC has lacked a supranational institutional focal point, and Parliament has failed to emerge as the EC's grand forum. Following the elections, Parliament's importance is likely to increase, not only in a decision-making sense, but also in respect of its role in creating a European political identity and furthering the idea of EC citizenship. For it to accomplish this, it will require the co-operation of the media.

More needs to be done by the Parliament to encourage the press, radio and TV to cover its work. However, it has first to ensure that its activities become more salient and newsworthy. Televising or broadcasting its proceedings on a regular basis would bring it to the attention of EC citizens, and help to make it more visible, intelligible and tangible. By mid-1978 the Parliament will have its own broadcasting unit with full technical facilities, which will greatly facilitate the work of the media. In addition, it is likely that the main media services will extend their coverage of the European Parliament's activities in preparation for, and following, the elections; that they will establish offices in Luxembourg or wherever the Parliament is eventually located on a permanent basis; and that they will appoint full-time correspondents to cover its work. Such developments are essential if the Parliament is to increase its ability to perform its communicative, educative and informative functions effectively. In the interim, however, the Commission is to concentrate 65 per cent of its information effort on making the EC's 180 million voters aware of Community issues and on promoting a high turn-out. The Commission's programme is to be implemented in association with the Parliament's information services in the interests of co-ordination and efficiency, and the elections were to be given priority in the Commission's information programme for 1977. To this end, the Commission decided to divert a proportion of the resources available for its 'normal' information programme to the special election programme. Given that the Commission's Information Programme had 'opinion-makers' as its focus, and given the fact that additional measures will be necessary to ensure that Parliament remains in the public eye after the elections, candidates and parties must learn to make better use of the media.

Candidates and parties contesting European elections will need to use the media if they are to transmit their messages and to project their images, aims and aspirations to mass audiences. Through the media they can heighten both their own visibility and saliency and those of EC affairs to citizens. In addition, parties and candidates might be expected to use the media to attempt to ensure that the electorate perceives them as different from their competitors not simply in terms of party labels

TABLE 8.8. Adequacy of information about elections to the European Parliament

Do you think that people like yourself get enough information or not from newspapers, radio and TV about the European Parliament and the forthcoming election of its members?

%	B	DK	D	F	IRL	I	L	NL	UK	EC*
Yes	44	33	34	37	48	22	54	41	29	32
No	41	51	47	52	44	65	38	49	64	55
Too much	1	2	1	3	3	2	2	2	2	2
No reply	14	14	18	8	5	11	6	8	5	11

*Weighted average.

Source: *Eurobarometer*, no. 7 (July 1977).

and individual personalities, but also in terms of those issues to which greatest inportance is attached. This is not to imply that voting may or will be policy-motivated but to emphasise the importance of clear differentiation among parties, candidates and issues to public perceptions of the European elections as unique and distinct from national politics.

Adroit use of the media will also enable candidates to 'politicise' voters[1] by making them aware of issues and of their ability to affect the political balance in the European Parliament. Via the media, candidates can also by-pass party organisations and make direct appeals for support to the electorate.[2] This may well be important to candidates whose national party is divided (as in the case of the British Labour Party) over membership of the EC as well as over the elections.

For a number of reasons, we believe that the use made of television by candidates will be particularly important, firstly in increasing public awareness of the European Parliament; secondly, in increasing public awareness of the opportunity for voting; and thirdly, in motivating voters to turn out. Table 8.8 shows that *Eurobarometer* surveys have found public dissatisfaction with the extent of information obtainable from the media about the Parliament and elections.

Television is likely to be a more effective medium than the press for increasing public awareness of, and interest in, the elections. On the one hand this is because of factors governing the selection of press copy, on the other because of the different type of newpaper-reading habits in the Nine. In Britain, for example, readership of national dailies is higher than it is in other member states. Not only are the publics in continental Europe less avid readers of the daily press than their British counterparts, but regional rather than national, and weekly rather than daily papers may be more influential in providing political information. In addition, a 1970 EC poll found that television ranked ahead of the radio and press as the source of news information in the Six. According to Rabier[3] about seven out of ten watched television news broadcasts every day (48 per cent) or several times a week (20 per cent). Only 12 per cent never watched the news. Exposure to television was found to be higher in the Netherlands and Germany than in other member states. By contrast, radio took second place as a source of information: six out of ten listened to the news daily (45 per cent) or several times a week (16 per cent); 17 per cent never listened to the news.

Where the press was concerned, four out of ten read the political news every day (27 per cent) or several times a week (14 per cent); 25 per cent never read the political news. As with exposure to television and radio news, Dutch and German publics were the keenest political news readers. Rabier's total exposure index to the information media (calculated by adding together the percentages of persons most exposed – maximum 300 points) placed the Netherlands and Germany first (201 and 194, respectively), and Luxembourg next. Exposure was below average for the EC in France, Italy and Belgium.

The media is not only an important source of information. It also affects voting turn-out. It has been shown important in turning out many unaffiliated or weakly affiliated voters who through exposure to the media come to vote for the candidate with whom they have become most familiar during an intensive media campaign.[4] Given that many candidates in the European elections may be 'unknown' to EC publics, and given that the size of constituencies will militate against extensive person-to-person and face-to-face contact which usually helps to overcome problems associated with a candidate's anonymity or invisibility in local elections, the use candidates make of the media – especially of local and regional radio and television stations – may well be important in decreasing their anonymity and hence heightening voters' senses of familiarity with them, and their willingness to support them. It may well be the case that the extent to which a voter is familiar with a candidate (familiar in the sense of being able to put a name to a face, to identify a candidate's party affiliation and possibly aspects of that party's manifesto) will be a more important determinant of party choice for those voters who in local and national elections may be regarded as unaffiliated, weakly affiliated or floating voters than will be issues and the content of manifestoes. While this would not in any case be particularly surprising in view of the European Parliament's and MEPs' limited ability to influence the content and outcomes of the EC's legislative process, it has a number of implications for the relationship of candidates to the media.

The ability of parties and candidates to secure television exposure over and above time allotted for party political broadcasts will depend on their ability to increase the salience of EC issues to television companies and to convince them that matters they wish to raise have high public interest values. If they fail in this respect, commercial television companies may wish to limit their coverage of such issues, especially if they fear (in view of past experience) a drop in viewing figures when coverage is given to the European Parliament's affairs. In such cases, parties and candidates may experience difficulty in securing 'free' coverage in news and documentary items.

The personalities of candidates and the way they project themselves will have to be taken into account since viewers may well decide to support the candidate towards whom they feel most empathetic rather than the candidate with whose 'policies' they are most in agreement. This likelihood is strengthened by the relative weakness of MEPs either to influence the nature and content of legislative proposals or to ensure the fulfilment of any objectives advanced in a party manifesto. This in turn may lead to campaigns dominated by personalities. There are both advantages and disadvantages to this.

The most obvious advantage of a personality-based campaign would be the rapidity with which effective links might be established between voters and MEPs. These in turn might help to promote horizontal integration. A second advantage would lie in the likelihood of increased media coverage attending such a campaign because competition and conflict between rival personalities would have elements of the 'human interest' type of 'story' and therefore be likely to appeal to and interest a larger section of the viewers than would less engaging and more factual items about the same parties' manifestoes. On an individual level, candidates with good television styles would benefit over those unable to project themselves effectively through this medium. Since this may be an acquired skill, a personality-dominated campaign would probably work to the advantage of those candidates either more experienced in dealing with the media or those whose eccentricities of manner, style or background capture the media's attention.

Disadvantages of personality-dominated campaigns may not become apparent in the short term but would surface in the long run. The projection of a dynamic personality may help a candidate to win election to the European Parliament if only because a dynamic personality would help to make a candidate more visible, but in the long term it might not help to increase the visibility of the European Parliament. In other words, while, during the election campaign, voters may well become aware of the fact that they were electing candidates to an institution known as the European Parliament, after the campaign, when neither the visibility of MEPs nor the chamber would be sustained simply by the fact of the elections, voters' awareness of their representative and the Parliament might steeply decline. In order to maintain voters' interest, a representative would have to project himself constantly in order to ensure his continuing visibility. In this he/she would not simply be handicapped by his/her distance from voters, but by the nature of Parliament's business. Once again, media interest in covering Parliament's and MEPs' activities would have to be stimulated. During the immediate aftermath of the elections, curiosity might well lead the media to investigate MEPs' activities. Later, however, MEPs might very well face similar problems to their predecessors from the indirectly elected European Assembly.

Moreover, at subsequent European elections, unless an MEP who had gained election largely on the basis of his/her personality managed to maintain a dynamic image while in Luxembourg and Strasbourg and thus preserve his/her visibility, he/she might face a situation in which voters barely remember him/her. In such a case, the voter might regard such an MEP as a 'flash in the pan', a 'one day wonder', and decide to 'give someone else a chance' in the next election. This could mean that an MEP's chances of re-election would rest not so much on the degree of success in performing parliamentary duties, but on the extent to which he/she succeeded in remaining in the public eye. At the same time, however, even an MEP who managed to remain consistently visible might fare badly at subsequent elections if certain conditions prevailed. For example, public dissatisfaction with the European Parliament – born both of incomplete understanding of its role and ability to meet public demands – might be projected on to incumbents so that there was an inclination among voters either to opt for a rival or to abstain in greater numbers than on the occasion of the first European elections. Similarly, European elections might be used by voters to record dissatisfaction with national governing parties and this could result in MEPs not being judged either on their performance or manifestoes but rather in terms of with which national party they happened to be affiliated. In order to minimise this possibility, MEPs will have to engage media attention consistently. Their performance of an educative, communicative and informative function will not, in other words, cease once votes have been counted and seats allocated. Instead, they will have to engage themselves in a continuous communicative process vis-à-vis the public. Clearly, MEPs' ability to maintain the interest of the media in covering their activities will be crucial.

Adroit use of the media, and especially of television, is not the sole way in which MEPs will seek to perform educative, informative and communicative roles – although it is perhaps one of the most immediate ways in which they could inform electors about their activities. A number of indirect channels exist through which information about their activities and the work of the European Parliament could be transmitted to voters. These include national party and parliamentary links, and service in national parliaments by MEPs holding a dual mandate. Let us, therefore, examine these in greater detail.

Notes

1. H. van Dalen and L. H. Zeigler, *Introduction to Political Science: People, Politics, and Perception* (Englewood Cliffs, N.J.: Prentice-Hall, 1977) p. 199.
2. J. C. Strouse, *The Mass Media, Public Opinion, and Public Policy Analysis: Linkage Explorations* (Columbus, Ohio: Merrill, 1975) p. 201.
3. J. J. Rabier, in G. Ionescu (ed.), *The New Politics of European Integration* (London: Macmillan, 1972) p. 155.
4. Strouse, *The Mass Media*, p. 241.

9 The Dual Mandate

The dual mandate has been compulsory for MEPs since the inception of the Communities. Members of the European Parliament had to be nominated by member governments from among the body of parliamentarians and according to the strength of parties represented in national parliaments. This system had a number of advantages and disadvantages, and the latter are usually believed to have outweighed the former. In defence of the dual mandate, it is usually asserted that it provided young, inexperienced or backbench MPs with experience in a forum where their activities would not, in the event of mistakes, redound to their disadvantage in national parliaments. In other words, service in the European Parliament was not seen as likely, in the short term, to jeopardise careers in the national arena or to prevent an MP attaining ministerial office later in his member state.

By contrast, opponents of the dual mandate have argued that the calibre of national delegations to the European Parliament reflected both the level of importance national governments attached to the EC, and the extent of their 'pro-Europeanness'. The standing of members of national delegations was seen as reflecting member governments' attitudes towards the European Parliament in particular, and the extent of their favourability towards European integration in general. MEPs have often consisted of lesser politicians.[1] Recruits to the chamber have often been a mixed lot consisting of senior political figures with few prospects of either holding future government office or advancing their political careers at home; individuals whose European enthusiasms have 'made them bores in the eyes' of their fellow-members of national parliaments[2] (although this is less the case today than it was during the 1960s); national parliamentarians of lesser calibre or potential; backbenchers having less onerous parliamentary and party duties than their more senior colleagues (and, because of their lower status, less opportunity of gaining front-bench attention and of influencing policy at the national level); and members recently elected to national chambers. MPs of higher calibre have tended to remain in the national parliament in order to pursue, for the most part, governmental careers. However, there are some important exceptions to this, and the tendency to avoid or seek appointment to the European Parliament has varied, in the past, with nationality. Whereas, for some, appointment to the European Parliament represented a political cul-de-sac, for others it has represented both an attractive opportunity for gaining experience likely to be valuable in any subsequent front-bench careers at home, and a chance to forge useful links with other parliamentarians. This was particularly true, for instance, of German SPD members during the 1950s and early 1960s.[3] More recently, MEPs have used the European Parliament as a forum in which to increase their national standing, at least in the eyes of their home party. This is, for example, true of some of the British and Dutch members.

It remains the case, however, that the European Parliament has largely failed to attract sufficient politicians with high national standing and authority. This in turn has been seen as justifying postponement of the extension of the European Parliament's powers and legislative competence. Interestingly, however, the prospect of European elections led a number of erstwhile prominent politicians (for example, Willy Brandt) to announce their candidature for the Assembly. This suggested that they regarded the forum as a place in which they could extend their political careers.

The advent of European elections has been thought of in the past as signifying the end of the dual mandate. Practical considerations coupled with incertitude over the nature of the relationships thereafter between national parliaments and their governing parties and the European chamber have, however, resulted in resistance to the abolition of the obligatory dual mandate. Indeed, some member states, specifically Denmark, insist upon its retention. What then are the disadvantages, advantages and alternatives to the dual mandate?

Disadvantages

Disadvantages of the dual mandate take effect at four main levels – the national and European, the individual and party.

The compulsory dual mandate places considerable strain on MEPs and lessens their ability to play full roles in either the European Parliament or national parliament. The strain of commuting between national parliaments, Luxembourg and Strasbourg for plenary sessions, and Brussels for committee sessions, is aggravated for members also having constituency duties to perform. Moreover, service in national parliaments and attendance at crucial debates where governmental majorities may be at stake has resulted in priority being accorded to national as opposed to European affairs. This has four important repercussions. Firstly, it conveys the impression that the European Parliament's activities are not only of secondary importance but generally insignificant. Secondly, it reinforces the image of MEPs as insignificant politicians who can be sent to and recalled from the European Parliament at will: in other words, their contributions to either chamber are not regarded as vital unless their vote could be crucial in swaying parliamentary majorities. Thirdly, it quite significantly reduces the number of MPs in the national parliaments (see Table 9.1).

TABLE 9.1. Size of national and European parliaments

	(1) No. of directly elected MEPs	(2) No. of members of lower (or only) chamber	(3) (1) as % of (2)	(4) No. of members in both chambers	(5) (1) as % of (4)
Belgium	24	212	11.3	394	6.1
Denmark	16	179	8.9	–	–
Germany	81	518	15.6	563*	14.4
France	81	490	16.5	773	10.5
Ireland	15	144	10.4	204	7.3
Italy	81	630	12.9	953	8.5
Luxembourg	6	59	10.2	–	–
Netherlands	25	150	16.7	225	11.1
UK	81	635	12.8	1625	4.9

*No member of the Bundesrat was delegated to the non-elected European Parliament. MEPs were delegated from the upper chambers of the other member states.

Source: Adapted from V. Herman, *Parliaments of the World: A Reference Compendium*, (London: Macmillan 1976) Chaps. 1 and 2.

A final disadvantage of the dual mandate is that it means the ability of MEPs to opt for a career in the European Parliament is contingent upon national considerations. Unless MEPs successfully pursue national commitments, they risk losing their seats in the national parliament. Without them they cannot be nominated to the European Parliament. In other words, while being expected to attend the European Parliament and pursue their duties there, their political contributions are evaluated in local rather than European terms. The danger of this lies not simply in an MEP's need to strike a balance between devotion to national and European politics, but in the fact that personal advancement will often be contingent upon the success with which national/constituency roles and duties are pursued. The incentive structure, therefore, works to the disadvantage of the European Parliament. Ambitious MEPs may use the chamber not so much with a view to increasing the effectiveness of its contributions to and its influence over EC policies, but as a forum in which to air controversial opinions with a view to gaining media attention for national purposes. In other words, a contribution in the European Parliament –such as the raising of contentious issues at Question Time – might enable enterprising MEPs to gain media coverage that they would otherwise not get at the national level, either because of their low status (as backbenchers and concomitant lower newsworthiness) or because the issue would not capture media attention at the national level whereas it would at the EC level.

This in turn means that the ambitious MEP is likely to use the European Parliament for advancing his national career; that for some the European Parliament is seen as a launching-pad for higher national offices rather than as a career in itself; that commitment to European duties is determined by the degree to which their accomplishment affords advancement at the national level; and that an MEP regards himself first and foremost as a national MP. In addition, if MEPs find themselves able to secure media exposure of their European Parliament activities, national parties might exert specific pressure on them to help them advance national rather than European causes. This is likely to weaken MEPs' self-identification with the European party group and reinforce predilections towards expressing nationally biased views.

On the other hand, if an MEP is seen by his national party as having been effective and as having acquired useful expertise in his European role, he is likely to be recalled to the national level where his party can make use of his experience. Ultimately, of course, he may reappear at the European level of decision-making in the Council of Ministers, or even as a Commissioner. Commenting on the negative aspects of the process of selecting MEPs from national parliaments, Dutch Labour MP Henk Vredeling noted that while, on the one hand, national parties tended to put forward 'only second-line politicians', there was, on the other hand, a tendency for the more influential to return, or be recalled, to national office – sometimes to ministerial positions and, hence, the Council of Ministers in some cases. He attributed these tendencies to the nature of the Parliament's powers.[4]

Additional disincentives to MEPs concentrating on their European-level activities derive from two considerations. Firstly, an MEP who effectively pursues his European duties, and in so doing contributes to modifying the EC's institutional balance in the Parliament's favour, may be penalised by his party or government when the Parliament's membership is renewed by not gaining nomination to the chamber. Alternatively, his visibility to colleagues in his national parliament may decrease the more he immerses himself in his European activities. This would endanger his career at the national level if it resulted in him not gaining the opportunity to secure a place on the government's front-benches or as a spokesman for his party if it is in opposition.

A second disincentive to concentrating on European activities derives from the non-coincidence of national parliamentary elections both between the member states, and with the sessions of the European Parliament. In other words, the fate of MEPs and their European work can be determined by national elections. If at any point in their term of office MEPs are defeated in an election at home, they are usually automatically precluded from continuing their work in the European Parliament. An MP forfeits two roles, thereby, and the European

Parliament loses a member whose work (and its continuation) may have been particularly valuable to it.

A third disincentive to concentrating on European issues lies in the lack of rewards at the national level for most MEPs, for either effective performance of European duties, or the acquisition of expertise on EC matters. This can be directly attributed to the constraints and logistics of the dual mandate. MEPs' frequent absence from national parliaments means that any expertise they have on EC matters cannot be put to effective use in either national parliaments' committees dealing with EC matters or in plenary debates, or at Question Time. To take just one example, in the Bundestag committees MEPs do not act as rapporteurs on EC questions in which they specialise. While this is primarily due to the time constraints and excessive workload imposed by the dual mandate, it must be borne in mind that there is competition for places on Bundestag committees and that service on the most prestigious is normally regarded as important to career advancement.

At the same time, however, a further deterrent to MEPs making effective use of any European expertise at the national level lies in the fact that time pressures probably mean that only the most diligent MEPs have sufficient knowledge of both national and European aspects of particular issues to command the respect of their national colleagues. Their absence from the national arena obviously leaves them open to the charge – if advancing a pro-EC or integrationist argument – of being ill-acquainted, through absence, with national needs. Since national needs tend to take priority at the national level and since, moreover, parties win support by their performance at the national level, the MEP will only rarely be regarded by his home party as an asset, electorally speaking. As a rule, an MEP's European achievements will only be publicised by national parties when it is felt that they redound to their favour, and are basically in line with national and/or party thinking. Thus, for example, the late Sir Peter Kirk's achievements in terms of Question Time in the European Parliament were acclaimed at the national level.

Over and above the disadvantages in personal terms of the dual mandate in national politics, a number of additional disadvantages are apparent at the European level.

Firstly, the dual mandate increases the chances of there being a relatively high turnover of personnel delegated to the European Parliament. This has a number of subsidiary effects for individual members and the party groups. For the former, it militates against the development of a politically rewarding career structure within the European Parliament; and for the latter, it inhibits the development, on the one hand, of genuine autonomous European political parties, and on the other hand, of coherent party programmes. Both of these cannot simply be attributed to the limited nature of the European Parliament's powers.

Secondly, the dual mandate inhibits the maintenance of personal relationships among MEPs in the same party group that could be advantageous in giving the party either visible coherence, or in providing a stable basis for the elaboration of medium- or long-term schemes to improve Parliament's powers and its effectiveness vis-à-vis the other institutions. If it is the case that lower-status MPs have in the past been delegates to the European Parliament, then it may also have been the case that these MEPs' national positions were less stable than others in the sense that they may have had more marginal seats, or been lower down on party lists, than their colleagues. This may also have been a potential source of a greater rate of turnover among the Parliament's personnel.

Thirdly, the dual mandate has inhibited the development and projection by MEPs and the European party groups of European identities and images. This, as we noted in Chapter 7, has contributed to the Parliament's relatively low visibility over the years.

This tendency may, moreover, have been exacerbated by the degree of importance attached to service in the European Parliament by national parties. Thus, for example, if low importance were attached to it, and if performance in national arenas were the criterion by which a politician's performance and suitability for higher national office was evaluated, then MEPs may have perceived it to be contrary to their own self-interest to project European images. Moreover, for the ambitious in the larger member states, although 'doing a stint in the European Parliament' early in their careers might have been helpful in establishing their potential capabilities, few would have wanted to have a protracted period in the forum when faced with the prospect of colleagues in the national arena developing European expertise competing with their own and, possibly, reducing their chances of ful-filling their European political ambitions at the national level. While this possibility must not be overstated, since performance in European bodies appears to have been more favourably evaluated by individuals and parties in the smaller EC states, it draws attention to the potentially disruptive effect of the dual mandate on the possibility for greater continuity in the Parliament's membership.

Advantages

Given the many disadvantages of the dual mandate, it is perhaps surprising that some member governments should, when faced with the prospect of European elections, have advocated its retention. The advantages that have been associated with its retention relate primarily to the way in which it is believed the dual mandate would serve as a ready-made institutional device between the European and national parliaments on the one hand, and European and national parties on the other. In addition, it is thought that it would facilitate the exchange of information between the two fora and sets of politicians. Potential advantages of the dual mandate such as these have been recognised by both the Political Affairs Committee of the European Parliament and bodies in the member states. If, however, the views of both groups are compared, it becomes apparent that the latter have very different reasons than the former for isolating advantages.

The European Parliament's Political Affairs Committee noted that the main advantage of the dual mandate lay in the fact that the delegation of members of national parliaments to the European Parliament automatically established a useful link between the parliaments as institutions and the political groups and parties. In other words, for the Committee, the advantage lay in the automaticity of the communicative link between the two sets of parliamentarians.[5]

The member states, on the other hand, and more especially the British and Danish who had reservations against abolishing the compulsory dual mandate, clearly saw a major advantage of the dual mandate to lie in the opportunities it afforded national parliamentarians and parliamentary parties to scrutinise, monitor and, to a certain extent, control the activities and opinions expressed by their delegations to the European Parliament. Their emphasis on the dual mandate as a vehicle of control indicated that MEPs were primarily regarded as delegates to a European forum; as extensions of national parliamentary parties and subject to usual parliamentary party discipline; and as politicians participating in a European forum but remaining primarily concerned with national duties. In other words, the dual mandate's advantage lay in the potential it afforded national parliamentary parties (and by extension national governments) to inhibit the development of autonomous European parties. This could not be directly achieved, of course, but disciplinary action could be hinted at, if not taken, against non-compliant delegates to the European Parliament or those whose European enthusiasms were deemed too exuberant for comfort. The overall effect of the national parliamentary parties' covert control potential over MEPs has thus been to contribute to inhibiting the development of a career structure in the European Parliament.

The advantages of the dual mandate from the point of view of control were perhaps best summed up in the British White Paper on European elections of April 1977. Under the section summarising the advantages of the compulsory dual mandate, it was stated:

A compulsory dual mandate would ensure that United Kingdom Assembly members had as their primary base their position at Westminster and in their Westminster constituencies; it would minimise the risk of divergencies between Assembly members and other Westminster members of the same party; and it would discourage the development in Britain of European parties with federalist aims which might undermine the position of our national parties.[6]

Why should the British Government have deemed it necessary to 'minimise the risk of divergencies between MEPs and Westminster members' and to discourage the development of European parties? What does this suggest about the advantages of the dual mandate in the other member states?

Firstly, for domestic political reasons born of intra-party divisions over the desirability not only of holding European elections by direct universal suffrage but also of Britain's continued membership of the EC, the Labour Government may well have reasoned that the best way of maintaining some control over the expression of such dissent at the European level would be via the medium of the dual mandate. This would have been seen as necessary given that some of its members of the Council of Ministers were well-known anti-Marketeers. The public criticism of a Council member by his party compatriots and political inferiors in terms of national politics would not only have created a poor impression of government unity and stability but would also have posed a challenge to a minister and been a source of additional pressure to modify his course. For example, were British Labour MEPs to have disputed a British Labour minister's contention in the Council that he was following a course of action designed to advance EC goals while protecting national interests, and to have suggested to the contrary that he was merely concerned with maximising British national interests, they would have given a fillip to other member states intent upon persuading the British minister to make a concession in their favour. This, in turn, would have provided the Conservative Opposition at Westminster and in the European Parliament with electoral ammunition.

Secondly, through the dual mandate parliamentary parties can maintain some degree of control over the extent to which their delegates to the European Parliament feel free, or have time, to engage in activities likely to lead to the emergence of autonomous European parties to which national MPs might not only owe allegiance in the European Parliament, but from whom they might take their cues. In other words, through the dual mandate it has been possible to inhibit the development of a party system at the European level capable of rivalling national parties for MEPs' allegiances. That the British perceived the dual mandate as counterbalancing any such tendency was made clear in the White Paper:

Without a compulsory dual mandate, Assembly members who were not also members of the Westminster Parliament would tend to be out of touch with developments at Westminster and might regard themselves as owing a primary allegiance to European rather than national Parties.[7]

This highlights the importance of control considerations to advocates of the compulsory dual mandate. It demands that MEPs, and/or candidates contesting European elections, observe the demands of national as well as European parties, and support the former where the two disagree. However, so long as the compulsory dual mandate is retained, national parties will continue to have a monopoly over those who successfully gain seats in the European elections. This is because the dual mandate demands that MEPs hold seats in the national and European chambers and, thereby, effectively means that only members of national parliamentary parties will gain election to the European Parliament.[8]

Any incentive European parties may have to contest European elections on an autonomous basis independent of national parties in a member state where the dual mandate is compulsory is eliminated. Even if a candidate gained election on a European party ticket, it is almost certain that he or she would not be able to take up a seat in the European Parliament unless he or she had also won a seat in the national parliament. Since it is fairly unlikely that candidates could successfully contest national elections as members of European parties, European parties are effectively discouraged from developing party and electoral machines independent of national parties. The emergence of European party figures capable of rivalling national politicians for media and public attention, and allegiance, is also inhibited. Thus, the main advantages of a compulsory dual mandate are seen to lie with the opportunities they afford national parties and governments to manage, oversee and control developments likely not only merely to promote political integration but also to stimulate the emergence of a supranational political centre of authority whose programmes, ideals, aspirations and public appeal may rival their own.

In so far as such rivalry might be curbed or precluded by retention of the compulsory dual mandate, national governments and parliamentary parties may see some merits in it. In addition, however, the question of rivalry raises a more basic question than that of national party control over MEPs. It draws attention to the possibility of the legitimacy of the collective role of member governments in the Council of Ministers in the EC's decision-making process being ultimately questioned. If European rather than national parties were to contest European elections, then not only would the directly elected MEPs be able to claim that they were the democratically elected and responsible representatives of EC citizens, but they would also be able, and likely, to point to the incongruity of a decision-making process which afforded a non-elected body more extensive decision-making powers (including the power to reject Commission proposals) than an elected chamber.

While the Council of Ministers' decision-making processes and role are already criticised, these would appear even more anachronistic in the above situation. In other words, the long-range implications of abolishing the compulsory dual mandate are more extensive than is either commonly recognised or stated: they call into question the whole distribution of authority among the EC's institutions. This, from the member governments' point of view, must be a more awesome prospect and provide more persuasive arguments against the immediate outlawing and abolition of the compulsory dual mandate than any of the disadvantages and practical difficulties attending its retention. In this context, the White Paper acknowledged:

> The strain of performing the double task could be great – though some of this might be avoided through changes in procedure in the House of Commons ... it would be necessary to provide for the situation where an Assembly member lost his Westminster seat at a national election which did not coincide with elections to the Assembly.... [F]ollowing direct elections, the dual mandate concept might be much more difficult to operate than hitherto. At present the United Kingdom sends 36 delegates, some of whom come from the House of Lords; but after direct elections we shall send 81 members, all of whom would have to come from the House of Commons ... [w]hen the European Assembly is directly elected and the over-whelming majority of its members do not sit in a national legislature, the Assembly is likely to have a more intensive scheme of business which pays little regard to the times of sittings of the various national legislatures.[9]

Changes in the arrangements of the House of Commons' business and voting procedures were seen as possible ways of overcoming this last point, even though the introduction of proxy voting was seen as involving 'formal recognition that Assembly members' votes were being cast without their having participated in debates, and would disturb long established conventions.'[10] The alternative possibility – the automatic pairing at Westminster of Assembly members – would, while overcoming any reservations about proxy voting, tend to augment pressure on MEPs holding dual mandates to toe national parliamentary party lines.

The final advantage some member governments associate with the dual mandate is the automatic link it maintains between the European and national parliaments. However, it is a moot point whether this link really is as useful in enhancing national parliamentarians' awareness and understanding of EC affairs as is sometimes purported. This is due, as we have noted already, to the backbench status of most MEPs and often to their exclusion from national parliamentary committees concerned with EC affairs. Thus, we suspect that the 'usefulness' of the

link afforded by the dual mandate lies in the opportunity it gives to
national parliamentary parties and governments to put direct pressure
on MEPs drawn from among their number.

If the dual mandate neither formally, nor informally, enhances the
ability of MEPs to increase national MPs' appreciation of EC affairs
and 'Euro' solutions to specific problems, then the main argument
advanced in favour of the dual mandate is undermined. Indeed, the
willingness of the majority of member governments to resist retention
of a compulsory dual mandate suggests that the argument of it being the
best link between the European and national parliaments is not
particularly persuasive. However, it has been the most important, if not
the sole, structural link between the two parliamentary levels. What
alternatives could be established?

Alternatives

The abolition of the compulsory dual mandate and the presence of
fewer MEPs holding a dual mandate in the European Parliament need
not eliminate, although it will weaken, personal and structural links
between parties and members of the European and national parliaments.

A number of specific proposals exist as to how these personal links
can be maintained. These can be divided into two groups.[11] The first
consists of variations on the existing form of simultaneous membership
and includes proposals for the setting-up within the national parliaments of a group of representatives of the European Parliament who
would be excused committee duties and authorised to delegate their
voting rights. Another possibility is that the main duties and
responsibilities of MEPs in the national parliaments and in their
constituencies would be undertaken by substitutes. A final variation on
existing practices is for the creation of extra seats in the national
parliaments for all or some of the MEPs.

The second set of proposals covers arrangements that would ensure
that if the dual mandate were abolished, the national parliaments
would be able to benefit from the experience and knowledge of MEPs.
Among the various possibilities are suggestions that MEPs should be
additional members of the national parliaments with full rights; be
additional members with status akin to that of the Berlin deputies in the
Bundestag; or be additional members of the national parliament with
speaking but not voting rights.[12] Concerning membership of
committees in the national parliaments, MEPs could have full voting
and speaking rights; or be allowed to attend and speak at committee
meetings on agenda items which dealt with European matters; or be
invited as experts on European affairs to attend national parliamentary
hearings; or have links with the rapporteurs of the committees in the
national parliaments.

The status of MEPs and their membership of national parliamentary political groups would also be affected by the abolition of the dual mandate. As regards the status of MEPs, they may be given their own offices in the national parliaments, have access to the library and documentation services of the parliament, and have the right of assigning tasks to the research services. In their links with national parliamentary parties, MEPs may have membership with full voting and speaking rights, or have only the right to speak, or be members of the political groups' working parties.

The dual mandate is but one way of maintaining links between the European and national parliaments. Other structural links already exist or could easily be developed, and as the obligatory dual mandate is abolished these are likely to take on increasing importance. The two sets of parliamentary institutions could be linked through establishing ties between the various subject-matter committees of the national parliaments and the relevant committees of the European Parliament. Indeed, the Vedel Report proposed joint meetings of European and national parliamentary committees.[13] The difficulty here, however, lies with the timing of such meetings. Bilateral meetings would increase the strain on MEPs, whereas a joint meeting of all committees would be difficult to co-ordinate because of national parliamentary activities. In addition, if all member states were to participate in a joint session with their counterparts in one of the European Parliament's committees, the size of the meeting would make any effective work, over and above a rather superficial exchange of information, impossible. It might be necessary, therefore, to limit the membership of such transnational committees to the chairman, vice-chairmen and rapporteurs of the national and European committees, accompanied perhaps by an expert or official. Such arrangements would considerably facilitate the exchange of information, and take account of the particular circumstances prevailing in the different regions and member states.

An alternative way of maintaining structural links between the European and national parliaments could be through European committees. These were referred to in the final communiqué of the Rome Conference (of the Presidents or Speakers of the European Parliamentary Assemblies) which mentioned the setting-up in the national parliaments of 'committees for liaison with the European Parliament and for the co-ordination of European affairs'.[14] More than half of the national parliaments of the Community have no committees with special responsibility for such co-ordination. In many of the national parliaments the Foreign Affairs Committee is the committee which deals with EC affairs, and EC matters are debated in plenary sessions during consideration of the budget and not on separate occasions.

The experiences of national parliaments which do have such committees differ. In the Belgian Chamber of Deputies and in the

Bundestag the overlapping in the relevant committees of matters relating to the European Community with those concerning the Council of Europe and the Western European Union has sometimes complicated the committees' work. The Select Committee on Secondary European Legislation in the British House of Commons has not been able to cope effectively with the volume of legislative matters put before it (see Table 9.2), and initially it had difficulties in impressing on the House the importance of its work.[15] By contrast, the Market Committee of the Folketing has established itself as an efficient controlling body, and it has been suggested that it may serve as a model for the other national parliaments.[16]

The main functions of such parliamentary committees might be to ensure effective exchanges of information concerning their respective activities, and the extent and effectiveness of national parliamentary control of the EC executive. This would be invaluable given that national parliaments have lost a good deal of power to the Council of Ministers as a result of the EC Treaty's implementation, and such losses have not been recouped at the supranational level by the European Parliament. National parliaments have resisted the accretion of the European Parliament's powers largely because they associate it with a further diminution of their own powers – a view most frequently embodied in the 'loss of sovereignty' argument. The tendency to perceive the European Parliament as responsible for, or the beneficiary of, such losses must be corrected if effective parliamentary control of the EC executive – and especially of the Council of Ministers – is to be achieved.

Indeed, both the national and European parliaments have a role to play in respect of EC legislation. For example, in the case of regulations – which are directly enforceable in the Community – the position of the national parliaments is weaker than that of the European Parliament which may give an opinion and which has to be consulted on major questions. However, in the case of directives, national parliaments are regularly called on to make implementing arrangements for the adaptation of existing national law to the directives concerned. In both instances it would be in the interests of the national and European parliaments were each one's points of view, proposals and objectives made known. Thus, European and national parliaments might co-operate in monitoring and scrutinising the impact of EC legislation on parliamentary controls at the national and supranational levels with a view to ensuring that any erosion at the national level is compensated for at the European level.

Regular conferences of the Presidents or Speakers of the EC's parliamentary assemblies and the European Parliament would also facilitate contacts, as would exchanges between the rapporteurs of specified committees. In addition, better use might be made of data-processing facilities. The European Parliament might, for example,

TABLE 9.2. Reports from House of Commons Select Committee on European Secondary Legislation

Session	Meetings of Committee	Reports including Special Reports	Documents considered*	Documents recommended for debate	Debates in House of Commons†	Debates in Standing Committee‡
1974 (Mar–Sep)	14	14	192	21	2	—
1974–5 (Oct 74–Nov 75)	42	41	701	69	26	—
1975–6 (Nov 75–Apr 76)	18	17	243	49	7	8

*This figure includes documents noted by the Committee as having already been adopted by the Council.
†On some occasions several documents have been debated together.
‡The option of holding debates in Standing Committee was introduced by the Order of the House of 3 November 1975. On some occasions several documents have been debated together.

Source: Annex to the Spénale Report, 'The development of relations between the European Parliament and the national parliaments', PE 45.223/Ann. 1. (1976) p. 54.

play an important part in co-ordinating national parliaments' access to the EC's CELEX system. All would benefit from having their own source of information on, for instance, the extent to which EC directives have been implemented or incorporated into national legislation. Such information is essential to the exercise of control over the executive at both the national and European levels.[17]

Whatever structural and personal links are maintained between the European and national parliaments in the absence of (or supplementing) the dual mandate, ultimately both the relationship between the European Parliament and Council of Ministers and their roles in EC decision-making must be reconsidered.

Notes

1. H. Vredeling, 'The Common Market of Political Parties', *Government and Opposition*, VI (1971). 448–61, at p. 455.

2. W. Pickles, 'Political Power in the EEC', *Journal of Common Market Studies*, II (1963) 63–84, at p. 66.

3. J. Lodge, *The European Policy of the SPD* (Beverly Hills and London: Sage, 1976) pp. 20–36.

4. Vredeling, op. cit., pp. 449–50.

5. Political Affairs Committee 'Draft report on relations between the European Parliament and the parliaments of the member states' (PE 47.239, Dec 1976).

6. *White Paper on Direct Elections to the European Parliament*, Cmnd. 6768 (London: HMSO, 1977).

7. Ibid., pp. 8–9.

8. 'The office of representative in the Assembly shall be compatible with membership of the Parliament of a Member State.' Article 5, Act concerning the Election of Representatives of the Assembly by Direct Universal Suffrage.

9. *White Paper on Direct Elections to the European Parliament*, p. 9.

10. Ibid., Annex D.

11. See Georges Spénale, 'The development of relations between the European Parliament and the national parliaments in the light of the development of the Community since the last conference' (of the Presidents or Speakers of the European Parliamentary Assemblies) (PE 45.359, 1976).

12. In its report *Direct Elections to the European Parliament*, the Joint Committee on the Secondary Legislation of the European Communities of the Irish Parliament (the Oireachtas) stated:

> The experience of the Members of the Joint Committee who are also members of the present European Parliament suggests that dual membership will, in fact, be *difficult to sustain* particularly when the powers of the European Parliament are extended. In line, therefore, with its declared objective of maintaining a close link between the members of the European Parliament and the political structure at home the Joint Committee considers that the benefit of those members' knowledge and experience of European Affairs should continue to be available to the Houses of the Oireachtas. Accordingly, it recommends that where a member of the

European Parliament is not a member of the Oireachtas he should be given a *right of audience* in the Dail (House of Representatives) and Seanad (Senate) and in appropriate Committees of both Houses. It believes that this objective could be achieved by making appropriate provisions in the Standing Orders for both Houses.

13. *Vedel Report* (Brussels, Bulletin of the European Communities, Suppl. 4/1972).

14. Final communiqué of the Rome Conference of the Presidents or Speakers of the European Parliamentary Assemblies, 1975.

15. M. Kolinsky, 'Parliamentary Scrutiny of European Legislation', *Government and Opposition*, X (1975) 46–69. The Committee's Order of Reference is:

to consider draft proposals by the Commission of the European Economic Communities for secondary legislation and other documents published by the Commission for submission to the Council of Ministers and to report their opinion as to whether such proposals or other documents raise questions of legal or political importance, to give their reasons for their opinion, to report what matters of principle or policy may be affected thereby, and to what extent they may affect the law of the United Kingdom, and to make recommendations for the further consideration of such proposals and other documents by the House.

16. See S. Auken *et al.*, 'Denmark Joins Europe', *Journal of Common Market Studies*, XIV (1975) 1–36; and J. Fitzmaurice, 'National Parliaments and European Policy-Making: The Case of Denmark', *Parliamentary Affairs*, XXIX (1976) 310–26.

17. Political Affairs Committee, 'Introductory memorandum on relations between the European Parliament and the national parliaments – elements of a motion for a resolution' (PE 43.709, Feb. 1976).

10 The Case for a Bicameral Parliament

... si le fédéralisme présuppose toujours l'existence de collectivités publiques dotées d'une certaine autonomie d'action, son originalité consiste également en ce qu'il cherche à faire participer ces dernières à l'exercice des pouvoirs conférés aux organes supérieurs communs. Or sur ce plan-là aussi, les Communautés font une place importante à la préoccupation fédéraliste.

François Cardis, *Fédéralisme et Intégration Européenne* (1964) p. 225

It is commonly argued that direct elections will affect the institutional balance in the Community in a number of significant ways. This argument derives from a belief that the direct election of the European Parliament *per se* will be sufficient justification for the accretion of its powers. The ways in which the Parliament's powers are expected to be increased are seen by some as necessitating formal amendments to the Treaty of Rome, and by others as demanding little more than a fuller exploitation of its current rules of procedure and existing practices. MEPs themselves have contended that the Parliament's influence can be expected to increase even in default of formal Treaty amendments (to which some national governments are believed to be opposed) by virtue of the enhanced status and direct rather than derivative legitimacy that direct elections are expected to afford the Parliament. Irrespective of formal changes to the distribution of powers among the Community's institutions, pressures to augment the Parliament's role in the decision-making and legislative processes can be expected to grow. If the Parliament both seeks and acquires greater influence in the formulation of EC policy, and if practices are developed to increase its participation in the pre-decisional stages of the legislative process (that is, during the phase of consultation and bargaining preceding the final submission of Commission proposals to the Council of Ministers for approval), then a gradual shift in the EC's legislative power base will be effected. As such practices become institutionalised, pressure for a formal acknowledgement and confirmation of the accretion of the Parliament's powers is likely to arise.[1]

It is usually assumed that the accretion of the Parliament's legislative powers is desirable in the name of democracy.[2] This assumption derives from the notion of no taxation without representation. As the Community's taxation powers and its 'own resources' grow, it is argued, there should be a concomitant development to ensure that those taxed are represented at the EC level and that their representatives assume some financial control powers in respect of Community expenditure.[3] Control at the EC level is, moreover, warranted given that national parliaments neither exercise control over their country's contribution to the EC budget, nor over the EC's *ressources propres*. The European Parliament is usually seen as the proper, if not only, vehicle for accomplishing this since it is regarded as the institution that represents the peoples of the Community.[4] Both the extent to which the Parliament can claim to be directly representative of EC citizens, and the extent of its recently acquired scrutiny powers over the Community budget, are modest. However, following the Parliament's direct election it is expected that claims for increased legislative, financial and control powers for the Parliament will be regarded as more legitimate than hitherto.[5]

While the extension of the Parliament's powers is expected to alter the Community's institutional balance – especially the relationship between the Commission, Council and Parliament – the precise nature of the change, the purpose of and ways in which the chamber's powers, and the legislative roles of the other institutions, should or could be modified, remain unclear.[6] The confusion derives in part from the ambiguous nature and functions of the Council. Fitzmaurice and Coombes have likened it to a legislature, while Allott sees it as an executive-type body. Since without the Council's assent in all bar a few instances, Commission proposals could not become part of EC law, the analogy with a legislative organ is perhaps more useful for our purposes. Indeed, it is this conception of the Council that dominates many considerations of the effects of direct elections on the EC's institutional balance in general and on the Council's powers in particular. Typically, it is suggested that the overall effect will be a curtailment of the Council of Ministers' autonomy and dominant role in the legislative process. In part it is assumed that this curtailment will be self-imposed as it is argued that the Council of Ministers will feel obliged (morally, if not legally) to heed the views of parliamentary members elected by the people and claiming to express their interests.[7] There are a number of ways in which the Council of Ministers could demonstrate its readiness to pay attention to and act upon the Parliament's views. It could, for instance, await the Parliament's opinion or vote before passing Commission proposals; or its President could record these prior to the Council taking its decision, thereby making clear that the Parliament's views had been taken into consideration even though those of the Council may have remained different and prevailed. Whatever way the Council were to demonstrate greater receptiveness and attention to the Parliament's views, a shift in the effective exercise of legislative power would have taken place. While the Council can refuse to sanction the extension of further rights of co-decision to the Parliament (although probably at the peril of its own legitimacy being called into question), and while it can continue to ignore the Parliament's views for the time being, the question of the role of the Parliament in the Community's development and decision-making requires re-examination. This inevitably demands a reappraisal of the role of the Council of Ministers given the Parliament's aspirations to becoming the Community's legislature.

In considering the role of, and relationship between, the two institutions, we shall argue that a bicameral parliamentary arrangement is implicit in the Community's existing institutional set-up, and attempt to elucidate the paradoxical allocation of powers between the Parliament and Council with a view to suggesting the type of bicameral arrangement that would satisfy demands for the Community's 'democratisation' and, at the same time, afford the Parliament greater legislative power.

The federalist tendencies in the Community incline us towards the view that a bicameral arrangement would be appropriate. Existing federalist tendencies within the Community have been variously commented upon.[8] Bowie regards the European experience as an 'effort to achieve federalism by a unique process adapted to the peculiar needs and situations existing in postwar Europe'. For him, the distinctive feature of this process has been the development of federal institutions 'stage by stage, through successive agencies, wielding limited powers in specific fields' and relying on 'a cumulative process of growth and gradual fulfilment'.[9] The institution that is generally seen as most symbolising federalist tendencies is the European Parliament.[10]

Spinelli regards the Parliament's powers, and specifically its power to censure the Commission, as an 'almost purely formal concession made by the treaty negotiators to the democratic-federalist approach'.[11] He points out that its predecessor, the Common Assembly, 'was not in the logic of the functionalist plan, in which the institutional mechanism consisted essentiallly in the dialogue between Eurocrats who proposed and governments which disposed'.[12] This notwithstanding, Article 138 of the Rome Treaty has been widely interpreted as indicative of federalism (and democracy) in the Community. The article provides for the Parliament's election by direct universal suffrage in accordance with a uniform procedure in all member states, and it has been the notion of direct elections which has been regarded as signifying a transfer or pooling of sovereignty at a level above the nation-states.[13] The European Parliament, as the locus of popular sovereignty, is regarded as the embodiment of sovereignties formerly vested in national parliaments, and as symbolising the subordination of member governments to a supranational Euro-polity.

Fears lest the members of a European Parliament possessing powers characteristic of the member states' popular chambers would both aspire to becoming the EC's executive –to forming the EC's cabinet from among their number – and to usurping the role and powers of national governments and parliaments in EC affairs have been coupled with an inadequate appreciation of both the position of regional parliaments in federations and of the political nature of federalism itself. One of the major problems stems from the view that, unlike federalism within single nation-states, federalism at an international level implies centralisation rather than decentralisation, and less rather than greater decisional autonomy for the component units. Predicated on the classical definition of federalism as an arrangement where powers are so divided that 'the general and regional governments are each, within a sphere, co-ordinate and independent',[14] this view associates political integration in the EC with the progressive emasculation of the member states on a zero-sum basis. Thus, member states are expected to come to exercise no more than a set of residual powers left over to them by the supranational agencies. This is certainly what integration along *functional* lines implies,[15] but it is not necessarily the terminal condition[16] of integration along *federalist* lines. That it should have been thought to be so derives from confusion of the two processes, and from inferences made about the relative financial powers of central and regional governments and centripetal tendencies imputed to the latter in federal systems.[17] In other words, it has usually been implicitly assumed that federalism in the Community would lead to the creation of a unitary state. However, both Wheare and Friedrich indicate that neither greater centralisation nor evolution towards a unitary state necessarily follow in federal systems.

Wheare argues that federal government can be considered appropriate for a group of states or communities if 'at one and the same time, they desire to be united under a single independent general government for some purposes and to be organised under independent regional governments for others . . . they must desire to be united but not to be unitary'.[18] While Wheare nevertheless adheres to the notion of the need for a strict division of competences between two levels of government (and therefore upholds principles of classical federalism), Friedrich suggests that federalism can be seen as the 'process by which a number of separate political organisations, be they states or any other kind of associations, enter into arrangements for making decisions on joint problems'.[19]

Both perceive a need for regulating decision-making and disagreements between central and local authorities and ensuring the representation of their interests. Similar considerations are reflected in the practice of supranationalism, although this has usually been accomplished within an administrative framework[20] (specifically through the processes of *engrenage*[21] and the COREPER[22]), or at an intergovernmental level where interests are traded-off within the Council of

Ministers. However, within both fora the process involves not so much trade-offs between the corporate interests of the member states and the supranational authorities, as trade-offs between the member states themselves. This is not to deny that the member states may have corporate interests to represent against the supranational authorities, but it is to highlight an incongruity of EC decision-making, for it is the Council of Ministers that is charged with both ensuring the passage of supranational legislation and with performing the potentially contradictory task of advocating member state interests.

The nature of the Community's legislative process makes the pursuit of contradictory objectives inescapable since the one institution is accorded the sole right to pass Commission proposals[23] while being, by virtue of its composition and the absence of any other organ empowered to defend national interests or to represent Community interests, predisposed towards maximising national interests or minimising any deleterious consequences for individual member states of Commission proposals. While the Council of Ministers was conceived of as a check on the integrationist pace established by the Commission which is independent of national governments (Article 157), it can effectively prevent the passage of Commission proposals submitted to it for decision. This has often led to the Council being regarded as a brake to integration, and to it being condemned for decelerating integration through its insistence upon protection for specific national interests and its tendency to make decisions on the basis of the lowest common denominator rather than upgrading the common interest.[24] Such criticisms are, however, based on the assumption that the defence of national interests at the Community level is dysfunctional to the progress of integration, and is to some extent undesirable and illegitimate if it interferes with the advancement of Community goals. We intend to suggest that, to the contrary, the representation and protection of national interests at a Community level is desirable and legitimate, but that it might be more effectively accomplished were the dualist functions of the Council of Ministers to be reappraised and its relationship with the Parliament reconsidered.

Let us examine, then, the attributes of the Council of Ministers and Parliament with a view to establishing which is better suited to the representation of member states' interests. Let us also suggest that, given federalist tendencies within the Community and associated with its parliamentary institution, and given the close association of federalism with bicameralism,[25] bicameral arrangements for the Community can be usefully explored.

Generally, in bicameral parliaments, lower chambers possess greater powers than upper chambers.[26] The latter are often conceived of as 'watchdog' devices over central governments in federal systems. They are vigilant over the activities of central governments and are charged specifically with protecting the interests of component units. They represent the corporate interest of those units or members, and in some instances rules of procedure may be such as to ensure that the members of component states may vote, as in the case of *Länder* representatives in the Bundesrat, *en bloc* only. Upper chambers may share legislative functions with the lower house and be empowered to prevent the passage of legislation into law under certain circumstances. In some countries their role may be largely consultative, while in others they may have the right to introduce financial and non-financial legislation on an equal basis with the lower chamber.[27] Still others may reserve the right to introduce financial legislation to the lower chamber on the grounds that the authorisation of expenditure and imposition of taxation must be the preserve of the House elected by universal suffrage since the people must consent to financial burdens they will bear.[28]

Originally conceived of as chambers protecting the interests of an aristocracy against those of the 'general will', upper chambers are often seen as having extended their 'watchdog' role in order that they might operate as an effective check against the judgements of the lower chamber and executive. For this to be necessary presupposes the existence of divergences between the two chambers and a propensity for the upper chamber to adopt contrary stances to those of the lower chamber. For this to be effective, on the other hand, presupposes that executive accountability to the upper chamber exists and that this affords a more effective check against executive actions than does its need to retain the confidence, in parliamentary democracies, of governing parties in the lower chamber. It also presupposes that the upper chamber has the power to prevent the passage of legislation.

In only three of the EC's bicameral states – Belgium, Italy and the Netherlands – is the executive accountable to both houses of parliament. Only in the Netherlands does the upper chamber have a decisive right to secure the adoption or rejection of a bill passed by the lower chamber in cases of disagreement between the two; it cannot, however, amend such a bill. In the other bicameral member parliaments the lower chambers' views dominate for the most part, although in Belgium the *navette*[29] is designed to promote conciliation until agreement is reached, and in the United Kingdom a bill is dropped if agreement cannot be reached between the House of Commons and the House of Lords by the end of the session. However, the Lords cannot delay the passage of money bills for more than one month, or prevent the passage of any other bill (other than one to extend the maximum duration of Parliament) if passed by the Commons in two consecutive sessions.

If the respective powers of upper and lower chambers in the EC's bicameral member states are compared, it becomes apparent that the powers of upper chambers are for the most part less extensive than those of lower chambers, and that the ability of the upper chamber's members to maximise their control functions vis-à-vis the executive and lower chamber is sometimes contingent upon their being able to exploit their powers when a government's parliamentary majority in the lower house is slender, and non-existent in the upper house. While it is often suggested that governmental stability is promoted when the powers of bicameral parliaments are dissimilar, the Bundesrat has in recent years demonstrated that it can be a source of disequilibrium.[30]

If we now compare the powers of Community bodies involved in the EC's legislative process with those of legislative bodies in member states, a lack of fit between the two, and the paradoxical nature of the allocation of powers between the Council of Ministers and the European Parliament, will be noticeable.

While the powers of the EC's member states' bicameral parliaments are not identical in every respect, similar functions are performed by them. In each member state the executive is responsible to the lower chamber; collective accountability to lower chambers obtains in all member states, and individual accountability in Denmark, Germany, the Netherlands and the United Kingdom. Through a vote of no confidence or a motion of censure, lower chambers can force the resignation of the government. All bar the Dail and the House of Commons have some power to amend the budget. None has the power of self-dissolution; all must be dissolved by the head of state. All have the power to legislate – to initiate and decide upon legislative proposals – and all have some control over the budget. In addition, all perform analogous roles vis-à-vis the public. All are elected by universal suffrage, and their members play communicative, educative and informative functions vis-à-vis the voters.[31] In most member states the name of the lower chamber expresses its elective function. By contrast, neither the powers nor nomenclature of the European Assembly suggest that it is a popularly elected legislative chamber.

The nomenclature of legislative chambers is of importance for a number of reasons. In the first place, the choice between the terms 'parliament' and 'council' or 'assembly' may indicate, as Wheare suggests,[32] the difference between a body with authority to decide and a body with authority to advise – between a general government and a general conference. In the second place, the name may indicate the relationship of the chamber to the citizens in a given political entity; it thus has some symbolic meaning. Although the European Assembly, when adopting its rules of procedure in May 1962, decided to refer to itself as the 'European Parliament' rather than 'the Assembly' as per treaty, member governments continue to refer to it as 'the Assembly'. Among the Community's other institutions only the Council of Ministers has avoided adopting the nomenclature 'European Parliament'. The member governments' and Council's reticence to call the Parliament by its chosen name is often interpreted as indicative of resistance to the notion that the chamber should evolve into anything more than a debating chamber, and of an unwillingness to admit that the Community embodies federal and hence political, as well as functional characteristics. Against this, however, it might be suggested that avoidance of the nomenclature 'European Parliament' is indicative of a feeling that the Community's institutional configuration is incomplete and the nature of the 'legislature' rudimentary. One can speculate as to whether or not the framers of the Rome Treaty recognised, and allowed for in their choice of name for a popular chamber, that in existing unitary and federal systems only unicameral systems referred to the popular chamber as 'parliament'. In all others the term 'parliament' was the corporate reference for a bicameral legislature. In other words, was a bicameral evolution implicitly assumed?

Since its inception the European Parliament has endeavoured to secure changes in the methods of the selection of its members.[33] Consisting of delegates nominated by the national parliaments from among their members, the Parliament has pursued the goal of direct elections in order that its claims to being the legitimate representative of the peoples of the Community could be realised. It conceives of itself as a Community organ representing Community interests rather than as a chamber through which national parliaments defend national interests. To this its rules of procedure, working arrangements and party-group activities attest.[34]

However, even after direct elections the composition of the Parliament, and specifically the implications of the retention of a system of national quotas of members drawn from each of the member states, may suggest that the Parliament represents national *qua* member parliaments' political biases rather than the common will and opinions of EC citizens. The reasons why members of the Parliament both now and after direct elections may be regarded as representing national rather than European interests derives in part from the lack of genuine, autonomous transnational European parties[35] possessing the right and ability to nominate candidates for election on a single party ticket throughout the member states; partly from some member governments' intentions to manage the degree of independence accorded MEPs by national parliamentary parties (and therefore to ensure that the chamber consists of some instructed delegates); and in part from the existence, and any continued use, of the dual mandate.

The British White Paper of April 1977 recorded advantages of the dual mandate as, firstly, ensuring that 'United Kingdom Assembly members had as their primary base their position at Westminster and in their Westminster constituencies'; secondly, as minimising 'the risk of divergencies between Assembly members and other Westminster members of the same party'; and thirdly, as discouraging 'the development in Britain of European parties with federalist aims which might undermine the position of our national parties'.[36] More importantly, perhaps, if a member state's MEPs are subject to the discipline of their home parties, then efforts might be undertaken to facilitate a coincidence of national views between specific groups of

MEPs and their respective national ministers in the Council. Generally, however, MEPs should be expected to continue voting along either transnational party grouping or regional lines. MEPs committed to promoting Europeanism and integration are also likely to resist pressures from national parties, governments and parliaments to conform to national prescriptions (although those opposed to the Community and its policies may adhere more rigidly to national party lines). Indeed, their support for direct elections lies with their belief that they will thereafter be the legitimate representatives of European voters and under obligation to promote their interests; that the Parliament will be the expression of popular sovereignty[37] and the 'general will', and that in it numerical majorities will find expression. These are deemed important both for giving direction to the EC and for its institutional balance and, specifically, Commission-Parliament relations.

MEPs' conception of the Parliament is commonly taken to be one of a lower chamber representing the interests of the people. For them, the interests of the member states are articulated in the Council of Ministers in which each state is autonomous, has *equal representation* and equal rights – three of the principles Wheare deems necessary attributes of upper chambers in federal systems. However, the Connecticut Compromise of equal representation for unequal states indicates, that this principle is neither necessary nor sufficient for bicameral chambers in federations. However, it remains an important principle in the EC where the 'big states' are not, by virtue of either their size or international political influence, afforded special prerogatives or rights over smaller members to determine EC policy. In principle, within the Community, each state has an equal voice, and the weighted majority voting procedure is so calculated to guard against the 'big states' asserting their interests over those of the smaller members.

Unlike the lower chambers of other bicameral parliaments, the Parliament lacks the power to approve executive proposals. This power is invested with the Council of Ministers alone. The Parliament also lacks the power to initiate legislation, that power resting with the Commission alone.

The Parliament's powers are 'advisory and supervisory' (Article 137). In the legislative process its role is largely limited to the right to deliberate upon and scrutinise legislative proposals. It also has the right to exercise certain, albeit limited, budgetary powers in conjunction with the Council of Ministers. Its legislative powers are therefore imperfectly developed, especially when these are compared with those of national parliaments. However, it possesses two powers typically associated with lower chambers: namely, the right to control the executive and the right to reject the budget.[38] Both powers are limited.

Under Article 144 the Parliament is empowered to censure the activities of one arm of the bicephalous executive – the Commission. If a motion of censure is carried by a two-thirds majority the Commission is obliged to resign *en bloc*. This is seen as evidence of the collective responsibility of the Commission to the Parliament. The idea that individual Commissioners should be made accountable to the Parliament has been periodically raised but rejected.[39] So long as the Parliament lacks any real authority in respect of the nomination and appointment of individual Commissioners (this right being reserved for the member governments and Council of Ministers under Articles 158, 159 and 160), the power to censure the Commission does not greatly enhance the Parliament's powers. Moreover, the Parliament lacks the kind of authority that would devolve upon it were it directly elected. As things are, one non-elected body exercises control over another.

Although power to censure the Commission is frequently criticised as being 'nuclear',[40] the fact of its possession by the Parliament does to some extent anticipate and provide for elements of lower chamber–executive relationships common to the member states.[41] With the exception of France, the lower chambers of the member states exercise control powers vis-à-vis the executive and its head. (In France the National Assembly cannot exercise a control function over the actions of the President, but can do so over those of the Prime Minister.)

Like members of other lower chambers, MEPs have the right to question members of the executive. Commissioners are formally obliged, under Article 140, to reply orally or in writing to questions put by the Parliament or its members. The Council of Ministers has also agreed to answer questions put by the Parliament, and the latter has recently established the right to put questions to the Conference of Foreign Ministers within which the Nine co-operate on matters not directly specified in the Treaty. Generally, however, the Council of Ministers is in no way accountable to the Parliament for its decisions. With the exception of matters arising out of the presentation of the draft budget,[42] the Council of Ministers is neither obliged to heed nor to act upon Parliament's opinions or views emitted after committee scrutiny of legislative proposals. However, the President of the Council of Ministers may seek advice and opinions of the Parliament by submitting a request for advice to the assembly's President.[43]

As a rule, the influence which the Parliament's opinion has on Council deliberations on an item of legislation varies from case to case. When explicitly sought by the Council, the Parliament's advice might be expected to carry greater weight than when its opinions are considered by the Council and Commission under Article 190. While the Parliament's opinions may lead the Commission to reappraise proposed measures, the draft legislation may, nevertheless, not be modified as a result. In 1976, of 162 opinions delivered on Commission proposals, 110 were favourable, 31 suggested amendments were accepted by the Commission, and there were 21 amendments on which the Commission was unable to act. In these cases the Parliament accepted the Commission's explanations for its inability to do so.[44]

The right to emit opinions and give advice, like the right to discuss the Commission's Annual General Report, does not appreciably increase either the Parliament's role in the legislative process, or its power of control over the executive, even though the right to discuss the Annual General Report is often claimed to be 'an essential condition for the effective control of the executive's activity'.[45] Similarly, the practice established since 1970 of the President of the Commission presenting to the Parliament an annual programme of the Communities' activities neither augments its legislative functions nor represents a significant control function vis-à-vis the executive. It merely affords the Parliament the opportunity to comment publicly on the framework and main principles of the Commission's priorities and programme before, rather than after, their implementation.

The import of these rights may be seen as lying more with the parallels they represent with existing executive–lower chamber practices than with the ways in which they augment the Parliament's powers. Both in France and Germany, where there is no formal parliamentary vote of investiture, the Prime Minister and Federal Chancellor respectively present a declaration of policy to the National Assembly and Bundestag at the start of each parliamentary session. The debate on the Commission's programme parallels the latter. A variety of procedures have been suggested both to improve the contextual significance of the censure motion and to strengthen the imputed executive–lower chamber relationship existing, or being established, between the Commission and the Parliament. Leo Tindemans has argued in favour of the Commission President being appointed by the European Council; his making a policy statement to Parliament and being confirmed by its vote; and his then appointing his colleagues in consultation with the Council.[46] Were such a procedure to be adopted, the Council would effectively and collectively perform the role of the head of state, and the Commission President that of Prime Minister or head of government, in respect of, firstly, the nomination of a 'government' and, secondly, the appointment of 'ministers'. Both in terms of securing his own endorsement by the Assembly and in his choice of colleagues, the Commission President's sensitivity to parliamentary opinion and majorities might be expected to increase given his need to secure and retain the Parliament's confidence and support. Alert to this, Thomas has suggested that, prior to the definite appointment of the Commission, national governments await the investiture of their proposed Commission members by the Parliament.[47] Apart from the constitutional implications of such suggestions, their significance lies in their anticipating the evolution of the Parliament as a lower chamber playing a role similar to those of the member states' popular chambers.

The Parliament's increased powers in respect of the budget confirm this.

Control of the EC's budget is jointly exercised by the Parliament and Council of Ministers. The Commission is responsible for preparing, for each calendar year, a preliminary draft budget which is then considered by both the Council and the Parliament in two 'readings',[48] as we have explained above. Since 1975 the Parliament has possessed the power to reject the budget as a whole. But to the extent that the Council retains control over the greatest portion of the EC's budget, the Parliament's control over expenditure might be regarded as insignificant. However, two facets of the budgetary control procedure enhance its role.

Provision exists for a 'conciliation committee', consisting of representatives of the Council and a delegation from the Parliament with Commission participation, to be called into being to facilitate consultation over and reconcile divergences between the Parliament and Council.[49] Either the Parliament or the Council may initiate such consultation. This is a relatively recent innovation and represents an increase in the Parliament's powers in so far as, like the lower chambers in the Nine, it now has the right to hold up the passage of the budget, and the ultimate right to reject it *in toto.*

The corollary of budgetary control is vigilance over subsequent expenditure. It is in this area that the Parliament's role has also grown and might be regarded as indicative of its acquisition of functions assumed by other lower chambers in the EC. On 15 June 1976 the Parliament set up a public accounts committee as a sub-committee of its Committee on Budgets. To some extent its tasks are analogous to those of committees charged with considering the budget in the member state parliaments.[50] Its creation coincided with the decision to establish the European Court of Auditors. It is charged with working in co-operation with the Audit Board and Court of Auditors, checking expenditure for discrepancies and fraud, and conducting special in-depth enquiries. That this form of *a posteriori* control can be useful is well established.[51] More importantly, as Coombes suggests, the significance of budgetary control powers lies in the effects of their exercise by parliament on the executive and on effective and open government.[52] It is the contribution that the Parliament's exercise of budgetary control makes towards increasing the visibility of decision-making processes in the EC to publics and elites (especially given that Council decisions are reached in secret session) that also underlines its position as a putative second chamber. It is the chamber not only of public debate but increasingly the one in which, through a variety of mechanisms, the executive can be held answerable for its decisions. An element of Council responsibility to the Parliament results from the fact that its President takes part in the Parliament's budget debates; and a Council representative takes part in meetings of the Parliament's Committee on Budgets during the budgetary procedure. This is obviously not synonymous with formal control over the actions of both arms of the executive but represents a step towards ameliorating the nature of executive accountability to the Parliament. Moreover, the Council of Ministers or EC observers might interpret Parliament's rejection of the budget as a vote of 'no confidence' in it. Faced with this possibility, the Council might feel constrained to accord Parliament's views greater attention in order to avoid such an eventuality.

Let us now consider the attributes and powers of the Council of Ministers. That these have been regarded as paradoxical was evinced by the late British Secretary of State for Foreign and Commonwealth Affairs, Mr Anthony Crosland, in his first speech to the European Parliament on 12 January 1977. Referring to the role and *modus vivendi* of the Council, he noted that its tasks were partly legislative and akin to those of a parliament, but mainly executive, policy-making and negotiating and here akin to those of a cabinet.[53] We intend to suggest that not only are the powers and role of the Council of Ministers in EC decision-making paradoxical, but that, as we shall see, the Council can to some extent be regarded as possessing some of the attributes and potentialities of an upper chamber.

The Council comprises ministers from the member states which are equally represented. Its composition is not constant as it varies according to the subject-matter before it. To the extent that it groups together members of national cabinets for purposes of decision-making, it may seem appropriate to view it as an extension of national cabinets. However, since the number of ministries represented at any one session is rarely more than two or three, and since the Council lacks a number of attributes normally associated with national executives, this analogy is not particularly instructive.[54] Moreover, members' participation is based not so much on the representation of one functional interest against another as on the promotion and protection of specific national interests. Members are the envoys of national governments (Article 146) charged with ensuring that EC legislation contrary to specific national interests is either modified in an appropriate manner or not passed. Retention of the veto, consensus-building behaviour and decision-making by unanimous assent are predicated on this view of the functions of delegates to the Council, and on the belief that each member has an equal right and opportunity to influence outputs irrespective of the size of the state he represents.

The latter is also a basic principle of federal/bicameral arrangements where the principle of the equality of the citizens finds expression in and through a federal popular chamber and where the territorial collectivities, although unequal in terms of population, receive equal representation in an upper chamber. The success with which the equality or near-equality of territorial collectivities is demonstrated in upper chambers varies from country to country.[55] What matters is not so much the numerical parity between the component units as the

existence of provisions or practices attesting to the principle of their
equal right to be heard in decision-making. This principle is honoured
in the Council of Ministers and finds expression in the retention of the
veto, and the way in which majorities are weighted.

Under Article 148(2) of the EEC Treaty, as amended by Article 14 of
the Act of Accession Treaty, and modified by Article 8 of the
Adaptation Treaty, it is affirmed that:

> Where the Council is required to act by a qualified majority, the votes
> of its members shall be weighted as follows:
>
> | | |
> |---|---|
> | Belgium | 5 |
> | Denmark | 3 |
> | Germany | 10 |
> | France | 10 |
> | Ireland | 3 |
> | Italy | 10 |
> | Luxembourg | 2 |
> | Netherlands | 5 |
> | United Kingdom | 10 |
>
> For their adoption, acts of Council shall require at least: forty-one
> votes in favour where this Treaty requires them to be adopted on a
> proposal from the Commission; forty-one votes in favour, cast by at
> least six members, in other cases.

This prevents the four large states in coalition imposing their will on
the smaller states. Voting on a Commission proposal they need the
support of at least one and in other instances at least two of the smaller
states.[56]

A survey of some of the functions of the Council of Ministers under-
scores the extent to which an analogy with national cabinets is
misleading.

The Council of Ministers is the Community's supreme legislative
organ. It has, in all matters bar the adoption of the budget, the sole right
to pass legislation.[57] It therefore possesses the one power normally
associated with the legislatures of the member states. It also possesses a
related power: the right to reject legislative proposals. Article 149
states:

> Where in pursuance of this Treaty, a formal measure is taken by the
> Council on a proposal from the Commission, the Council may only
> take a measure amounting to an amendment of the proposal if its
> decision is unanimous.

If unanimous, then, the Council can reject and require a proposal's
amendment. In all other cases the Commission is empowered to amend
the proposal in such a way as to enable it to secure the Council's
approbation.

Like parliaments, the Council can require the re-drafting of proposal, and by requiring their amendment hinder their passage into law. This latter power is one associated with upper chambers in bicameral systems; and the power of an upper chamber to delay or require reconsideration of bills has been thought of as an advantage of bicameralism.

Unlike members of parliaments, on the other hand, Council members have no right of initiative in legislative matters, this being the prerogative of the Commission. If the Council deems action on a specific issue desirable, the most it can do is request the Commission under Article 152 'to undertake any studies which [it] considers desirable for the achievement of . . . common objectives, and to submit to it any appropriate proposals.' It can neither determine nor directly influence the content of any such proposals given the Commission's sworn autonomy under Article 157. Nor can it determine their timing. At most the Council may request the submission of reports by specified dates. Similarly, national governments may influence the timing of EC and Commission activities via the European Council's decisions.

The Council therefore has the right to pass but not to initiate legislation. Its right to pass legislation juxtaposes the basic dilemma regarding its position in EC decision-making. On the one hand, its members individually represent the member states and their individual interests (a fact which may partly explain its lack of accountability to any other EC or national institution). On the other hand, its primary function is to act as the EC's legislative body. The two functions are incompatible and dysfunctional to effective decision-making and integration since the same set of people are charged with performing contradictory tasks. The incongruity in EC decision-making lies with the granting of powers normally distributed between two chambers in federal systems to the one institution. The Council, therefore, approximates neither a lower nor an upper chamber, nor a cabinet. This is also evidenced by its lack of formal collective accountability for its decisions to either EC citizens, or Community or national-level bodies.

Individual ministers may be obliged to explain their decisions to national cabinets and/or parliaments, but there is no way in which they can be held accountable for passing or rejecting EC legislation at the supranational level. Apart from the fact that, within national settings, national ministers are responsible to national parliaments in their capacity as members of national governments, *not* as members of an EC body *per se*, national parliaments eschew disavowal of a national minister's actions in the Council when he can purport to have acted in the 'national interest'.[58] Because no individual and visibly no recognisable person can be held responsible for a lack of integrative decisions, 'anonymous neo-absolutism' results.[59] Although acting collectively, the Council is not collectively accountable for its decisions. Because it acts collectively, no provision exists for individual accountability for its outputs. Comprising delegates of national governments rather than directly elected representatives, it cannot be held responsible to publics.

The solution to the Council's irresponsibility is often seen as lying in making its members accountable on an individual or collective basis to the Parliament. A number of objections to this exist. The most important reservation must be that the basic dilemma as to the appropriate role and functions of the Council and its members would not be resolved by increasing their accountability at the European level, even though it would indubitably mitigate criticisms of the 'undemocratic' nature of current decision-making practices. If the dilemma is to be resolved, a number of questions must be asked. What is, or should be, the Council's role? Should it be the corporate representative of member state interests, or should it be the EC's primary legislative body? Recent developments indicate some circumscription of its legislative power and a shift towards power-sharing. Since the conciliation procedure has also been adopted to deal with disagreements between the Parliament and Council on matters other than those of a budgetary nature, an increase in the sharing of legislative responsibility and functions may be predicted, especially after direct elections.

However, the extent and implications of this sharing are problematic. If they are not extensive, and if – more importantly – greater legislative power is not devolved to the Parliament, then it is unlikely that the Council's role will be reappraised. If, on the other hand, the Parliament can credibly claim to represent European rather than national voters after direct elections,[60] then the quintessential 'national' characteristics of the Council will be highlighted. This in itself would not be undesirable provided that (a) the Council was not expected to continue to determine, via its legislative functions, the pace and direction of integration; and (b) the Council was in a position to advance national interests with impunity. Were legislative power-sharing greater, then the Council's advocacy of national interests would seem less reprobate since it would be balanced by the integratively inclined Parliament. In other words, we advocate the Council becoming the representative of the *member states*, not – as it is at present – the representative of the *member governments*.

This is not to deny that the latter may want representation at the supranational level (which they have already in the European Councils *qua* summits) but to emphasise the role of the Council as a chamber of member states. Such a development would be consonant with the terms of the appointment of members to the Council under Article 146 which stipulates that the Council 'shall consist of representatives of the Member States'. Article 146 further stipulates that each government shall 'delegate to it one of its members'. While Council practice, its nomenclature and composition until now suggested that governments have chosen to interpret this as meaning that the Council shall consist of a representative from each government of the member states, alternative interpretations are possible.

We suggest that the Council's membership could be expanded within the terms of Article 146 such that member governments' delegates to it were complemented by representatives of the member states. The latter could be drawn from a number of sources. They could emanate from national parliaments, regional or local councils if it were deemed important that the Council continue to comprise politicians only. Alternatively, they could be drawn from functional and interest groups, or the Council's membership could be expanded to include members from the Nine's Permanent Representatives. The Permanent Representatives remain and function in the supranational arena as spokesmen for their national governments even though they may also advocate 'European' solutions within national settings.[61] Their inclusion in the Council would meet demands for greater technical expertise in that body and would go some way towards making those administrators who have decision-making capabilities under the 'Points A' procedure more clearly visible and accountable to the Council[62] (and specifically to member governments' representatives) than they are at present. In addition, an expanded Council might include European ministers.[63]

A variety of procedures could be adopted in the selection of Council members. Some might be popularly elected – as is the case with half the members of the Belgian Senate; some might be co-opted, and some appointed. Among the advantages of increasing the Council's membership would be the element of permanence that the institution would acquire through its membership being, in part, constant for the duration of a session. Whereas the member governments' delegates would vary according to the questions under scrutiny, representatives from the member states would have a permanence that would enable them to develop useful links with other institutions in the Community. To ensure that delegates and representatives to the Council remained firmly committed to the articulation, promotion and defence of national over European interests, a system of bloc voting, like that of the Bundesrat's, could be instituted so that the nationals of each member state would be dissuaded from splitting their vote.

It would be difficult to prescribe an optimum size for an upper chamber in the EC. The sizes of existing upper chambers in the member states offer little guidance, ranging as they do from 49 to almost 1100. While some formula relating the allocation of seats to population size might be found, if the smaller states are to retain their influence, and if their equality is to be respected, a formula akin to that devised for determining weighted majority voting (see above) might be adopted. Thus, the Council's expanded membership might be 58.

Let us now consider appropriate powers for the Council in its guise as upper chamber. We should like to suggest that it retain its legislative functions but that these be exercised in conjunction with the

Parliament. This need not involve wholesale deviations from current practice. However, if decision-making is to be effective, it will be imperative that, provided the CPR is subjected to some form of democratic control, the more technical items come under the 'Points A'[64] procedure so that the Council and Parliament are freed to concentrate on the more salient and substantive issues facing the Community.

In the past it has been suggested that in the event of institutional reform in the EC, the Council should assume a ratifying function in a capacity as an upper chamber. This is not a feasible proposition since it assumes that the Parliament would be given the legislative functions currently exercised by the Council, and that necessary Treaty amendments could be obtained. However, let us suggest that the Council be given a veto power in legislative matters but that legislative competence be shared between the Parliament and the Council either on a co-equal basis or on a basis that would permit the Parliament gradually to acquire greater legislative authority. For example, under existing practice Commission proposals could be passed to both chambers, their decisions communicated to each other and to the Commission, and the conciliation procedure brought into operation to resolve differences. In the event of irreconcilable positions being adopted by both chambers the Council's vote could be decisive on a second or third reading, or the proposal could be dropped at the end of the session in the last resort. Alternatively, the conciliation committee could, with the Commission's assistance, be charged with finding a solution. Under the *navette* procedure, for instance, exchanges between the two houses could continue until a mutually acceptable position were reached.

Institutional changes of the type suggested above would go some way towards satisfying demands for 'democratisation' of decision-making, and increasing the efficiency and effectiveness with which EC and member state interests are represented. The problem of the nature of the Council's accountability would also be partly resolved by its sharing of decision-making powers with the, then elected, Parliament. This, we suggest, would also be a less sensitive way of dealing with the problem than requiring its accountability to the Parliament to be demonstrated in a manner similar to the Commission's. It would obviate imputations of the Council's subordination to a body comprising members from national parliaments having backbench, and hence junior, status but exercising 'inappropriate' powers (relative to their national status) over their seniors in the Council.[65]

In order that the Council's control and supervisory powers vis-à-vis the Commission would be not less than those of the Parliament, it might be considered advisable to afford the Council a censure right over the Commission. However, we do not consider this necessary since, in the member states, executives are in practice generally responsible to lower chambers.

The EC's institutional balance would inevitably be modified by a move towards bicameralism. The executive would become a unicephalous organ unless the European Council (summit) were to intensify its 'guidance' role.[66] In other words, this body – having already been institutionalised – might be expected to perform its directive functions with greater efficiency were its role in the EC's institutional set-up more clearly perceived and accepted as legitimate.

By advocating a bicameral arrangement for the EC in which the composition and role of the Council of Ministers is transformed, we reject the suggestion (sometimes canvassed by those seeing a need to accord functional bodies greater decision-making and legislative competences in a 'technocratic' Community) that the ESC should become the second 'parliamentary' chamber. Such a suggestion overlooks the political and potentially federal nature of the Community. Clearly, any transformation of the Council of Ministers' role in the Community would have to be accomplished gradually. As a first step towards increasing its membership, it might be useful simply to ensure that, with a view to minimising compartmentalisation of decision-making, ministers from more than one or two departments were present and able to participate. However, this suggestion alone raises a number of difficulties, not least of which would be establishing days on which all the relevant ministers from the Nine would be able to attend.

If a bicameral arrangement for the EC were to be accepted, then it would become imperative for the European Parliament to be located alongside any upper chamber. Unless the Council of Ministers were to be situated in Strasbourg or Luxembourg, the Parliament should, as Patijn has suggested, be moved to Brussels and preferably located in the rue de la Loi.[67] Indeed, bicameralism would strengthen arguments in favour of a centralisation of the Community's institutions.

Notes

1. No formal reference is made to the COREPER in the Rome Treaty but it is accepted as an EC institution and its powers have been expanded.

2. A. Spinelli, *The European Adventure* (London: Charles Knight, 1972) p. 173.

3. A. Spinelli, *The Eurocrats* (Baltimore: Johns Hopkins Press, 1966) p. 162.

4. Developed in W. N. Hogan, *Representative Government and European Integration* (Lincoln: Univ. of Nebraska Press, 1967).

5. S. Henig, 'New Institutions for European Integration', *Journal of Common Market Studies*, XII (1973) 129–37; see also his 'The Institutional Structure of the European Communities', *Journal of Common Market Studies*, XII (1974) 373–409.

6. Spinelli has attempted to outline a model for the EC's institutional development: see his *The European Adventure*.

7. Ibid., p. 180.

8. See, for example, R. Mayne, *The Institutions of the European Community* (London: PEP/Chatham House, 1968); also R. Pryce, *The Political Future of the European Community* (London: Marshbank/Federal Trust, 1962) pp. 58–65.

9. R. R. Bowie, 'The Process of Federating Europe', in A. W. MacMahon, *Federalism: Mature and Emergent* (New York: Doubleday, 1955) p. 508.

10. The Court of Justice is also regarded by some as the EC's 'most federal' institution.

11. Spinelli, *The Eurocrats*, pp. 151–2.

12. Ibid., p. 153.

13. See Pryce, *The Political Future of the European Community*; also M. Steed, 'The European Parliament: The Significance of Direct Election', *Government and Opposition*, VI (1971) 462–76.

14. K. C. Wheare, *Federal Government* (London: Oxford Univ. Press, 1946) p. 11.

15. See D. Mitrany, *The Functional Theory of Politics* (London: Martin Robertson, 1975); also A. J. R. Groom and P. Taylor, *Functionalism* (London: Univ. of London Press, 1975).

16. In Etzioni's sense of the word: see A. Etzioni, *Political Unification* (New York: Holt, Rinehart & Winston, 1965).

17. For a discussion of this see D. J. Elazar, 'Fiscal Questions and Political Answers in Intergovernmental Finance', *Public Administration Review*, XXXII (1972) 471–8.

18. Wheare, *Federal Government*, p. 36.

19. C. Friedrich, 'Federal Constitutional Theory and Emergent Proposals', in MacMahon, *Federalism*, p. 510.

20. The Court of Justice also has a special role not discussed here.

21. For a discussion of this see D. Coombes, *Politics and Bureaucracy in the European Community* (London: Allen & Unwin, 1970) pp. 86–100.

22. For details see É. Noël, 'The Committee of Permanent Representatives', *Journal of Common Market Studies*, V (1967) 219–51.

23. We are not concerned here with those areas in which the Commission can decide on and pass measures, usually of an administrative nature.

24. Spinelli, *The European Adventure*, pp. 180 ff.

25. V. Herman, *Parliaments of the World: A Reference Compendium* (London: Macmillan, 1976) p. 4.

26. G. Smith, *Politics in Western Europe* (London: Heinemann, 1972) p. 328; also see E. Machek, *Die Österreichische Bundesverfassung* (Vienna: Cura Verlag, 1965) p. 40; P. M. Williams, *The French Parliament: 1958–1967* (London: Allen & Unwin, 1968) p. 29; and Herman, *Parliaments of the World*, pp. 585–94.

27. For a series of comparative studies see D. Coombes *et al.*, *The Power of the Purse: The Role of European Parliaments in Budgetary Decisions* (London: Allen & Unwin/PEP, 1976).

28. Herman, *Parliaments of the World*, p. 586.

29. Ibid., for an explanation of this.

30. See G. Smith, 'West Germany and the Politics of Centrality', *Government and Opposition*, XI (1976) 393.

31. See J. Lodge, 'Citizens and the EEC: The Role of the European

Parliament', *The Parliamentarian*, LVIII (1977) 176–81; also J. Lodge and V. Herman, 'Citizenship, Direct Elections and the European Parliament', *Res Publica*, XIX (1977) 579–605 and G. Zellentin, 'The Function and Form of the Opposition in the European Parliament', *Government and Opposition*, II (1967) 418.

32. Wheare, *Federal Government*, p. 11.

33. See *The Case for Elections to the European Parliament by Direct Universal Suffrage* (Luxembourg: Directorate-General for Parliamentary Documentation and Information, 1969); also J. Lodge, 'The Reform of the European Parliament', *Political Science*, XXV (1973) 58–78; the Vedel Report. *Report of the Working Party Examining the Problem of Enlargement of the Powers of the European Parliament* (Brussels, 1972); and A. Shlaim, 'The Vedel Report and the Reform of the European Parliament', *Parliamentary Affairs*, XXVII (1974) 159–70.

34. For details see Sir Barnett Cocks, *The European Parliament* (London: HMSO, 1973).

35. For a discussion of this see H. Vredeling, 'The Common Market of Political Parties', *Government and Opposition*, VI (1971) 455.

36. *White Paper on Direct Elections to the European Assembly*, Cmnd 6768 (London: HMSO, 1977) Annex.

37. Luxemburgensis, 'The Emergence of a European Sovereignty', *Government and Opposition*, IX (1974) 79–95.

38. On budgetary powers see Cocks, *The European Parliament*, pp. 20–4.

39. Discussed in J. Lodge, 'Parliamentary Reform in the EEC', *The Parliamentarian*, LV (1974) 254–5.

40. Spinelli, *The Eurocrats*.

41. *The European Parliament* (Luxembourg: Directorate-General for Information and Public Relations, 1976) p. 7.

42. For details of this see D. Strasser, 'La Nouvelle Procédure Budgétaire des Communautés Européennes et son Application a l'établissement du Budget pour l'exercise 1975', *Revue du Marché Commun*, no. 182 (1975) 79–87; also C.-D. Ehlermann, 'Applying the New Budgetary Procedure for the First Time (Article 203 of the EEC Treaty)', *Common Market Law Review*, XII (1975) 325–43.

43. Cocks, *The European Parliament*, pp. 105 ff.

44. *Commission Report* (Brussels, 1976) p. 31.

45. Cocks, *The European Parliament*, pp. 19–20; see also the Derringer Report (Document 74, Session 1962–63).

46. *European Union: Report by Mr Leo Tindemans* (Brussels, 1975).

47. H. Thomas, *Europe: The Radical Challenge* (London: Quartet, 1973) p. 24.

48. *Budgetary Powers of the European Parliament* (Luxembourg; Directorate-General of Information, 1975) p. 1.

49. V. Herman and J. Lodge, 'The European Parliament and the "Decline of Legislatures" Thesis', *Politics* XIII (1978) (forthcoming).

50. For details of procedures in other countries see Herman, *Parliaments of the World*, pp. 755–91.

51. Coombes *et al.*, *The Power of the Purse*, p. 370; see also E. L. Normanton, *The Audit and Accountability of Governments* (Manchester: Manchester Univ. Press, 1965).

52. Coombes *et al., The Power of the Purse*, p. 390.

53. *The Times*, 14 Jan 1977.

54. Mayne, *The Institutions of the European Community*, p. 29, points out that the Council is an 'Executive' 'in the limited sense that its role in the Community is to take decisions; but it has neither the legal freedom of movement nor the practical agility of most national governments'.

55. See A. Grosser, 'The Evolution of European Parliaments', *Daedalus*, XCIII (1964) 153–78.

56. Had Norway acceded to the EC the five small member states would have had the power together to block proposals favoured by the large states.

57. We are not concerned here with the Commission's decisional powers in respect of daily amendments to levies, etc.

58. J. Lodge, *The European Policy of the SPD* (Beverly Hills & London: Sage, 1976) pp. 66–7.

59. K. Meyer, 'Integration and its Institutions', *Aussenpolitik*, XXIII (1972) 61–82.

60. See report of Sir Christopher Soames' speech at Whitchurch on the subject of direct elections and accountability in *European Community*, Oct–Nov 1976, pp. 6–7.

61. Noël, op. cit.; see also É. Noël and H. Étienne, 'The Permanent Representatives Committee and the "Deepening" of the Communities', *Government and Opposition*, VI (1971) 422–47.

62. D. Norrenberg, 'Un modèle institutionnel déficient: la communauté européenne', *Res Publica*, XVIII (1976) 210.

63. For discussions of the role of the European ministers see *Revue du Marché Commun*, no. 146 (1971) 355–60; see also the Vedel Report in *Bulletin of the European Communities*, Supplement 4/72 (Brussels; 1972) p. 78.

64. Explained in footnote 45 in H. Wallace, *National Governments and the European Communities* (London: PEP/Chatham House, 1973) p. 59.

65. Steed, op. cit.

66. For details of this see J. Lodge, 'Towards the European Political Community: EEC Summits and European Integration', *Orbis*, XIX (1975) 626–51.

67. *European Report*, 18 Feb 1976.

Bibliography

This list includes some but not all of the works cited in the endnotes as well as further related works, and a selection of some of the most useful official documents.

M. Abelein, 'Die Neuregelung der Finanzverfassung der Europäischen Gemeinschaften und die Erweiterung der Haushaltsbefugnisse des Europäischen Parlaments', *Öffentliche Verwaltung*, XXIV (1971) 298-301.

C. Ake, A Theory of Political Integration (Homewood, Dorsey, 1967).

M. Albertini, 'Il Parlamento Europeo: Profilo storico, giuridico e politico', *Politico*, XXXVI (1971) 754-74.

P. Allott, 'The Democratic Basis of the European Communities: The European Parliament and the Westminster Parliament', *Common Market Law Review*, XI (1974) 298-326.

——, 'Britain and Europe: A Political Analysis', *Journal of Common Market Studies*, XIII (1975) 203-23.

J. A. Armstrong, *The European Administrative Elite* (Princeton: Princeton Univ. Press, 1973).

R. Aron, 'Is Multinational Citizenship Possible?', *Social Research*, XLI (1974) 638-56.

W. Averyt, 'Eurogroups, Clientèla and the European Community', *International Organisation*, XXIX (1975) 949-72.

M. Bangemann and R. Bieber, *Die Direktwahl: Sackgasse oder Chance für Europa* (Baden-Baden: Nomos, 1976).

S. H. Barnes, 'Participation, Education and Political Competence', *American Political Science Review*, LX (1966) 348-53.

W. Behrendt (ed.), *The EC's Own Resources and the Budgetary Powers of the European Parliament: Selected Documents* (Luxembourg, 1972).

R. Bieber, 'Offene Fragen direkter Wahlen zum Europäischen Parlament', *Europa Archiv*, XXXI (1976) 707-16.

——, 'Funktion und Grundlagen direkter Wahlen zum Europäischen Parlament im Jahre 1978', *Zeitschrift für Parlamentsfragen*, VII (1976) 228-44.

——, and M. Palmer, 'Power at the Top: The EC Council in Theory and Practice', *The World Today*, XXXI (1975) 310-18.

—— and ——, 'A Community without a Capital', *Journal of Common Market Studies*, XV (1976) 1-8.

W. Birke, *European Elections by Direct Suffrage* (Leiden: Sijthoff, 1961).

J. Blondel, *Comparative Legislatures* (Englewood Cliffs, N.J.; Prentice-Hall, 1973).

N. C. Braun, *Commissaires et Juges dans les Communautés Européennes* (Paris: Librairie Générale de Droit et de Jurisprudence, 1972).

179

K.-H. Buck, 'Die Haltung von KPI und KPF gegenüber Direktwahl und Funktionen des Europa-Parlaments', *Zeitschrift für Parlamentsfragen*, VII (1976) 209–19.

J. L. Burban, 'Les anglais et l'élection du Parlement européen au suffrange universel direct', *Revue du Marché Commun*, no. 151 (1972) 157–61.

——, 'Relations entre Parlement européen et Parlements nationaux', *Revue de Marché Commun*, no. 160 (1972) 780–90.

——, 'Le nouveau projet d'élection du Parlement européen au suffrange universel: du projet 'Dehousse' au projet 'Patijn' *Cahiers de Droit Européen*, XI (1975) 455–63.

——, 'Les gaullistes et l'élection du Parlement européen au suffrage universel direct', *Revue de Marché Commun*, no. 193 (1976) 75–85.

——, 'Les communistes et l'élection du Parlement au suffrage universel', *Revue du Marché Commun*, no. 199 (1976) 373–80.

J. A. Caporaso, *Functionalism and Regional Integration: A Logical and Empirical Assessment* (Beverly Hills and London: Sage, 1972).

——, *The Structure and Function of European Integration* (Pacific Palisades, Calif.: Goodyear, 1974).

F. Cardis, *Fédéralisme et Intégration Européenne* (Lausanne: Centre de Recherches Européennes, 1964).

W. H. Clark, *The Politics of the Common Market* (Englewood Cliffs, N.J.: Prentice-Hall, 1967).

Sir B. Cocks, *The European Parliament* (London: HMSO, 1973).

D. Coombes, *Politics and Bureaucracy in the European Community* (London: Allen and Unwin, 1970).

——, 'The Implications of British Entry to the European Community for the Party Groups in the European Parliament', *Lo Spettatore Internazionale*, no. 3–4 (1972) 135–46.

D. Coombes *et al.*, *The Power of the Purse: The Role of European Parliaments in Budgetary Decisions* (London: Allen & Unwin/PEP, 1976).

—— and I. Wiebeke, *The Power of the Purse: The Budgetary Powers of the European Parliament* (London: PEP/Chatham House, 1972).

E.-O. Czempiel, 'The Citizen's Society: Lessons from Europe', *Social Research*, XLI (1971) 746–68.

R. Dahrendorf, 'The Foreign Policy of the EEC', *The World Today*, XXIX (1973) 47–57.

——, 'Citizenship and Beyond: The Social Dynamics of an Idea', *Social Research*, XLI (1974) 673–701.

F. Dehousse, 'Réflexions á propos des élections européennes de demain', *Revue de Marché Commun*, no. 182 (1975) 49–56.

——, 'Vers des élections européennes', *Studia Diplomatica*, XXIX (1976) 65–86.

M. Dell'Omodarme, 'Ruolo e azione del Parlamento europeo per l'elezione a suffragio universale diretto dei suoi membri', *Politico*, XXXVI (1971) 775–81.

H. Dessloch, 'Europäische Wahlen 1978?', *Politische Studien*, no. 232 (1977) 117–26.

I. E. Druker, *Financing the European Communities* (Leiden: Sijthoff, 1975).

M. Edmond (Ed.), *European Parliament Digest* (Lewes: New Educational Press, 1974).

C.-D. Ehlermann, 'Ein Schritt auf dem Wege zur Demokratisierung der Europäischen Gemeinschaften: Die Vorschläge der Kommission zur Stärkung des Europäischen Parlaments', *Europa Archiv*, XXVIII (1973) 821–30.

——, 'Applying the New Budgetary Procedure for the First Time (Article 203 of the EEC Treaty)', *Common Market Law Review*, XII (1975) 325–43.

A. Etzioni, *Political Unification* (New York: Holt, Rinehart & Winston, 1965).

J. Feidt, 'L'activité du Parlement européen en 1975', *Revue de Marché Commun*, no. 198 (1976) 330–45.

W. J. Feld and J. K. Wildgen, 'Electoral Ambitions and European Integration', *International Organisation*, XXIX (1975) 447–68.

—— and ——, 'National Administrative Elites and European Integration: Saboteurs at Work?', *Journal of Common Market Studies*, XIII (1975) 244–65.

H. Ferdinand, 'Die erste Gewalt in der Europäischen Union: Uberlegungen auf Grund von Erfahrungen in den europäischen Versammlungen', *Politik und Zeitgeschichte*, XLVIII (1974) 3–16.

W. E. Fischer, 'An Analysis of the Deutsch Sociocausal Paradigm of Political Integration', *International Organisation*, XXIII (1969) 254–90.

G. FitzGerald, 'Ireland and the European Parliament', *Lo Spettatore Internazionale*, no. 3–4 (1972) 147–59.

J. Fitzmaurice, *The Party Groups in the European Parliament* (Farnborough: Saxon House, 1975).

P. Fontaine, *Le Comité d'Action pour les Etats-Unis d'Europe de Jean Monnet* (Lausanne: Centre de Recherches Européennes, 1974).

M. Forsyth, *The Parliament of the European Communities* (London: PEP, 1964).

——, 'The Political Objectives of European Integration', *International Affairs*, XLIII (1967) 483–97.

J. R. Frears, 'The French Parliament and the European Community', *Journal of Common Market Studies*, XII (1975) 140–56.

C. J. Friedrich, *Europa: Nation im Werden?* (Bonn: Europa Union Verlag, 1972).

J. A. Frowein, 'Zur institutionellen Fortentwicklung der Europäischen Gemeinschaften', *Europa Archiv*, XXVII (1972) 623–32.

H. Furler, 'Europäisches Parlament und europäische Politik', *Aussenpolitik*, XI (1960) 789–97.

J. Galtung, 'A Structural Theory of Integration', *Journal of Peace Research*, V (1968) 375–95.

——, *The European Community: A Superpower in the Making* (London, Allen & Unwin, 1973).

P. Gerbet and D. Pepys, *La Décision dans les Communautés Européennes* (Brussels: Presses Universitaires de Bruxelles, 1969).

P. Ginestet, *Le Parlement Européen* (Vendôme: Presses Universitaires de France, 1970).

P. Green and S. Levinson, *Power and Community: Dissenting Essays in Political Science* (New York: Random House, 1970).

N. D. Gresh, 'Die supranationalen Fraktionen im Europäischen Parlament', *Zeitschrift für Parlamentsfragen*, VII (1976) 190–208.

A. J. R. Groom and P. Taylor, *Functionalism: Theory and Practice in International Relations* (London: Univ. of London Press, 1975).

A. Grosser, 'The Evolution of European Parliaments', *Daedalus*, XCIII (1964) 153–78.

V. Guizzi, 'L'azione del Parlamento italionao in favore dell'elezione a suffragio universale de Parlamento europeo', *Politico*, XXXVI (1971) 782–91.

E. B. Haas, *The Uniting of Europe: Political, Social and Economic Forces, 1950–57* (Stanford: Stanford Univ. Press, 1958).

——, *The Obsolescence of Regional Integration Theory* (Berkeley: Univ. of California Press, 1975).

W. Hallstein, *Europe in the Making* (London: Allen & Unwin, 1972).

F. C. Heidelberg, 'Parliamentary Control and Political Groups in the Three European Regional Communities', *Law and Contemporary Problems*, no. 3 (1961) 430–7.

S. Henig, 'New Institutions for European Integration', *Journal of Common Market Studies*, XII (1973) 129–37.

——, 'The Institutional Structure of the European Communities', *Journal of Common Market Studies*, XII (1974) 373–409.

—— and J. Pinder (eds.), *European Political Parties* (London: Allen & Unwin, 1969).

G. Heraud, *Les Principes du Fédéralisme et la Fédération Européenne: Contribution à la théorie juridique du fédéralisme* (Paris: Presses d'Europe, 1968).

V. Herman, *Parliaments of the World: A Reference Compendium* (London: Macmillan, 1976).

—— and J. Lodge, 'Is the European Parliament a Parliament?', *European Journal of Political Research*, VI (1978) forthcoming.

W. N. Hogan, *Representative Government and European Integration* (Lincoln: Univ. of Nebraska Press, 1967).

——, 'Political Representation and European Integration', *Integration*, IV (1970) 288–97.

A. M. Houdbine, 'Sociologie du Parlement européen', *Politique*, no. 7–8 (1964–5) 9–23.

R. Inglehart, 'Cognitive Mobilisation and European Identity', *Comparative Politics*, III (1970) 45–70.

——, 'Public Opinion and Regional Integration', *International Organisation*, XXIV (1970) 764–95.

——, 'Changing Value Priorities and European Integration', *Journal of Common Market Studies*, X (1971) 1–36.

——, 'Long Term Trends in Mass Support for European Unification', *Government and Opposition*, XII (1977) 150–77.

G. Ionescu (ed.), *The New Politics of European Integration* (London: Macmillan, 1972).

R. D. Kaiser, 'Toward the Copernican Phase of Regional Integration Theory', *Journal of Common Market Studies*, X (1972) 207–32.

P. J. G. Kapteyn, 'The European Parliament, the Budget, and Legislation in the Community', *Common Market Law Review*, IX (1972) 386–410.

H. C. Kelman, 'Patterns of Personal Involvement in the National System: A

Social-Psychological Analysis of Political Legitimacy', in J. N. Rosenau (ed.), *International Politics and Foreign Policy* (New York: Free Press, 1969) pp. 276-88.

H. H. Kerr, Jr, 'Changing Attitudes through International Participation: European Parliamentarians and Integration', *International Organisation*, XXVII (1973) 45-83.

P. Kirk, *Motion for a Resolution on the Establishment of a Temporary Committee of the European Parliament to Examine the Procedure and Practices of the Parliament, together with an explanatory memorandum* (Luxembourg: European Parliament, Conservative Group, 1973).

B. Kohler, 'Direkte Wahlen zum Europäischen Parlament', *Europa Archiv*, XXVI (1971) 727-38.

M. Kolinsky, 'Parliamentary Scrutiny of European Legislation', *Government and Opposition*, X (1975) 46-69.

H. G. Kundoch, 'Le recours en carence comme moyen juridique de promouvoir l'élection directe du Parlement européen', *Cahiers de Droit Européen*, XI (1975) 425-52.

K. Kyle, 'The European Parliament', *The World Today*, XXVIII (1972) 530-7.

E. Lakeman, *Nine Democracies: Electoral Systems of the Countries of the European Economic Community* (London: Arthur McDougall Fund, 1973).

J. M. Lamblin, S. Lô and J. van de Calseyde, *Les Parlementaires des Pays Membres de la CEE et l'Intégration Européenne* (Bruges: Collège d'Europe, 1975).

C. Lassalle, 'L'initiative parlementaire dans la procédure normative communautaire', *Cahiers de Droit Européen*, VII (1971) 127-45.

R. Legrand-Lane, 'Elire des députés européens', *Etudes*, (Paris, June, 1976) 789-807.

J. F. Leich, 'The Italian Communists and the European Parliament', *Journal of Common Market Studies*, IX (1971) 271-81.

M. Lévi, 'Physionomie d'un Parlement européen', *Politique Étrangère*, I (1966) 86-97.

R. Liguori, 'Risorse proprie delle Communità Europee e poteri del Parlamento europeo', *Communità Internazionale*, XXVI (1971) 35-41.

L. N. Lindberg and S. A. Scheingold, *Europe's Would-Be Polity* (Englewood Cliffs, N.J.: Prentice-Hall, 1970).

—— and ——, *Regional Integration: Theory and Research* (Cambridge, Mass.: Harvard Univ. Press, 1971).

K. Lindsay, *European Assemblies* (London: Stevens, 1960).

J. Lodge, 'The Reform of the European Parliament', *Political Science*, XXV (1973) 58-78.

——, 'The Role of EEC Summit Conferences', *Journal of Common Market Studies*, XII (1974) 337-45.

——, 'Parliamentary Reform in the EEC', *The Parliamentarian*, LV (1974) 250-7.

——, 'Britain and the EEC: Exit, Voice or Loyalty?', *Cooperation and Conflict*, X (1975) 199-216.

——, 'Towards the European Political Community: EEC Summits and European Integration', *Orbis*, XIX (1975) 626-51.

——, *The European Policy of the SPD* (Beverly Hills and London: Sage, 1976).

——, 'Citizens and the EEC: The Role of the European Parliament', *The Parliamentarian*, LVIII (1977) 176–81.

——, 'Towards a Human Union: EEC Social Policy and European Integration', *British Journal of International Studies*, IV (1978) 47–74.

——, 'Loyalty and the EEC: The Limitations of the Functionalist Approach', *Political Studies*, XXVI (1978) 268–84.

Luxemburgensis, 'The Emergence of a European Sovereignty', *Government and Opposition*, IX (1974) 79–95.

A. W. MacMahon, *Federalism: Mature and Emergent* (New York: Doubleday, 1955).

C. J. Mann, *The Function of Judicial Decision in European Economic Integration* (The Hague: Nijhoff, 1972).

M. Manning, 'Direct Elections to the European Parliament: Some Implications for Irish Politics', *Administration*, XXII (1974) 384–99.

H. Manzanares, *Le Parlement Européen* (Paris: Berger-Levrault, 1964).

R. Mayne, *The Institutions of the European Community* (London: PEP/Chatham House, 1968).

B. Mennis and K. P. Sauvant, 'Describing and Explaining Support for Regional Integration: An Investigation of German Business Elite Attitudes toward the European Community', *International Organisation*, XXIX (1975) 973–96.

P. H. Merkl, 'European Assembly Parties and National Delegations', *Journal of Conflict Resolution*, VIII (1964) 50–64.

R. L. Merritt and D. J. Puchala (eds.), *Western European Attitudes on Arms Control, Defense and European Unity 1952–1963* (New Haven: Yale Univ. Press, 1966).

K. Meyer, 'Integration and its Institutions', *Aussenpolitik*, XXIII (1972) 61–82.

J. Meynaud and D. Sidjanski, *L'Europe des Affaires: Rôle et structure des groupes* (Paris: Payot, 1967).

J. D. B. Mitchell, 'The Tindemans Report: Retrospect and Prospect', *Common Market Law Review*, XIII (1976) 455–84.

D. Mitrany, *The Functional Theory of Politics* (London: Martin Robertson, 1975).

K. Neunreither, 'Das parlamentarische Element im Entscheidungsprozess der Europäischen Gemeinschaften', *Europa Archiv*, XXI (1966) 811–22.

——, 'Bemerkungen zum gegenwärtigen Leitbild des Europäischen Parlaments', *Parlamentsfragen*, II (1971) 321–43.

——, 'Legitimationsprobleme in der Europäischen Gemeinschaften', *Zeitschrift für Parlamentsfragen*, VII (1976) 245–58.

M. Niblock, *The EEC: National Parliaments in Community Decision-Making* (London: PEP/Chatham House, 1971).

É. Noël, 'The Committee of Permanent Representatives', *Journal of Common Market Studies*, V (1967) 219–51.

——, 'The Institutional Problems of the Enlarged Community', *Government and Opposition*, VII (1972) 413–25.

——, 'The Effect of the Enlargement of the EEC on the Institutional Evolution of the Community', *Government and Opposition*, IX (1974) 253–62.

——, 'The External Relations of the EEC and its Internal Problems', *Government and Opposition*, X (1975) 159–65.

——, *Les Rouages de l'Europe* (Paris: Fernand Natham, 1976).

—— and H. Étienne, 'The Permanent Representatives Committee and the "Deepening" of the Communities', *Government and Opposition*, VI (1971) 422–47.

D. Norrenberg, 'Un modéle institutionnel déficient: la communauté européenne', *Res Publica*, XVIII (1976) 203–14.

J. S. Nye, *Peace in Parts: Integration and Conflict in Regional Organisation* (Boston: Little Brown, 1971).

G. van Oudenhove, *The Political Parties in the European Parliament* (Leiden: Sijthoff, 1965).

M. Palmer, 'The Role of a Directly Elected European Parliament', *The World Today*, XXXIII (1977) 122–30

—— and J. Lambert, *European Unity* (London: Allen & Unwin/PEP, 1968).

A. Papisca, 'Communità europa: dal consenso permissivo alla partecipazione politica', *Revista Italiana di Scienza Politica*, VI (1976) 289–330.

A. Parry and S. Hardy, *EEC Law* (London: Sweet & Maxwell, 1973).

W. E. Paterson, *The SPD and European Integration* (Farnborough: Saxon House, 1974).

S. Patijn (ed.), *Landmarks in European Unity: 22 Texts on European Integration* (Leiden: Sijthoff, 1970).

C. Pentland, *International Theory and European Integration* (London: Faber & Faber, 1973).

P. Pescatore, 'Les exigences de la démocratie et la légitimité de la communauté Européene, *Cahiers de Droit Européen*, X (1974) 499–514.

W. Pickles, 'Political Power in the EEC', *Journal of Common Market Studies*, II (1963) 63–84.

G. Pridham, 'Transnational Party Groups in the European Parliament', *Journal of Common Market Studies*, XIII (1975) 266–79.

W. A. Proctor, 'The European Parliament', *The Parliamentarian*, LIV (1973) 71–79.

R. Pryce, 'The Future of the European Parliament', *Parliamentary Affairs*, XV (1962) 450–60.

——, *The Political Future of the European Community* (London: Marshbank/Federal Trust, 1962).

——, *The Politics of the European Community* (London: Butterworths, 1973).

——, 'Legitimacy and the European Integration: The Role of Information', *International Political Science Association Paper* (Edinburgh, 1976).

D.J. Puchala, 'National Distinctiveness and Transnationality in West European Political Opinion, 1954–1962', *Integration*, IV (1970) 273–87.

——, 'Patterns in West European Integration', *Journal of Common Market Studies*, IX (1971) 117–42.

——, 'Of Blind Men, Elephants and International Integration', *Journal of Common Market Studies*, X (1972) 267–84.

——, 'Domestic Politics and Regional Harmonisation in the European Communities', *World Politics*, XXVII (1975) 496–520.

J.-J. Rabier, 'Europeans and the Unification of Europe', *Government and Opposition*, VI (1971) 477–501.

A. Ranney, *The Doctrine of Responsible Party Government: Its Origins and Present State* (Urbana: Univ. of Illinois Press, 1962).

186

Bibliography

H. Rattinger and M. Zängle, 'Distribution of Seats in the European Parliament after Direct Elections: A Simulation Study', *European Journal of Political Research*, V (1977) 201–18.

E. Reister, 'Bemerkungen zum ersten parlamentarischen Misstrauensvotum in den Europäischen Gemeinschaften', *Zeitschrift für Parlamentsfragen*, IV (1973) 208–12.

A. H. Robertson, *European Institutions: Cooperation, Integration, Unification* (London: Stevens, 1973).

M. T. W. Robinson, 'The Political Implications of the Vedel Report', *Government and Opposition*, VII (1972) 426–33.

S. Rokkan (ed.), *Citizens, Elections and Parties* (New York: David McKay, 1970).

C. Russell, 'The European Parliament: Commitment and Challenge', *Parliamentary Affairs*, XXIV (1971) 251–61.

B. M. Russett, 'Transactions, Community and International Political Integration', *Journal of Common Market Studies*, IX (1971) 224–45.

M. Ryan and P. Isaacson, 'Parliament and the European Communities', *Parliamentary Affairs*, XXVIII (1975) 199–215.

A. Sánchez-Gijón, 'Las limitaciones de soberanía por la integración en la Communidad Económica Europa', *Revista de Estudios Políticos*, no. 183–184 (1972) 279–90.

D. Sanders and V. Herman, 'The Stability and Survival of Governments in Western Democracies', XII, *Acta Politica* (1977) 346–77.

J. H. Schaar, 'Legitimacy in the Modern State', in P. Green and S. Levinson (eds.), *Power and Community: Dissenting Essays in Political Science* (New York: Random House, 1970).

U. Scheuner, 'Bestandaufnahme und Prognose zur Fortentwicklung des Europäischen Parlaments', *Zeitschrift für Parlamentsfragen*, III (1972) 498–515.

K. P. Schulz, 'Widerstand gegen ein "Volksfront"-Europea', *Politische Meinung*, no. 165 (1976) 27–35.

J. J. Schwed, 'Les Questions écrites due Parlement Européen á la Commission', *Revue du Marché Commun*, no. 135 (1970) 365–8.

——, 'Quelques considérations sur l'avenir des institutions des Communautés européennes', *Revue du Marché Commun*, no. 152 (1972) 221–8.

——, 'Le Parlement européen et son élection au suffrage universel', *Revue du Marché Commun*, no. 192 (1976) 20–7.

C.-C. Schweitzer, 'Election du Parlement européen au suffrage universel' *Documents* (Cologne), XXX (1975) 26–35.

R. J. Shepherd, *Public Opinion and European Integration* (Farnborough: Saxon House, 1975).

A. Shlaim, 'The Vedel Report and the Reform of the European Parliament', *Parliamentary Affairs*, XXVII (1974) 159–70.

A. Shonfield, *Europe: Journey to an Unknown Destination* (Harmondsworth: Penguin Books, 1973).

P. Shore, *Europe: The Way Back* (London: Fabian Society, 1973).

D. Sidjanski and D. H. Handley, 'Aperçu des sondages d'opinion sur l'intégration européene 1945–69', *Bulletin du Centre Européen de la Culture*, XIII (1970) 118–39.

J. Siotis, 'Some Thoughts on the European Parliament', *Lo Spettatore Internazionale*, no. 2 (1971) 113–31.

J. H. Sloane, 'Political Integration in the European Community', *Canadian Journal of Political Science*, I (1968) 442-61.

G. Smith, *Politics in Western Europe* (London: Heinemann, 1972).

——, 'West Germany and the Politics of Centrality', *Government and Opposition*, XI (1976) 387-407.

Social Surveys Ltd, *British Attitudes towards the Common Market 1957-1972* (London: Gallup Poll, 1972).

D. Spanier, *Europe, Our Europe* (London: Secker & Warburg, 1972).

A. Spinelli, *The Eurocrats* (Baltimore: Johns Hopkins Press, 1966).

——, *The European Adventure* (London: Charles Knight, 1972).

M. Steed, 'The European Parliament: The Significance of Direct Election', *Government and Opposition*, VI (1971) 462-76.

A. Stevens, 'Problems of Parliamentary Control of EC Policy', *Millennium*, V (1977) 269-81.

M. Stewart, 'Direct Elections to the European Parliament', *Common Market Law Review*, XIII (1976) 283-301.

P. G. Stillman, 'The Concept of Legitimacy', *Polity*, VII (1974) 32-56.

D. Strasser, 'La Nouvelle Procédure Budgétaire des Communautés Européennes et son Application a l'établissement du Budget pour l'exercise 1975', *Revue du Marché Commun*, no. 182 (1975) 79-87.

P. Taylor, *International Cooperation Today* (London: Elek, 1971).

——, 'The Politicis of the European Community: The Confederal Phase', *World Politics*, XXVII (1975) 336-60.

H. Thomas, *Europe: The Radical Challenge* (London: Quartet, 1973).

R. Vaughan, *Post-War Integration in Europe* (London: Edward Arnold, 1976).

G. Vedovato, 'Assemblee europee e parlamenti nazionali', *Revista di Studi Politici Internazionali*, XLII (1975) 593-625.

J. Vergès, 'Les pouvoirs financiers du Parlement européen', *Cahiers de Droit Européen*, VIII (1972) 3-42.

H. Vredeling, 'The Common Market of Political Parties', *Government and Opposition*, VI (1971) 448-61.

J. K. Vree, *Political Integration: The Formation of Theory and its Problems* (The Hague: Mouton, 1972).

H. Wallace, 'The Impact of the European Communities on National Policy-Making, *Government and Opposition*, VI (1971) 520-38.

——, *National Governments and the European Communities* (London: PEP/Chatham House, 1973).

—— and W. Wallace, 'The Impact of Community Membership on the British Machinery of Government', *Journal of Common Market Studies*, XI (1973) 243-62.

——, W. Wallace and C. Webb (eds.), *Policy-Making in the European Communities* (London: John Wiley, 1977).

S. J. Warnecke, *The European Community in the 1970s* (New York: Praeger, 1972)).

K. C. Wheare, *Federal Government* (London: Oxford Univ. Press, 1946).

K. von Lindeiner-Wildau, *La Supranationalité en tant que Principe de Droit* (Leiden: Sijthoff, 1970).

J. K. Wildgen and W. J. Feld, 'Evaluative and Cognitive Factors in the Prediction of European Integration', *Comparative Political Studies*, IX (1976) 309-34.

J.-C. Willame, 'Le rapport Tindemans et les élections européennes', *Res Publica*, XIX (1977) 345–71.

C. Wilson, *Parliaments, Peoples and the Mass media* (London: Cassell, 1970).

S. Z. Young, *Terms of Entry: Britain's Negotiations with the European Community, 1970–72* (London: Heinemann, 1973).

G. Zampaglione, 'L'elezione del Parlamento europeo a suffragio universale diretto', *Comunità Internazionale*, XXIV (1969) 583–603.

G. Zellentin, *Europa 1985* (Bonn: Europa Union Verlag, 1972).

Official Publications

(*a*) *Commission of the European Communities*
  Official Journal of the EC
  Report by the Ad-hoc Committee Studying the Problem of Expanding the Authority of the European Parliament (Vedel Report) (Brussels: Bulletin of the European Communities, Supplement 4/1972).
  Strengthening of the Budgetary Powers of the European Parliament (Brussels: Bulletin of the European Communities, 9/1973).

(*b*) *European Parliament*
  Debates
  Working Documents
  European Parliament: Report
  European Parliament: The Sittings
  The Case for Direct Elections to the European Parliament by Direct Universal Suffrage (Luxembourg: Directorate-General for Parliamentary Documentation and Information, 1969).
  Selected Texts of Resolutions: I. Resolutions on General Reports of the Executives 1958–71; II. Resolutions on the Extension of Powers of the European Parliament 1963–70 (Luxembourg: European Parliament, 1971).
  Statement to the European Parliament Made by Monsieur F. Malfatti in Strasbourg on 15 September, 1970 (Luxembourg: Office for Official Publications of the European Communities, 1970).
  European Integration and the Future of Parliaments in Europe, Papers and Report of Proceedings of a Symposium held at Luxembourg, 2–3 May 1974 (Luxembourg: European Parliament, 1975).
  Report on Behalf of the Political Affairs Committee on the Adoption of a Draft Convention Introducing Elections to the European Parliament by Direct Universal Suffrage (Patijn Report) (Luxembourg: European Parliament, Doc. 368/74).
  The European Community; Our Common Cause (Luxembourg: European Parliament, Conservative Group, 1974).
  Elections to the European Parliament by Direct Universal Suffrage: Draft Convention with Explanatory Statement (Luxembourg: European Parliament, 1975).
  History and Development of the Political Groups in the European Parliament (Luxembourg: European Parliament, Christian-Democrat Group, Doss. 2, 1975).

(*c*) *British Government*
   The Treaty of Rome (London: HMSO, 1967).
   Third Report from the Select Committee on Direct Elections to the European Assembly, Cmnd 6623 (London: HMSO, 1976).
   Direct Elections to the European Assembly, Cmnd 6399 (London: HMSO, 1976).
   White Paper on Direct Elections to the European Assembly, Cmnd 6768 (London: HMSO, 1977).

Index

Accession Treaty, 49, 170
Act concerning the Election of
  Representatives to the Assembly,
  1, 73, 155n
Adaptation Treaty, 170
Aigner, H., 49, 51, 52, 53, 54, 61n
Alice Through the Looking Glass, 25
Allegiance, 8, 108
Allott, P., 31, 46, 81, 85, 86, 158
Annual General Report, Commission, 48,
  56, 58, 59, 62n, 65, 123, 167
Annual Report, EEC, 25
'anonymous neo-absolutism', 171
Association for a Democratic and
  Socialist Europe, 106
Authority, 1, 5, 6, 7, 14, 66, 74, 77, 78, 81,
  82, 83, 86, 98, 163, 166
Autonomy, 4, 6, 7, 8, 21, 77, 158, 159

Bagehot, W., 15, 16, 22n, 94, 95
Bangemann, M., 52
Belgium
  Chamber of Deputies, 152
  navette, 162, 174
  Senate, 173
Bentham, J., 120
Bertrand, A., 53, 111
Beyme, K. von, 15, 16
Bicameralism, 161, 171, 175
  bicameral chambers, 165
  bicameral legislatures, 33, 164
  bicameral parliament, 4, 161, 162, 163,
    165
  bicameral parliamentary arrangement,
    159, 161, 169, 175
  bicameral systems, 45, 171
Blondel, J., 17
Blumenfeld, E., 134
Boano, M., 101
Bowie, R. R., 159
Brandt, W., 142
Britain
  anti-marketeers, 135
  Cabinet, 47, 55
  Conservatives, 110
  Crown, 55

dual mandate, 147, 148
elections to European Parliament, 110,
  111
House of Commons, 15, 23n, 47, 66, 81,
  111, 150, 153, 154, 163
  select committees, 111, 153, 154
House of Lords, 4, 150, 162
Labour government, 3, 110, 127, 128,
  133, 148
Labour MPs, 88, 124, 128, 129
Labour Party, 136
Liberals, 110, 111
Prime Minister, 39, 110
Referendum, 116, 124, 125
Westminster, 81, 111, 127, 147, 148,
  150, 164
Budgets, 18, 19, *see also*, Commission of
  European Communities, Council
  of Ministers, European
  Community, European Parliament
Buerstedde, E., 25
Bundesrat, 33, 143, 162, 163, 173
Bundestag, 15, 24, 153, 167
  Berlin Deputies, 151
  committees, 145
Bureaucracy, 18, 24
Byars, R. S., 103

Cabinet, 23n, 24, 46, 47, 55, 56, 86
Cardis, F., 157
Central government, 13
Chapman, D., 16
'Cheysson' fund, 43n
Chicken-and-egg, 3, 67
Citizens
  and direct elections, 2, 4, 5, 7, 8, 9, 16,
    67, 73, 74, 77, 78, 79, 80, 83, 85, 90,
    94, 95, 96, 97, 98, 99, 104, 105, 111,
    113, 114, 116, 117, 122, 123, 135,
    158, 164, 171
Cocks, Sir B., 25, 56
Cointat, M., 49, 52, 53, 54
Colombo, E., 1, 134, 168
Commission of European Communities,
  21, 25, 83, 98, 121, 134, 144
  Acts, 28

agricultural instruments, 42n
appointment, 45, 59n
authority, 50
budgetary powers, 37, 38, 39, 40, 168
butter sales to Eastern Europe, 52
collegiate nature, 46
Commission-Council dialogue, 30, 31, 124
Commissioners, accountability of, 46, 47, 59, 166
democratic legitimacy, 75
democratic responsibility, 48
Eurocrats, 159
European identity, 96
European Parliament, relationship with, 26, 28, 29, 32, 67, 88, 89, 117, 124, 125, 158, 165, 166, 167, 168, 174
General Directorate, 46
information programme, 114, 116
information services, 101
initiative powers, 8, 30
integrationist pace, 161
legislative powers, 8, 27, 28, 29, 30, 31, 32, 33, 85, 165
legitimacy, 66
President, 49, 51, 52, 68n, 89, 97, 123, 127, 133, 167
proposals, 29
'undemocratic organisation', 48
Committee of Permanent Representatives (COREPER), 3, 20, 85, 160, 173, 174, 175n
Common Agricultural Policy (CAP), 53
Common Assembly, 25, 91, 106, 159
'Concertation procedure', 29, 32, 33, 42n, 67
Conciliation committee, 32, 33, 42n, 168, 174
Conciliation procedure, 89, 174
Conference of Foreign Ministers, 57, 166
Connecticut Compromise, 165
Consensus, 78
Constitution, 78
constitutional practices, 15
constitutional system, 17
'constitution of EC', 24
Constitutional Code, 120
The English Constitution, 15
Consultative Assembly, 25, 26
Coombes, D., 13, 30, 34, 35, 158
Copenhagen Summit Declaration, 10n
Council of Europe, 153
Council of Ministers, 3, 20, 35, 83, 95, 98, 144, 160
accountability, 21, 46, 74, 171, 174

Acts, 28
ambiguous nature, 158, 159
appointment, 45
autonomy, 4, 7, 21, 158, 159
'brake to integration', 161
budgetary powers, 37, 38, 39, 40, 41, 169
collegiate nature, 46
democratic legitimacy, 75
European identity, 96
European ministers, 173
and European Parliament, 26, 28, 29, 32, 57, 67, 88, 89, 117, 124, 125, 154, 155, 158, 161, 165, 166, 167, 168, 169, 172, 173, 174, 175
'executive', 178n
expansion of membership, 173
initiative power, 8
legislative powers, 5, 6, 8, 27, 28, 29, 30, 31, 85
no confidence motion, 46
power, 153, 155, 165, 169, 170, 171
President, 58, 68, 126, 166, 168
'qualified majority', 36, 43n, 170
responsibility
collective, 45, 59, 86, 171, 172
individual, 46, 59
'reversed majority rule', 43n
selection, 173
supreme decision-making body, 4, 30, 53, 149, 161, 169, 170, 174
unanimous voting, 169, 170
veto power, 33
weighted majority voting, 170
Council of State, 24
Court of Justice, 47, 60n, 63n, 98
Crosland, Rt. Hon. A., 119n, 169
Culture, 96

Decision-making, 2, 4, 6, 9, 30, 53, 54, 65, 67, 74, 77, 81, 85, 86, 89, 99, 113, 117, 149, 161, 169, 170
'Decline of legislatures' thesis, 17, 18, 19, 20, 21
Dehousse, F., 3
Delegated legislation, 14, 28, 33
Delvaux, M., 16
Democracy, 2, 3, 30, 80, 94, 157, 159
and European Community, 159
and European Elections, 74, 77
and European Parliament, 157
democratic consent, 79, 82
democratic-federalist approach, 159
democratic legitimacy, 5, 9, 14, 66, 74, 75, 76, 78
democratic politics, 74

democratic polities, 76
democratic responsibility, 24, 47, 48
democratising decision-making, 174
representative democracy, 17
Denmark
Folketing, 153
Diarchy, 45, 47
Direct Elections, 1, 2, 4, 5, 7, 8, 9, 32, 56,
    68n, 73, 74, 75, 76, 159
and citizens, *see* Citizens
and democratic legitimacy, 77
and EC institutional balance, 158
and legitimacy of European
    Parliament, 78, 94, 157, 164, 165
and political integration, 104
procedure, 3
see also, Direct Universal Suffrage,
    European Elections, European
    franchise, Members of the
    European Parliament
Direct Universal Suffrage, 1, 2, 3, 58, 66,
    73, 82, 91n, 148, 159
Dual mandate, 4, 40, 58, 87, 110, 135, 139,
    141, 164
advantages, 146, 147, 148, 149, 150, 151
alternatives, 151, 152, 153, 154, 155
compulsory mandate, 148, 149
disadvantages, 142, 143, 144, 145, 146
Dunwoody, Hon. G. P., 134
Durieux, J., 53
Dykes, H., 134

Easton, D., 78
Economic and Social Committee
    (ECOSOC), 29, 48, 85, 98, 175
Ehlermann, C.-D., 36
Electoral systems
proportional representation, 110, 111
simple majority, 111
Elites, 83, 97, 168
'Engrenage', 160
Eurobarometer, 99, 101, 102, 103, 116,
    118n, 121, 136, 137
Euro-beer, 120
Europe, 1, 2
European Assembly, 24, 25, 73, 163
see also, European Parliament
European Atomic Energy Community
    (EURATOM), 25, 106
European Broadcasting Union (EBU),
    121
European citizenry, 8, *see also*, Citizens
European Coal and Steel Community
    (ECSC), 24, 25, 91n, 106
European Community (EC)
Audit Board, 39, 43n, 168

authority structure, 77, 78, 82, 83, 112
autonomy, 77
awareness-building, 96, 97, 98, 102, 103,
    105, 112, 114, 115, 116, 117, 122, 123
bicameral arrangements, 161, 175
bicameral evolution, 159, 164
bicameral states, 162, 163
bicephalous executive, 44, 49, 85, 165
budgetary process, 21, 26, 35, 36, 37, 38,
    39, 40, 41, 43n, 52, 168
CELEX system, 155
citizens, *see* Citizens
citizens charter, 9, 96
citizenship, 109, 135
Commission, *see* Commission of
    European Communities
constitution, 24
Council, *see* Council of Ministers
Court of Justice, *see* Court of Justice
decision-making, 2, 4, 6, 9, 30, 53, 54,
    65, 67, 74, 77, 81, 85, 86, 89, 99, 113,
    117, 149, 169, 170
democracy, 66, 73, 74, 77, 94, 159
democratic legitimacy, 9, 73, 75, 79
ECOSOC, *see* Economic and Social
    Committee
electors, 78
élites, 83, 97, 168
European Council, 85, 96, 124, 167, 171,
    172, 175
European Investment Bank, 85
European Parliament, *see* European
    Parliament
executive power, 30
expenditure, 35, 36, 37, 38, 43n, 168, 169
federalism, 159, 160, 161, 163, 164, 175
future, 1, 50, 75, 174, 175
goals, 40, 161
government, 91
identity, 8, 9, 95, 96, 108, 114, 115, 123,
    135, 146
institutions, 8, 13, 47, 58, 64
accountability, 57
authority, 66, 73, 74, 78, 82, 83, 150
balance, 49, 50, 68, 77, 108, 117, 158,
    165
centralisation, 175
Commission, *see* Commission of
    European Communities
Court of Justice, *see* Court of Justice
democratic legitimacy, 74, 75, 76
ECOSOC, *see* Economic and Social
    Committee
European Investment Bank, 85
European Parliament, *see* European
    Parliament

executive-legislative relations, 91
grand forum, 82
incomplete configuration, 164
intangibility, 68, 82, 83, 98, 122
intelligibility, 68, 82, 83, 85, 120
legitimacy, 66, 76, 80, 81, 82, 83, 94
'own resources', 35, 157
presidential/parliamentary nature, 47
reform, 66, 67, 157–175
role after direct elections, 117,
    157–175
structure, 30, 61n, 66, 75, 80, 85
sui generis, 85
integration, *see* Integration
legislation, 5, 27, 28, 85, 86, 87
legislative process, 29, 161, 163, 164
legitimacy, 13, 66, 74, 75, 76, 77, 78, 79,
    80, 81, 82, 83, 91, 117, 175
linguistic diversity, 95, 96, 97, 98, 105
management committee, 27
nationhood, 9
party system, 106, 107
passport, 9, 96
people, 68, 75, 81, 85, 86, 94, 95
political maturity, 97
public, 1, 8, 83, 84, 86, 87, 88, 90, 91, 95,
    97, 101, 108, 109, 115, 116, 120,
    121, 122, 134, 168
revenue, 35, 157
rule-making, 28
upper chamber, 173, 174
voters, 97, 99, 102, 103, 104, 105
European Council, 85, 96, 124, 167, 171,
    172, 175
European Elections, 5, 67, 68, 74, 80, 88,
    89, 95, 106
arguments against, 73
awareness of, 101, 108, 109
campaign, 90, 91, 101, 112, 113, 114,
    115, 116, 122
and citizens, *see* Citizens ·
common electoral system, 111
constitutional significance, 109, 110
and dual mandate, 142
electoral procedures, 73, 109, 110, 111,
    112
and European parties, 107, 108
European party programmes, 113
functions, 90, 91
influence on institutional balance, 117
and legitimacy, 76, 77, 79, 81, 82, 83, 84
manifesto, 18
and media, 135
and MEPs, 134, 138, 139
and national party tickets, 113
and non-voting public, 105

objectives, 113
opponents, 75, 77, 86, 108
and political communication, 97, 98, 99,
    100
preparations, 104, 107
problems, 73, 148
and proportional representation, 110,
    111
prospects of, 107, 108
proxy and postal provisions, 111
results, 117
right to vote, 111
and simple majority system, 111
supporters, 75, 77, 83, 86, 108
supranational campaign, 73, 97
turn-out, 91, 94, 98, 99, 101, 104, 109,
    115, 116, 117, 135
uniqueness, 97, 136
voters attitudes, 101, 135
see also, Direct Elections, Direct
    Universal Suffrage, European
    franchise, Members of the
    European Parliament
European franchise, 94, 95, 96, 97
European Investment Bank, 85
European Parliament (EP)
accretion of powers, 2, 3, 4, 5, 6, 7, 135,
    153, 157
audio-visual section, 123
authority, 6, 73, 98, 105, 117, 166
awareness-building, 135, 146
budgetary powers, 3, 8, 24, 26, 34, 35,
    36, 37, 38, 39, 40, 41, 46, 49, 50, 64,
    65, 125, 165, 168
and citizens, 73–117, *see also*, Citizens
Commission, relationship with, 26, 28,
    29, 32, 67, 88, 89, 117, 124, 125,
    158, 165, 166, 167, 168, 174
committees, 48, 58, 59, 120
    finance and budgetary committee, 49,
        168
    membership, 62n
    parliamentary control sub-
        committee, 52
    plenary sessions, 29, 31, 56, 93n, 142,
        146
    political affairs committee, 3, 147,
        155n, 156n
    scrutiny role, 6, 59, 89, 158, 165
    selection, 107
    visibility, 89
control powers, 44–59
Council of Ministers, relationship with,
    26, 28, 29, 32, 67, 88, 89, 117, 124,
    125, 154, 155, 158, 161, 165, 166,
    167, 168, 169, 172, 173, 174, 175

debates and questions, 56, 57, 58, 142, 145
decision-making, 66, 77, 78, 99, 109, 117, 155, 157
democratic legitimacy, 66, 79, 82
and direct elections, 78, 83, *see also*, Direct Elections, European Elections, Members of the European Parliament
evolution, 67, 167
extension of powers, 2, 3, 5, 74, 117, 167
functions, 13, 18, 64, 65, 66, 67, 68
  communication, 22, 68, 95, 98, 117, 122
  education, 22, 68, 95, 98, 101, 102, 109, 117, 122
  expressive, 95, 98
  information, 21, 68, 95, 98, 101, 102, 109, 117, 122
  legitimation, 22
  representation, 22
grand forum, 82, 83, 84, 89, 90, 135
history, 25
intelligibility, 82, 83, 84, 85, 86, 90, 97, 98, 112
is EP a parliament?, 24–41, 59, 64, 65, 84
legislative powers, 2, 5, 6, 8, 18, 20, 21, 24, 26, 27, 28, 29, 30, 31, 32, 33, 34, 64, 66, 67, 109
legitimacy, 8, 73, 74, 77, 78, 82, 83, 84, 86, 89, 90, 91, 94, 98, 157, 158, 165
location, 84, 120, 175
and media, 121–39
and motion of censure, 48, 49, 50, 51, 52, 53, 54, 55, 56, 65
nomenclature, 24, 25, 26, 85, 163
party groups
  autonomous parties, 113, 148, 164
  awareness-building, 103, 105
  British Labour delegation, 124, 128, 129
  and campaign, 108, 112, 113, 114, 115, 116
  Communists, 107
  composition, 45
  enlarged bureau, 107
  European Conservatives, 50, 107, 108
  European Federalists, 108
  European Progressive Democrats, 107
  functions: communication, 106, 108; education, 106, 109; information, 106, 109
  identity-building, 105, 108, 112
  information service, 101
  intelligibility, 112

Liberal-Democratic Federation, 112
  Liberals, 107
  manifestos, 98, 107, 112
  'non-inscrits', 107
  organisation, 107, 108
  Socialists, 107, 108
  tangibility, 112
  transnational parties, 105, 113, 164, 165
  and turn-out, 111
  visibility, 88, 108, 112
  voting patterns, 54
and people, 75, 164
and political socialisation, 96
powers, 1, 2, 3, 5, 6, 8, 9, 13, 18, 20, 21, 22, 24, 26, 27, 28, 29, 30, 31, 32, 33, 34, 35, 36, 37, 38, 39, 40, 41, 44–59, 64, 65, 66, 67, 68, 74, 75, 78, 83, 84, 88, 89, 109, 125, 135, 158, 165, 166, 167
President, 1, 40, 58, 68n, 134
relationship with Commission, 26, 28, 29, 32, 67, 88, 89, 117, 124, 125, 158, 165, 166, 167, 168, 174
relationship with Council, 26, 28, 29, 32, 57, 67, 88, 89, 117, 124, 125, 154, 155, 158, 161, 165, 166, 167, 168, 169, 172, 173, 174, 175
relationship with National parliaments, 26, 150, 155
representativeness, 66, 68, 74, 94, 98, 109
rules of procedure, 57, 107, 164
salience, 68, 88, 90, 112, 120, 121
size, 106
sovereignty, 159
tangibility, 97, 98, 112, 121
turn-out, 99, 109, 111, 116
visibility, 86, 87, 88, 89, 97, 98, 112, 116, 120, 121, 122, 146
'voice of the people', 98
European Parliamentary Assembly, 25
European People's Party, 106
European union, 1, 94, 129
Executives, 14, 16, 17

Fabrini, F., 50
Federal community, 7, 163
Federal government, 110, 160
Federalism, 1, 7, 148, 157, 158, 159, 160, 161, 163, 164, 165, 175
Fédéralisme et Intégration Européenne, 157
federal parliament, 4
federal popular chamber, 169

federal systems, 160, 161, 162, 163, 164, 165
Federal Trust, 80
Federal union, 7
Federations, 7, 160, 165
Fellermaier, L., 53, 60n
Fitzmaurice, J., 25, 30, 53, 66, 86, 158
Flesch, C., 16, 50
France
    government opposition to EP, 3
    Houses of Parliament, 33, 38
    National Assembly, 166, 167
    National Assembly's Foreign Affairs Committee, 119n
Friedrich, C. F., 78, 160
Funtionalism
    funtional approach, 15, 16
    functional characteristics, 164
    functional lines, 160
    functional plan, 159
    functional premise, 1, 8

Genscher, H.-D., 73
Gerlach, H., 52
Germany, Federal Republic of, 7, 110, 162, 167
    CDU/CSU, 110
    FDP, 110
    Federal Chancellor, 167
    Federal elections, 125
    Land election, 110
    Länder, 162
    SPD/FDP government, 110
Giorni d'Europa, 123
Gladwyn, Lord, 111

Hague conference, 1
Hallstein, Dr W., 9n
Henig, S., 55, 80
Hennis, W., 24
High Authority, 24, 25
Hogan, W. N., 90
Humpty Dumpty, 26

Integration, 8, 40, 75, 88, 98, 99, 103, 161, 171, 172
    and European Parliament, 117
    horizontal, 95, 138
    in-depth, 89
    literature, 74, 76
    and media, 123
    and member governments, 141
    and MEPs, 145, 165

political, 104, 108, 149, 160
    public attitudes towards, 113
    and role of information, 79, 80
    West European, 74, 113
Intergovernmental practices, 7
International cooperation, 8
International organisation, 1, 13, 26
Ireland
    Irish parliament, 33, 38, 155n
        Dail, 156n, 163
        Seanad, 156n
Italy
    Parliament, 33, 38

Jenkins, R., 52, 89, 97, 102, 116, 123, 127, 133
Judiciary, 129
Juliet, Shakespeare's, 26

Kapteyn, P. J. G., 38
Kirk, Sir P., 49, 50, 51, 53, 54, 126, 129, 145
Kooning, J. de, 51

Legislatures, 14, 16, 17, 18, 21, 29, 94, *see also*, European Parliament, National Parliaments
Legitimacy, 8, 13, 14, 22, 66, 73, 74, 75, 76, 77, 78, 79, 80, 81, 82, 83, 84, 90, 91, 94, 98, 103, 117, 157, 165, 175
Liberal Party Federation, 106
Liberal state, 16
Lindberg, L. N., 78
Linguistic diversity, 95, 96, 97, 98, 105
Locke, J., 17
Loewenberg, G., 20
Loyalty
    and political system, 81, 103
    transfer of, 80, 81, 82, 83
Luxembourg
    Chamber of Deputies, 16

Mansholt, S., 49, 50
Media
    and Commission, 87
    and Council of Ministers, 87
    and European Elections, 101, 122, 135, 136
    and European Parliament, 87, 88, 90, 120–39
    and MEPs, 87, 89, 120, 134, 135, 136, 137, 138, 139, 143

and MPs, 19
and public, 19, 122, 137, 138, 139
Member governments, 8, 9, 45, 68, 77, 101, 109, 141, 159
Member states
    autonomy, 6, 7, 165
    and EP electoral procedures, 109, 110, 111, 112
    governments, 1, 3, 4, 5, 7, 8, 146, 147, 161
    independence, 6
    legislative processes, 5, 8, 44, 163
    sovereignty, 6, 7, 8
Members of the European Parliament (MEPs), 4, 5, 9, 54, 65, 87, 88, 89, 111, 164
    accountability, 2, 3, 21, 74, 90, 116, 117
    allegiance, 148, 149n
    authority, 66, 78
    awareness-building, 115, 146
    British Labour, 148
    candidates, 97, 98, 104, 105, 113, 114, 115, 116, 117
    career, 144, 145
    and citizens, 117, 134
    and Commission, 90
    constituencies, 114
    and dual mandate, 141–155
    and European elections, 91
    and floating- voters, 137
    functions: communication, 98, 105, 115, 116, 117, 139; education, 97, 105, 109, 117, 139; information, 97, 105, 109, 116, 117, 139
    legitimacy, 66
    and media, 87, 89, 120, 134, 135, 136, 137, 138, 139, 143
    and power in EC, 77
    scrutiny power, 117
    selection, 2, 144
    self-image, 104, 105, 115, 117, 134
    visibility, 112, 113, 114, 115, 116
Members of Parliament (MPs), 2, 4, 5, 7, 18, 19, 20, 31, 36, 38, 57, 88, 114, 141
Monarchic principles, 78
Montesquieu, C. de S., 17, 30
Motion of Censure, 19, 45, 48, 49, 50, 51, 52, 53, 54, 55, 56, 59, 65, 88, 89, 95, 159, 165, 166
Mueller, C., 77, 78
Multinational corporation, 13

Nation, 15, 44, 79
National governments, 6, 7, 14, 16, 18, 20, 67, 81, 171

National identity, 8
National interest, 4
National parliament, 2, 5, 8, 26
    authority, 7, 14, 20, 81
    autonomy, 6, 7
    cabinet, 56
    control of executive, 166
    decline, 17, 18, 19, 20, 21, 67
    financial power, 18, 19
    functions, 13, 14, 15, 16, 19, 20
    grand forum, 81
    individual responsibility, 60n
    legislative power, 29
    ministerial accountability, 55, 56
    party groups, 9
    powers, 7, 14, 18, 26
        of dissolution, 55
    procedures, 13, 19
    proceedings, 19
    and public, 20
    scrutiny powers, 6, 21
    sovereignty, 6, 7, 13, 21, 73, 153
    structure, 14
Nation state, 8, 97, 159, 160
Netherlands
    Minister of Foreign Affairs, 58
    Parliament, 58
Nine, The, 1, 30, 67, 73, 99, 166, 175
Non-parliamentary agencies
    Audit Office, 19
    Comptroller and Auditors General, 19
Nordic Assembly, 26
'No taxation without representation', 2, 82, 158

O'Dalaigh, President, 125
O'Hagan, Lord, 104
Ombudsman, 48
Ortoli, F.-X., 51, 52, 61n, 134

Palmer, M., 39, 57
Parliaments, 2, 5, 6, 7, 8, 9, 26, 29, 55, 60n, 66, 73, 97
    Belgium, 152, 162, 173, 174
    bicameral, 4, 161, 162, 163, 165
    Britain, 4, 15, 23n, 38, 47, 66, 81, 111, 150, 153, 154, 162, 163
    'decline of legislatures' thesis, 17, 18, 19, 20, 21
    Denmark, 153
    European Parliament, *see* European Parliament
    France, 33, 38, 119n, 166, 167
    functions, 13, 14, 15, 16, 17, 18, 19, 20, 44, 81, 94, 95

Germany, Federal Republic of, 15, 24, 143, 145, 151, 153, 162, 163, 167, 173
Ireland, 33, 38, 155n, 156n, 163
Italy, 33, 38
Luxembourg, 16
Netherlands, 58
Parliamentary democracy, 20, 67
'crisis' of, 14
Parliamentary government, 18
Parliamentary system, 24
Parliamentary time-table, 18
Parties
communicative role, 104, 105, 106, 107, 108
educative role, 104, 105, 106, 107; 108
informative role, 104, 105, 106, 107, 108
transnational, 101, 105
see also, European Parliament
Party systems, 16, 19, 103, 106, 107, 108, 109
Political authority, 22, 78
Political development, 75, 76, 101
Political institutions, 14, 26, 78, 79, *see also*, European Community
Political legitimacy, 76, 79, 81
Political power, 77, 78, 90
Political socialisation, 78, 95, 96, 98
Political structure, 66
Political systems, 13, 15, 82, 85, 164
and citizens, 80, 96
and direct legitimacy, 77, 78, 80, 83
and European elections, 90
intelligibility, 80
tangibility, 80
Political union, 80
Pompidou, G., 60n
Pressure groups, 13, 16, 20, 83, 116
Proportional representation, 110
Pryce, R., 79
Public accounts committee, 40
Public policy, 13, 44, 90

Rabier, J.-J., 137
Regional Development Fund, 39, 43n
Regional governments, 7
Regional parliaments, 7
Representative government, 79, 90
Representatives, 2, 5, 9, 17, 74, 81, 82, 164
Ribière, R., 50, 60n, 62n
Rome, Treaty of, 3, 6, 24, 25, 27, 28, 32, 36, 38, 40, 41n, 43n, 45, 46, 48, 50, 56, 57, 60n, 61n, 66, 75, 78, 89, 91n, 106, 110, 117, 153, 157, 159, 164, 165, 166, 169, 170, 171, 172, 173

Schaar, J. H., 78
Scheingold, S. A., 78
Scottish Nationalist Party, 111
Second World War, 13
Separation of powers, 29, 31, 34, 47, 64
Six, The, 49, 89, 99
Skimmed-milk, 51
Social contract, 78
Socialisation, 78, 95, 96, 98
Sovereignty, 3, 5, 6, 13, 15, 17, 21, 73, 165
limitations of, 75
loss of, 75, 153
of parliament, 81
of the people, 77, 78, 81
pooling of, 7, 20, 26, 159
transfer of, 7, 8, 20, 75
Speakers of the European Parliamentary Assemblies, 152
Rome conference, 152, 155n, 156n
Spénale, G., 49, 50, 53, 54, 58, 62n, 68n, 155n
Spinelli, A., 30, 159
Stability, 75
Statutes, 17
Stewart, Rt. Hon. M., 88
Stillman, P. G., 79
Stoel, M. van der, 68n
Summit meetings, 49, 172, 175, *see also*, European Council
Supranationalism, 160
supranational agencies, 160; authorities, 161; democracy, 74, 82, 85; élites, 105; Euro-polity, 159; government, 2; institutions, 135; legislation, 161; organisation, 8, 108; parliament, 7, 8, 21, 67, 105; party structures, 104; political centres of authority, 149; political parties, 107, 108; practices, 7; system, 67
Surveys, of public opinion, 19, 83, 99, 101, 103, 116, 118n, 121, 136, 137
Systems of domination, 77

The Power of the Purse, 34, 39, 40
Thomas, H., 167
Thomson, G., 32
Thorn, G., 126
Tindemans, L., 167
Tindemans Report, 1, 73, 94
Treaty of Luxembourg, 35
Treaty of Paris, 24, 91n
Tugendhat, C., 134

Unification of Europe, 75
Union, 3

United States
  Congress, 47
  President, 47

Vals, F., 50
Vedel, G., 65, 88
Vedel Report, 152
Vernaschi, V., 52
Voters, 3, 5, 90, 99, 113, 115, 117, 138
Votes of confidence, 19
Vredeling, H., 57, 62n, 133, 144

Western European Union (WEU), 153
Wheare, K. C., 160, 163, 165
White Paper on Direct Elections to the
  European Parliament, 147, 148,
  150, 164

Wilson, Rt. Hon. Sir H., 39

Zellentin, G., 94
Zero sum, 160

DATE			